The Golden Age of the
U.S.-China-Japan Triangle
1972–1989

Harvard East Asian Monographs 216

The Golden Age of the U.S.-China-Japan Triangle

1972–1989

Edited by
Ezra F. Vogel, Yuan Ming,
and Tanaka Akihiko

Published by the Harvard University Asia Center
and distributed by Harvard University Press
Cambridge (Massachusetts) and London 2002

Printed in the United States of America

The Harvard University Asia Center publishes a monograph series and, in coordination with the Fairbank Center for East Asian Research, the Korea Institute, the Reischauer Institute of Japanese Studies, and other faculties and institutes, administers research projects designed to further scholarly understanding of China, Japan, Vietnam, Korea, and other Asian countries. The Center also sponsors projects addressing multidisciplinary and regional issues in Asia.

Library of Congress Cataloging-in-Publication Data

The golden age of the U.S.-China-Japan triangle, 1972–1989 / edited by Ezra F. Vogel, Yuan Ming, and Tanaka Akihiko.
     p. cm. -- (Harvard East Asian monographs ; 216)
    Includes bibliographical references and index.
    ISBN 0-674-00960-6 (cl : alk. paper)
      1. United States--Foreign relations--China. 2. China--Foreign relations--United States. 3. United States--Foreign relations--Japan. 4. Japan--Foreign relations--United States. 5. United States--Foreign relations--1945–1989. I. Vogel, Ezra F. II. Yuan, Ming. III. Tanaka, Akihiko, 1954–. VI. Series.

E183.8.C5 G63 2002
327.73051'09'047--dc21

                                             2002024139

Index by Barbara Roos

⊗   Printed on acid-free paper

Last figure below indicates year of this printing
12 11 10 09 08 07 06 05 04 03 02

Acknowledgments

This volume is based on the second of three conferences between American, Chinese, and Japanese scholars examining their nations' relationship from 1945 until 2000. The purpose of these conferences was to provide a historical perspective on relations between the three powers likely to be most critical in determining the fate of East Asia over the next several decades.

The conferences also had a secondary purpose: to develop a common basis of understanding among research scholars in each country. They were organized under the direction of Professor Yuan Ming of Peking University, Professor Tanaka Akihiko of Tokyo University, and Ezra Vogel at Harvard University. At the time of the project, each was director, respectively, of a center in his own university: Ezra Vogel at the Fairbank Center, Yuan Ming of the Center for International Relations, and Tanaka Akihiko of the Institute of Oriental Culture.

The papers for the first conference, on the period 1945–71, are available on the Web site: www.fas.harvard.edu/~asiactr.

We gratefully acknowledge the assistance of the superb staffs of the Harvard Asia Center, especially Holly Angell and Anna Laura Rosow, and of the Fairbank Center. The conference was held at the International House of Japan in January 2000, with their usual graceful local arrangements under the direction of Kato Mikio.

The conference was made possible by the financial assistance of the Lee Folger Fund and the U.S.-Japan Foundation.

E.F.V.

Contents

Contents

Contributors

Gerald L. Curtis is a Professor and former Director of the East Asian Institute at Columbia University.

Jia Qingguo is Professor Dean of International Relations at Peking University.

Kamiya Matake is a Professor at the National Defense Academy of Japan.

Nakanishi Hiroshi is a Professor at Kyoto University.

The late *Michel Oksenberg* was a Senior Fellow at the Institute of International Studies Asia/Pacific Research Center at Stanford University.

Robert S. Ross is a Professor at Boston College and a Research Associate of the Fairbank Center, Harvard University.

Soeya Yoshihide is a Professor at Keio University in Tokyo.

Tanaka Akihiko is a Professor at Tokyo University.

Ezra Vogel is Henry Ford II Research Professor at Harvard University.

Yuan Ming is a Professor of International Relations and Director of the American Center at Peking University.

Zhang Baijia is a Researcher at the Central Party School of the Chinese Communist Party.

Zhang Tuosheng is a Researcher at the Chinese Institute of Contemporary International Relations in Peking.

The Golden Age of the
U.S.-China-Japan Triangle
1972–1989

Introduction

Ezra F. Vogel

East Asia not only lacks strong regional organizations like NATO and the European Community. It lacks the base for cooperation that European countries acquired from their common heritage of Roman law, the Latin alphabet, and Christianity, from centuries of relations between nation states, and from similarities in size and stage of development. The Association of Southeast Asian Nations (ASEAN) and the Asia-Pacific Economic Cooperation (APEC) have greatly reduced tensions between nations and increased regional cooperation, but in the decades immediately ahead, these loosely structured multilateral institutions cannot become strong enough to provide a regional security framework. In the absence of a strong regional organization, achieving peace and prosperity in East Asia will require the cooperation of the major powers of the region: the United States, China, and Japan. All three are proud nations and differ greatly in their history, values, and perceptions of national interests. Maintaining constructive relationships while the United States leads a revolution in military technology, China becomes stronger, and Japan reforms its institutions will be a Herculean task.

Yet during one period, from 1972 to 1989, the United States, China, and Japan enjoyed positive relations with one another. How and under what circumstances did this special era arise and why did it come to an end? To what extent did patterns of cooperation developed during this period survive, despite the instability that began in 1989? Is it possible in the early decades of the new century to achieve the spirit of positive cooperation of 1972–89 without the special circumstances of that period? To address such questions, this volume, a collaboration among scholars from all three countries, explores the nature of that special period—its origins, its development, and its demise.

The period 1972–89 is a striking contrast to the preceding century, when two of the powers were united against the third, and to the period of instability since 1989. From 1898 through the 1920s, Japan and the United States worked together to deal with the chaos in China. But from Japan's invasion of Manchuria in 1931 until after World War II, the United States first cooperated with and then allied itself with China to oppose the Japanese. Then, in another turnabout, from 1947 until 1972 the United States allied with Japan against Communist China as well as against the Soviet Union. Since 1989, Japan and the United States have remained allies, but their relationship with China has been tense and unstable.

The Strange, Unequal Triangle

Until now, each of the three countries has approached its relations with the other two primarily in bilateral terms. In tracing how they conceived of and structured their relations between 1972 and 1989, this volume must of necessity consider these bilateral relationships. In the 1970s and particularly in the 1980s, however, as China's economic relations with the outside world expanded, its economy also became more closely linked with those of the United States and Japan. As China expanded its political cooperation with other countries, its political influence grew, which in turn meant that bilateral political and security relations between Japan and the United States could no longer be dealt with effectively without considering the role of China. Thus, although the three nations still conceived of their relations with the other two in bilateral terms, they had in fact become an economic and political triangle. One assumption underlying the present volume is that previous conceptions need to change to allow more attention to focus on the new triangular reality and its importance.

This triangle is a strange one, unequal and constantly changing. Its corners (the three countries) and its sides (the three bilateral relationships) are unequal, and its overall nature (the capacity of the three countries to work together) has undergone considerable change in the last few decades. In the

1970s, China was still a very backward country with little capacity to take part in international trade or international politics. As China opened up in the 1970s and 1980s, it abandoned the idea of fomenting revolution abroad and came to accept the basic, previously established framework for regional and global cooperation. China's priorities since 1978 have clearly been to encourage domestic economic development and maintain good relations with other countries. Through access to foreign markets, China hoped to sell its raw materials and manufactured products and thus acquire the financial resources for new investment, new technology, and the development of new management skills. As its economy took off, its foreign trade grew even more rapidly, and by the end of the 1980s it was a major trading nation. Its influence in the regional and global economy continued to expand in the 1990s, and its entry into the World Trade Organization (WTO) will further hasten this process. China now has trained specialists who can analyze global developments and participate in international meetings, and this has facilitated its ability to expand its positive political participation. The broad network of people of Chinese ancestry throughout the world has helped China hasten its acquisition of information, investment, technology, and management skills, but it has also complicated China's relations with governments concerned about the loyalty of citizens of Chinese ancestry.

Yet even as a new century begins, China remains a developing country with an annual per capita income of less than a thousand dollars. Although coastal areas are rapidly approaching the standards of developed countries, inland areas lag far behind. During the 1970s and 1980s China began to lay the basis for modernizing its military, but it remains far behind the advanced nations in military technology. Unlike Japan, it has nuclear weapons as well as missiles and a military force of some three million, one of the world's largest, and its capacity already gives it considerable leverage over its smaller neighbors. More important, already in the 1980s, the prospects of China's continued economic growth and military modernization, its great size and its long history, and the past achievements of its civilization and future ambitions were leading other countries to treat it as the power it seemed likely to become. By the 1980s, even Japan and the United States, the major powers in Asia, began to express concern about what China might do with its increasing power, a view that would become more prominent in the 1990s.

Unlike China and the United States, which as continental powers have experience in managing considerable domestic diversity, Japan is a small, insular nation. The domestic unity and program for modernization that it achieved in the latter part of the nineteenth century, long before any other Asian country, have enabled it to acquire levels of skill, knowledge, capital, and technology far beyond those of its Asian neighbors and, in global terms, second only to those of the United States. But its early successes in military modernization, along with a power vacuum in Asia, made it possible for Japan, in the half-century beginning in 1894, to engage in conquest and colonization. Even half a century later, the legacy of hostility to Japan in East and Southeast Asia constrains its influence and power in the region. Japanese militarism has also left a domestic legacy of negative reaction against aggressive military action, further reinforced by the "anti–war making" constitution introduced by the occupying powers after World War II. This legacy has restrained Japan from acquiring nuclear and other potentially offensive weapons.

This policy of restraint on becoming a "normal military power" has not opened Japan to security threats because of its security agreement with the United States, which provides a nuclear umbrella and the assurance of support if Japan is attacked. Japan in turn contributes funds, logistic support, and bases for U.S. troops in Asia. Regional and domestic reaction against militarism, coupled with the leadership of the United States in international and regional affairs, has inhibited development of the kind of confidence necessary for building institutions and training people to think pro-actively about how to shape international structures. It has also left a residue of widespread frustration that Japan has not been able to play a political role in the international arena commensurate with its economic strength and modernization.

In addition, Japan is currently suffering political gridlock and economic stagnation: its domestic cold war political structure has collapsed and its economic institutions and structures, so well-suited to earlier phases of growth, are having difficulty adapting to fast-changing globalized markets, especially financial markets. Many Japanese are also pessimistic that Japan's century of leadership in Asia may yield to China's ability to combine low-cost labor with modern science and technology and its growing political role. Yet Japan remains arguably the world's cutting-edge manufacturer, the world's largest net creditor, and the world's second largest economy. It can claim one of the highest standards of living and modern technology second only to the United States. How successful Japan will be in overcoming its problems remains unclear, but as a country on the rise, during the period

1972–89 it seemed poised to overtake the United States as a source of modern technology and global capital.

Although in the 1990s the United States has distanced itself from its nearest rivals in high technology, leverage in global financial markets, and military capacities, in the late 1980s it was under threat of being overtaken by Japan in high technology and in domination of global capital markets. In the 1990s, the United States succeeded in turning back the Japanese challenge in such areas as semiconductors, automobiles, software, telecommunications, and financial services. The preeminence of major U.S. universities and think tanks and the global reach of American popular culture were already well established by the 1970s and 1980s. By the turn of the century, the only challenger seems to be China, but in the 1980s the major challenger still appeared to be Japan.

Although the United States is not an Asian country, its expanded trade, investment, and academic leadership in Asia, its presence in the Pacific and, since 1941, its enduring commitment to the security of the region, have made it an Asian power. Yet U.S. leaders, whose concerns are global, cannot concentrate their attention on Asia to the extent that the powers in Asia do, nor is the United States strong enough to maintain its power unilaterally. In the 1970s and 1980s especially, the United States was acutely aware of its reliance on Japan's cooperation in dealing with regional and global economic, energy, and security issues.

The bilateral relationships between the United States, China, and Japan, however, remain unequal. The U.S.-Japan relationship is by far the strongest, not only because of the security alliance, but because of the interface between institutions in all sectors of a democratic modern society that have been built up since the late 1940s. Mutual understanding, and with it, the mechanisms for cooperation, have also developed in all sectors and in all major regions of both countries.

The Sino-Japanese relationship has a deeply rooted cultural component arising from the geographic proximity of China and Japan; their common background of Confucianism, Buddhism, and use of Chinese characters; and the centuries of cultural contact between them. If the history of Japanese aggression in China has constrained personal relationships and limited the kind of initiatives Japan can take with China, the danger of an outburst of Chinese antiforeign nationalism has also caused many Japanese to keep a low profile and to approach China with caution. Yet in the many sectors and many localities where Japanese and Chinese interact, they have been able to develop effective working relationships. Paradoxically, in China's Northeast and in Shanghai, where Japanese colonialism was most deeply established, the contact was also deeper. In the 1980s, the United States was still far more important to Japan than China.

The Sino-American relationship in the 1970s and 1980s was basically positive, though distant, and mutual images were highly favorable. Strategic considerations played a major role. It was only in the 1990s, after the Tiananmen incident, that a number of factors—U.S. criticism of China's assault on human rights, the increased salience of China as a target for U.S. pressure groups, the complications arising from Taiwan's expanding democracy and pressures for independence, the growing concern of U.S. defense strategists over China's potential use of its increasing military power, and China's response to U.S. criticism—destabilized the relationship. Paradoxically, the range of freedoms within China continued to increase after the end of the cultural revolution in 1976, even as U.S. criticism of China's human rights record, relatively constrained before 1989, vastly increased.

The Origins of the Constructive Triangle, 1972–1989

A key starting point for Chinese Communist Party foreign policy strategists has been to identify the main enemy and then potential collaborators against the main enemy. From 1931 to 1945, the main enemy was Japan, from 1946 to 1949, the Chinese Nationalists, and from 1950 to 1969, the United States. In 1969, however, after two border clashes with the Soviet Union and the threat of further Soviet invasion, China concluded that the main enemy was then the Soviet Union. To reduce the danger of Soviet attack and improve its prospects for help from other countries, the Chinese government began to improve its relations with Western Europe, Canada, Australia and New Zealand, and the United States.

Richard Nixon and Henry Kissinger, who could initially determine China policy with little consultation either inside or outside the U.S. government, believed that China could be a useful ally against the Soviet Union and could also help terminate the Vietnam War. Thus began one of the most fascinating diplomatic efforts in the latter half of the twentieth century, in which Zhou Enlai and Kissinger, backed by Mao Zedong and Nixon, began to lay out a basis for strategic Sino-U.S. cooperation against the Soviet Union. In the process, Kissinger and his Chinese counterparts were able to exchange views on a broad range of global issues and forge a constructive relationship by identifying areas of common interest and setting aside divisive issues such as Taiwan.

When Kissinger secretly flew to China in 1971 and announced plans for a forthcoming Nixon visit, Japan initially felt betrayed. Under U.S. pressure, Japan had fought China's entry into the United Nations and restrained its trade with China. Suddenly, without notifying Japan, U.S. leaders were rushing to Beijing. In Japan some analysts explained that in the 1930s, the hostilities between the United States and Japan resulted from intense competition in the Chinese market and that Kissinger's secret diplomacy was designed to give U.S. business a head start as China began opening its markets to the outside world. In fact, Kissinger and Nixon not only failed to notify the Japanese, they also failed to notify their own State Department. The real reason they kept their plans secret was to prevent any possible leak that might have allowed the Taiwan lobby in the United States, working with Congress, to spoil their plans. Nixon shrewdly calculated that the excitement of his visit to Beijing would pull Congress along and that his firm anti-Communist credentials would deflect the "soft on Communism" label that had so bedeviled the Democrats since the late 1940s.

Once Nixon's visit had been announced, U.S. constraints on Japan to limit relations with China abruptly ended, and Japan urgently sought to gain prompt access to the Chinese market. Eisaku Sato, then the longest serving prime minister in Japanese postwar history, could not have achieved rapprochement because of his poor relations with China, and he was quickly replaced by a new prime minister, Tanaka Kakuei, who could work with China. To make sure that it did not fall behind the United States, Japan succeeded in normalizing relations with China in scarcely more than a year. For the United States, however, it would take seven years from the time of Kissinger's first visit to achieve the same goal.

During the years of the "constructive triangle," all three nations enjoyed good relations with each other. Once a geopolitical strategy brought them together, their economic, cultural, academic, and local community relations began to expand, slowly at first and then at an increased pace. Between 1971 and 1978, the growth of trust between China and the outside world paved the way for China's 1978 policy of "reform and opening." To advance modernization, China wanted a benign trading environment in which it could acquire technology and management skills and expand its export markets, in this way generating income to acquire more technology and investment capital. It is no accident that China announced its policy of reform and opening in December, the same month it joined with the United States to announce their agreement to normalize relations, or that both normalization and China's reform and opening began in January 1979.

The Destruction of the Constructive Triangle

The cordial political relationships between the United States, China, and Japan ended suddenly, beginning in 1989, because of the Tiananmen incident, the collapse of the Soviet Union, and the anxieties created by China's rapid economic and military growth. The collapse of the Soviet Union and the end of the cold war terminated the strategic rationale for the Sino-American and Sino-Japanese friendships. No longer did fear of the Soviet Union cause leaders in Washington, Beijing, and Tokyo to place such a high priority on mutual cooperation or to constrain their response on issues that might divide them.

The collapse of the Soviet Union also triggered a fundamental change in the rationale underlying U.S. foreign policy. As Henry Kissinger has emphasized, U.S. foreign policy has long involved some mixture of geopolitical strategy and the assertion of U.S. values. Theodore Roosevelt, for example, propounded a tough-minded geostrategic vision for expanding America's power, while Woodrow Wilson asserted American values. During the cold war, many U.S. liberals believed that supporting dictators to achieve geopolitical aims was a betrayal of U.S. values. With the collapse of the cold war, geopolitical pressures became less urgent. Now the United States could stop supporting dictators and pay more attention to its values.

The crackdown at Tiananmen Square on June 4, 1989, became the most poignant test of the new U.S. attention to values. Although the 1980 Kwangju Massacre in South Korea was of comparable scope, South Korea was at the time a U.S. ally, under threat from North Korea, and no Western TV cameras recorded the scene. As Richard Madsen has shown in his book *China and the American Dream*, the Tiananmen incident was a rude shock to Americans in general, who until then had received a favorable impression of China, and to liberals in particular, who had dreamed that the Chinese would gradually become more democratic, more "like us." The Tiananmen Square incident occurred just as the Soviet Union was collapsing, and the powerful impact of the television coverage throughout the world cast Chinese leaders, in the American mind, as the successors to Hitler and Stalin.

Overnight, the vivid image of a lone man standing in front of an oncoming tank in a country of such vast size and grandeur turned China into a lightning rod for U.S. groups concerned with human rights, political oppression, abortion, prison labor, religious intolerance, and the oppression of minorities. Ironically, foreign TV crews were in Tiananmen Square because freedoms in China were increasing; China was becoming more open just as Western criticism hardened.

The Japanese public was also upset by China's crackdown on Tiananmen, but it was far less moralistic than the American public. Aware of their own atrocities in China, the Japanese knew they were in no position to lecture China about morality. Acutely aware as well of the costs of chaos, which they had witnessed at first hand in China in the 1930s, the Japanese were more sympathetic to Chinese concerns about order. They also placed a higher priority on their economic interests in China, and although Japan responded to global pressures after the Tiananmen crackdown, restraining its trade and technology transfers to China, it was prepared to be more forthcoming. Likewise trying to break through the restraints of foreign sanctions after Tiananmen, China wished to maintain good relations with Japan. It was in this context that the Chinese welcomed Japanese Emperor Akihito in 1992 and sent President Jiang Zemin to visit Japan. The Japanese government felt that it was a propitious time for the emperor to travel to China in hopes of resolving the hostilities that had divided Japan and China since World War II. Unfortunately, this hope was to prove premature.

When China began its reform and opening in 1978, its economy and its military seemed too weak to present a serious threat to the United States and Japan. But China's rapid economic growth in the 1980s, and its projected trajectory of continued growth in GNP, trade, technology, and military power, had by the 1990s fueled anxiety in both countries. U.S. officials responsible for analyzing which powers might pose a potential threat naturally included China on the list. At the same time, international institutions like the World Bank began to measure GNP according to its purchasing power parity rather than according to what a given country could trade at current exchange rates. Calculated according to these new criteria, Chinese GNP was three or four times higher than the previous figures had indicated. Given particular assumptions about the measures of purchasing power parity, it might soon surpass that of Japan and, before many years, that of the United States. In fact, purchasing power parity is not a good measure of the international impact of a nation's economy, but the new figures heightened popular fears in the United States and Japan about China's potential threat, and placed constraints on the possibility of positive relations with China.

This new post-Tiananmen period of uncertainty in the Asian power triangle was further complicated by developments in Taiwan. After 1987, Taiwan took a large step toward democracy by ending its "military emergency" and announcing that opposition parties would be permitted. After Tiananmen, Taiwan could appeal to world opinion, contrasting Beijing's crackdown on dissidents with its own democracy. Domestically, expanded democratic rights allowed the Taiwanese majority, the "locals" whose ancestors had come from the mainland in the seventeenth century, to gain increasing power against the "mainlanders," who had fled China in the late 1940s, as the Communists were gaining power. Oppressed by mainlanders, who had greater links to China, the locals strongly desired independence.

Since the belief that Taiwan is part of China is so fundamental to China's conception of its national identity, Beijing vehemently opposes any effort by Taiwan to move toward independence. Officials in Beijing are convinced they must maintain a constant threat of military attack to ensure that Taiwan does not go down the road of independence. The United States, while recognizing the principle of one China, has long been on record as insisting that the issue of Taiwan be resolved peacefully, and it has pledged to help defend Taiwan in the event of an unprovoked attack from the mainland. This gridlock on the Taiwan issue further increases tensions and intensifies the risk of serious conflict between China and the United States.

China's response after 1989 to the new pressure from the United States and, to a lesser extent, Japan has been largely defensive. China's recognition of the importance of a peaceful international environment for economic growth and its limited economic and military power have placed restraints on its criticism of the West and led it to find ways of preventing a serious deterioration of relations with the United States and Japan. It has occasionally released dissidents and opened its institutions to foreign observers; but when foreign support for dissidents within China has threatened domestic order, China has cracked down while complaining vigorously about foreign interference. It has also complained about U.S. hegemony and begun to develop relationships with other countries that might constrain U.S. power.

As Michel Oksenberg points out in his essay, the 1970s and 1980s ushered in a new age when the policies of the three countries toward one another can no longer be determined by a small elite but involve more branches of the government, the Congress, and more private groups. An important legacy of the Golden Age of the Triangle, 1972–1989, is the vast increase in relations of all types between and among all three countries. These strongly rooted groupings—business, academic, cultural, religious, social, and local community—have continued during the period of uncertainty and still play a major role in restraining divisive tendencies.

The Structure of This Volume

DOMESTIC POLITICS

The first three essays in this volume trace the domestic environment that has influenced foreign policy in the United States, China, and Japan, respectively. Michel Oksenberg, research professor at Stanford University until his death from cancer shortly after completing this essay, in his paper traces the growing complexity of U.S. decision-making about China and Japan as the result of increasing foreign policy politicization and broader business and citizens' group involvement. A key consequence is a gradual loss of coherence in Asian policy, a trend further reinforced by the end of the cold war. Drawing in part on his experience as the Asian adviser to President Jimmy Carter and Zbigniew Brzezinski, Oksenberg gives an insider's view of how the various branches of government interact in the formation of Asian policy.

Zhang Baijia is a researcher at the Central Party School of the Chinese Communist Party. His father was the highly respected informal "dean" of the Chinese diplomatic corps officials dealing with English-speaking countries. Zhang presents a highly nuanced view of the role of the cultural revolution (1966–76) in shaping Chinese policy, but the key domestic factor, he points out, was the absolute authority of Chairman Mao and the highly centralized system of rule. Zhang then describes the impact of the period of reform and opening (begun in 1978 and basically completed by 1985) and the new emphasis given to accelerated economic development. Although Deng Xiaoping, who came to power in 1978, did not have Mao's absolute authority, he did wield considerable power; unlike Mao, in foreign affairs he played the dual role of decision-maker and implementer.

Kamiya Matake, a professor at the National Defense Academy of Japan whose father was a distinguished professor of international relations, traces the efforts of Nakasone Yasuhiro, the strongest of Japan's prime ministers over the last two decades, to forge a bolder foreign policy and increase Japan's military strength. Yet even Nakasone, who possessed a clear sense of foreign policy strategy and whose five-year tenure (1982–87) was, by Japanese standards, unusually long, had little impact on the underlying consensus that favored a strong alliance with the United States and only a modest military role. Unlike Mao, who held almost absolute power, and Deng, whose authority in Chinese foreign policy was considerable, even Nakasone had limited room for changing foreign policy. Even when the Liberal Democratic Party began to flounder in the years after Nakasone, eventually losing power in 1993, the basic foreign policy consensus continued. The major change of these years, the "opening" of China, was not a result of domestic factors.

U.S.-CHINA RELATIONS

Robert S. Ross and Jia Qingguo examine the U.S.-China relationship. As Ross, a professor at Boston College and a research associate at the Fairbank Center, Harvard University, makes clear, the dominant role of cold war strategy that shaped the opening between China and the United States pushed domestic politics to one side as relatively unimportant. The United States wanted to adjust its role in Asia after the Vietnam War and to unite with China against the Soviet Union. The opening of liaison offices following Nixon's visit to Beijing aided communication, and staff capacities gradually increased until in 1979 the Beijing office became a full-fledged embassy. Despite the turmoil in Washington during the Watergate crisis, Kissinger's involvement provided continuity throughout the Ford presidency, and China policy was relatively unaffected. The process of normalization took longer than the Chinese wished, however, and was only completed during the Carter administration. Although Ronald Reagan came to power determined to demonstrate his support for Taiwan, he soon developed a good relationship with China, and during his administration the security relationship with China was further stabilized.

Jia Qingguo, dean of International Relations at Peking University, looks at the repeated shifts between limited cooperation and limited confrontation. He describes the perspectives and circumstances that constrain how much the U.S.-China relationship can improve and the deep common interests that prevent its serious deterioration. When the Soviet Union and the United States approached nuclear parity, Sino-Soviet relations improved, since China's weight could now tip the strategic balance. Even in the 1970s there were continuing problems in the U.S.-China relationship: the United States was more willing to accept détente with the Soviet Union and China was unwilling to accept the U.S. request that it give up the use of force to resolve the Taiwan issue. Shortly after the normalization of relations with China, the U.S. Congress passed the Taiwan Relations Act, which further exacerbated relations, since it gave reassurances to Taiwan. But U.S.-China relations remained within bounds because both governments shared the belief that it was in their respective national interests to keep the relationship from collapse.

U.S.-JAPAN RELATIONS

Gerald L. Curtis, professor and long-time director of the East Asian Institute at Columbia, traces the strains on U.S.-Japan relations that resulted from the centralization of decision-making under Kissinger and Nixon and their secrecy, particularly on trade issues and U.S.-China relations. Kissinger gained Chinese acceptance of the U.S.-Japan security alliance on the grounds that it was the best way to prevent Japan from becoming a major military power. Nakasone's strong support for the U.S.-Japan alliance during the 1980s strengthened the basis for a positive U.S.-Japan relationship (symbolized by "Ron and Yasu"), which helped to compensate for trade tensions as Japan's trade surplus grew and many U.S. industrial sectors lost out to their Japanese rivals. Although the security alliance remained firm, the strains that developed over trade issues, coupled with the U.S. approach—to apply even more pressure—eroded the trust and goodwill between the two countries.

Nakanishi Hiroshi, a professor at Kyoto University, considers the consequences of Japan's growth as an economic power: increased exports and growing responsibilities in international affairs. Despite increasing tensions over trade and the United States' sudden China policy shift made without previously notifying Japan, U.S.-Japan relations remained relatively solid. The United States welcomed Japan's acceptance of expanded global responsibilities, symbolized in its participation in global summits beginning in 1975. The two nations came to consider theirs the most important bilateral relationship in the world.

SINO-JAPANESE RELATIONS

Since the major trends in Sino-Japanese relations that began in 1972 continued through the early 1990s, the two final contributions deal with the period until 1992. Zhang Tuosheng, a research scholar at the Chinese Institute of Contemporary International Relations, whose father played a key role in the Sino-Japanese friendship association, traces the broad-gauged improvement in relations that continued until the early 1990s. Once relations between China and Japan were reestablished in 1972, interaction and cooperation expanded on many fronts, including Japanese aid and investment in China, two-way trade, cultural exchanges, and local sister-city and provincial linkages. Good relations continued into the early 1990s, culminating, as noted earlier, with the visit of President Jiang Zemin to Japan and the visit of Emperor Akihito to China in 1992. Following the Tiananmen incident of 1989, China's relations with Japan were less affected than those with the United States. Sino-Japanese differences on historical issues, on Taiwan, on economic issues, and on the revival of Japanese militarism, which were to become sources of greater tension in the mid-1990s, were kept under control in the 1970s and 1980s.

Soeya Yoshihide, professor in the Faculty of Law at Keio University, shows that Japan did not think of its relationship with China primarily in global strategic terms, as the United States did. Instead, it regarded China as a large and special neighbor with a long political and cultural history, which had played, and would again play, a major role in Japan's foreign economic relations. Although many Japanese politicians and diplomats felt betrayed by the sudden rapprochement between the United States and China and thus moved quickly to normalize relations with China, in the process they worked closely with the United States to ensure that Japan's security relationship with the United States remained strong. The changing security environment created by normalization helped Japan and China conclude their Treaty of Peace and Friendship, finally, in August 1978. Because the Chinese had insisted on an antihegemony clause in the treaty but the Japanese wanted to avoid a serious deterioration in their relations with the implied hegemon, the Soviet Union, negotiations had dragged on until 1978. This treaty helped consolidate a positive Sino-Japanese relationship until new problems arose in the mid-1990s.

I

Domestic Politics and Triangle Relations

CHAPTER ONE

U.S. Politics and Asian Policy

Michel Oksenberg

In the early 1970s, for the first time in history, the United States developed constructive relations with both China and Japan simultaneously. This breakthrough was achieved because President Richard M. Nixon and a small group of advisers made a strategic decision to resolve the Vietnam War and respond positively to China's willingness to work with the United States against a major threat to both, the Soviet Union.

After 1971, as contacts with China expanded and trade issues with Japan heated up, broader areas of the government and the public became involved in East Asia policy, and the policymaking process moved to a new level of complexity. After 1978, when China decided to undertake "reform and opening" and the United States and China agreed to normalize their relations, the trend toward a more complex policymaking process was greatly accelerated. Washington's mood and the U.S. policymaking process changed further as a result of the events of 1989—the Tiananmen incident and the collapse of the Soviet Union and world communism.

Although by the early 1970s the United States' relations with Japan were already more complicated than its relations with China, the structure of U.S. policymaking toward Japan underwent a similar change. Until 1971 a relatively small group of officials in the White House, the State Department, and the Department of Defense (DOD) managed the U.S. relationship with Japan. But with the eruption of the textile wrangle in 1969–71, trade with Japan became more deeply embroiled in U.S. politics, and the U.S. Congress began to play a much larger role. In addition, as the Japanese economy grew, actors concerned with the global economy in such areas as energy also began to take a larger role in Japan policy. The White House, State Department, and DOD continued to manage the security relationship with Japan, but as the quantity of Japanese imports grew and affected a broader range of economic and regional interests within the United States, various pressure groups and the Congress became increasingly involved in trade issues.

The U.S. Policy Process and the Expansion of U.S.-China Relations

From 1949 to 1969, relations between China and the United States had been animosity ridden. The two nations were as isolated from each other as any two large nations could be in the twentieth century: they engaged in no direct trade and had little diplomatic contact; their militaries were bitter enemies. Then came the 1970–72 breakthrough engineered by President Nixon and Chairman Mao Zedong. Yet during the ensuing three decades, successive waves of ever higher expectations for a more positive relationship ended in dashed hopes, frustration, and mutual recrimination. Despite these oscillations, however, the once relatively narrow, simple relationship of the 1970s, which had been confined to a few arenas and involved relatively few people on either side of the Pacific, had become by the 1990s a multilayered, multifaceted relationship in which billions of dollars and major strategic interests were at stake. The fluctuations made the headlines, but the real story was one of growing complexity as the Sino-American relationship became more deeply embedded in the domestic policies of both countries. Barring armed conflict over the Taiwan issue, the relationship seemed to have lost its previous fragility. Achieving coordinated, coherent, and consistent policies, however, seemed beyond the reach of either side and likely to remain so.

In the 1970s the People's Republic had been the purview of a small number of government officials in the White House, the National Security Council, the State Department, the DOD, and the Central Intelligence Agency. Only a limited number of members of Congress (such as Senators Henry Jackson, Jacob Javits, and Edward Kennedy and Representatives Paul Findlay and John Brademus) and their staffs took an interest in China. In the private sector, four organizations (the National Committee on U.S.-China Relations, the U.S.-China Business Council, the Committee on

Scholarly Communications with the People's Republic of China of the National Academy of Sciences, and the U.S.-China Friendship Association) devoted themselves exclusively to the China relationship. A few others with broader interests (such as the National Council of Churches and the American Friends Service Committee) were involved in some activities especially devoted to China. Journalists covered China from Hong Kong or journeyed to China on short trips. A few businessmen and lawyers made the trek to Guangzhou and Beijing for the limited commercial opportunities the relationship offered.

For the most part, the U.S. community of government and nongovernment specialists knew one another. They perceived themselves as members of a small, pioneering group. When Pan American Airlines inaugurated its service to Beijing in 1980, most nontourist passengers used the occasion to gossip with each other about common concerns. Twenty years later, however, the relationship had broadened so extensively that even scholarly analysts of particular facets of contemporary China, those who focused, for example, on law, military affairs, environmental issues, economic reform, or local politics, had formed their own specialized networks. These identifiable subgroups, involving dozens of researchers in universities, corporations, think tanks, and government agencies, paid remarkably little attention to the lively debates going on in the other groups. This once rather coherent community of academic China specialists had become fragmented by disciplinary and professional interests.

Moreover, as the China issue gained in importance, new entrants joined the debate. The field was no longer the exclusive domain of the area specialist. Now, for example, specialists on Chinese law—those with language proficiency and training in Chinese philosophy, history, and traditional legal practices—had been joined by lawyers trained in international law, arbitration, or intellectual property rights. International relations generalists and specialists on topics such as arms control and theories of nuclear deterrence linked up with China specialists who focused on Sino-American strategic relations. And environmentalists began to work with China specialists to analyze issues ranging from the construction of the Three Gorges Dam to the protection of pandas.

While many Americans had strong vested interests in an expanding Sino-American relationship, others—especially the leaders and staffs of several single-interest groups—in fact benefited from confrontations with

China over the issues of concern to them. On the one hand, the development of costly weapon systems such as Theater Missile Defenses (TMD) and National Missile Defenses (NMD) would become more justifiable if one could posit an inevitable Sino-American military rivalry. Vendors of military weapons were poised to sell billions in arms to the Pentagon and Taiwan if the China threat were deemed sufficient to justify a U.S. response. On the other hand, the argument for engagement with China and for massive American investment and trade would become more persuasive if one assumed that contacts with the outside would inexorably lead China to a more just and democratic political system.

Interested parties—not only foundations but also corporations, labor unions, concerned citizens, and foreign governments (especially Taiwan)—were willing to provide funds to ensure that the policy debate in Washington was robust and, from the funder's point of view, informed. So important had China policy become that each of the major foreign-policy think tanks in Washington felt obligated to have at least one China specialist on its staff. By the 1990s, the Brookings Institution, the American Enterprise Institute, the Heritage Foundation, the Stimpson Center, the Nixon Center, the Institute of International Economics, the Center for Strategic and International Studies (CSIS), the Center for Naval Analysis, and the Carnegie Endowment had all launched China initiatives. Augmented by a growing number of retired military, intelligence, and foreign service officers who had specialized in China, a substantial number of dissident émigrés who had found employment in the area, and enhanced China studies programs at many universities, the Washington-based China policy community was now large, influential, and deeply knowledgeable about specific dimensions of contemporary China.

Meanwhile, the two societies were becoming intertwined. Several examples suffice. Over a hundred thousand Chinese visiting scholars and university students in the United States enjoyed the same extensive access to the advanced technologies on American campuses that all other faculty and students enjoyed. Thousands of Americans adopted very young Chinese children. Untold numbers of Americans married citizens of the People's Republic. Even more citizens of the People's Republic acquired green cards or became American citizens. Others migrated illegally in significant numbers. All these recent arrivals to the United States found employment and contributed to the American economy. Silicon Valley benefited particularly from the highly qualified scientific and technical personnel who received advanced training in American universities and joined the U.S. workforce. In addition, several thousand Americans lived and worked as expatriates in China. Children of American couples residing in various Chinese cities became so numerous that the private English-language schools aimed primarily at Americans could not expand rapidly enough to accommodate the growth in student enrollments. Finally, many Chinese corporations opened offices staffed by PRC citizens in the United States and entered American financial markets, raising capital through the sale of bonds or shares on U.S. stock exchanges.

From the Nixon opening until the mid-1980s, the White House oversaw the relationship and provided a measure of consistency, coherence, and clarity. Secret presidential initiatives were responsible for the Shanghai Communiqué and the 1979 normalization agreement. During the Nixon and the Carter years, the president's White House staff, especially his national security adviser, managed the relationship on his behalf. However, as the private sector inserted itself into the relationship, which now began to extend to interests beyond the strategic, it became the object of interest group, congressional, and bureaucratic politics, the familiar "iron triangle." By devoting close personal attention to China policy during the Reagan years, Secretary of State George Shultz achieved a fair degree of coherence. To be sure, many departments developed programs with counterpart Chinese bureaucracies following normalization during the Carter administration and then in the Reagan administration, but these diverse programs were integrated into a coherent, mutually supportive whole. The Congress was generally supportive of an expanding relationship. Initially, then, as policymaking spread through the executive branch to the iron triangle, executive leadership succeeded in maintaining a coherent policy.

After 1989, this coherence was lost. During the George Bush years, Democrats in Congress attacked the president's China policy mercilessly. The prior Washington consensus on China policy broke down, and many single-interest groups, long opposed to a constructive posture toward Beijing, now coalesced. This broad-based coalition included such disparate groups as anti-abortion activists, pro-Tibet organizations, hard-core anti-communists, and some environmentalist, trade union, protectionist, and pro-Taiwan elements. These diverse groups, which appealed to the relevant congressional committees, found eager allies among many Democrats and some Republicans.

In reality, however, Bush administration policy was more nuanced and complex than its critics portrayed it to be. Although the Bush administration sought to maintain a strategic dialogue with Beijing, sustain China's Most Favored Nation (MFN) status, and cooperate where possible, it also undertook many measures that vexed Beijing. Soon after the [Tiananmen] debacle of June 4, 1989, with mild congressional prodding (strong pressure would come weeks later), the administration imposed trade sanctions on China that included the suspension of arms sales. Particularly disturbing to Beijing, therefore, was the substantial 1992 sale of F-16s to Taiwan, which tested the limits of the August 1982 Sino-American agreement pledging a gradual reduction in the quantity and quality of U.S. arms sales to Taiwan as tension in the area diminished. During the Bush years, the relationship could no longer be portrayed as a strategic alignment.

Domestic Forces Underlying the Changing Relationship

What explains the expansion of Sino-American interactions from the strategically aligned, fragile, White House–dominated relationship of the 1970s into the more deeply rooted one of the 1990s, which was partly contentious, partly constructive, and deeply immersed in American domestic politics? Simply put, over the course of the three decades the factors shaping the relationship had changed. The initial period of the 1970s and 1980s entailed a recovery from the earlier period of estrangement prompted by the two nations' shared opposition to the Soviet Union. The period of the late 1980s, a watershed era, was marked by the Soviet-American and Sino-Soviet détente, the June 4, 1989, tragedy, and the collapse of the Soviet Union.

RECOVERING FROM ESTRANGEMENT IN THE 1970S AND 1980S

In the early 1970s Sino-American relations were highly artificial. These two large countries had been isolated from each other for over two decades. Some predicted that because their economies were complementary, trade was bound to flourish once restrictions were removed. But from Henry Kissinger's secret visit of July 1971 until the establishment of full diplomatic relations in 1979 under the Carter administration, relations remained quite fragile. They were conducted through liaison offices in anticipation of the establishment of full diplomatic relations. But in the absence of full relations, trade was tenuous and carried out without the usual governmental trade, tax, and investment agreements that protect merchants. Nor was either side confident that the Taiwan issue could be circumvented and a mutually satisfactory formula found to allow full diplomatic relations. Under these circumstances, it was imperative for the White House to maintain strict control over the U.S.-China relationship in order to ensure its meticulous management.

Once full diplomatic relations had been established, however, the two sides acted upon a number of shared interests, which the previous twenty years of hostility had obscured. The Carter White House, deliberately seeking to give each governmental agency a stake in the new relationship, mandated the establishment of joint committees between the Department of Commerce, the Treasury, and the government's scientific agencies headed by the Office of Science and Technology Policy (OSTP) and counterpart agencies in China. In 1979–80 nearly every U.S. cabinet-level official, from the heads of the Departments of Agriculture and Interior to those of the DOD and the CIA, visited China, and a parallel stream of Chinese officials visited the United States, a practice that continued throughout the Reagan administration. Immersing the bureaucracies of the two countries in the relationship was a deliberate strategy on the part of top leaders to thicken the ties between them.

The Sino-American animosity of the 1950s and 1960s had created a fault line in the region as the United States and its allies confronted China and its North Korean and North Vietnamese allies. Washington had restrained its allies and partners from forging ties with the People's Republic, and once the United States had dropped the barrier, most were eager to rush to Beijing. But the full ramifications of this transformation took many years to become fully evident, and South Korea, Indonesia, and Singapore were the last of the major pro-American Asian states to establish normal diplomatic relations with Beijing. The Soviet withdrawal from Afghanistan, the cessation of Moscow's support of the Vietnamese occupation of Cambodia, and the settlement of the Sino-Russian border dispute were the last steps in Asia's strategic transformation. For the first time in a hundred years, the five major powers involved in the vast region—China, Japan, Russia, the United States, and India—were simultaneously engaged in constructive relations with one another. This new configuration enabled the five powers to interact in various regional forums, thereby creating such new arenas for Sino-American interchange as the Asia-Pacific Economic Cooperation

(APEC) forum and the annual meeting of the Association of Southeast Asian Nations (ASEAN) regional forum.

China's embrace of reform and opening policies in the 1980s, and the resulting economic upsurge, was of course a second essential ingredient in the expanded Sino-American relationship. New policies inviting foreign investment and establishing special economic zones permitted growth in trade and foreign investment and facilitated China's entry into the World Bank and the International Monetary Fund. Membership in hundreds of other international governmental and nongovernmental organizations followed, which in turn provided further opportunities for interaction. In this altered context, moreover, the American private sector was able to become a more important actor on the Chinese scene. By the end of the 1980s, Beijing was host to the offices of newspapers, television networks, foundations, and the educational establishment as well as American corporations. Broadened contact, however, which brought in new actors from within the U.S. government and the private sector, greatly increased the complexity of resolving issues involving China.

THE 1989–1990 WATERSHED

Even during the expansion of the 1980s, seemingly trivial matters escalated into major confrontations. An invitation to the Reagan inaugural extended to representatives of Taiwan had to be withdrawn because of Chinese protests. The defection of the aspiring Chinese tennis player Hu Na, who was granted political asylum in the United States, also created a brief furor. More serious was the acrimony over Washington's possible development and sale of a new jet fighter, dubbed the FX, to Taiwan, a dispute that ended only when the Reagan administration abandoned the effort and reached the August 1982 agreement with China on arms sales to Taiwan. Beijing complained about lingering constraints on technology transfer to China and American protectionist impulses. The 1980s also saw the beginnings of a chronic American trade deficit with China and the first serious American condemnations of human rights problems in China, especially concerning forced abortion, religious oppression, and the export of commodities produced with prison labor. At the time, however, the two countries' shared opposition to the Soviet Union outweighed these differences. And despite periodic crackdowns on dissent, the evident trend toward political liberalization and reform quieted U.S. critics of China's human rights record.

The Tiananmen tragedy and the collapse of the Soviet Union dramatically altered the context. Millions of Americans watched on live television as the People's Liberation Army shot its way into the center of Beijing, wresting control of Tiananmen Square from the peaceful demonstrators who had occupied it over the preceding weeks. That one action on June 4, 1989, transformed the image of China's leaders in the minds of most Americans from one of progressive political reformers to one of hardline throwbacks to the Maoist era, willing and able to act with great brutality toward their own people. China's leaders meanwhile attributed the crisis in part to the subversive effect of American ideas. In the months following the tragedy, a coalition of opponents to the China policy of the Nixon-Carter-Reagan-Bush administrations arose that would persist throughout the 1990s. Centered in the Congress, it brought together liberal Democrats and conservative Republicans.

The Tiananmen tragedy occurred in the midst of the Soviet-American and the Sino-Soviet rapprochement of the late 1980s, thereby removing the sense of urgency in both China and the United States about surmounting the crisis. Nonetheless, neither Deng Xiaoping nor George Bush wished to cast aside the progress of the previous decade. Each had a historical appreciation of the significance of the relationship for the welfare of his country. The two fought valiantly against their domestic critics to maintain as much interaction between the two nations as possible. Both had a personal stake in the matter, Bush having served as head of the Liaison Office in 1974–75 and Deng having been responsible for normalized relations. Neither wished to relinquish control of the relationship to domestic critics, who were opportunistically seizing on the crisis to weaken the authority of each nation's preeminent leader. Yet both emerged from the events of 1989 sobered and weakened in their command over the issue.

In the end, both were able to achieve at least their minimum objective. The relationship survived and even continued to expand, particularly in the economic sphere. Nonetheless, the searing events of 1989 created the atmosphere of constructive contentiousness that characterized Sino-American relations over the subsequent decade. Having weathered a storm, the U.S.-China relationship became more durable and realistic. At the same time, however, as a high-profile issue pervading Washington, it also became subject to the iron triangle of the congressional committees, government bureaus, and interest groups.

How Japanese Exports Altered U.S. Policymaking Toward Japan

After Japan's defeat in 1945, its economy was so weak that when it became a cold war ally in 1947, the United States was pleased to help with its economic revival. Since Japan had no natural resources and hardly enough food to feed its population, it developed an industrial strategy to encourage exports and thus to ensure that it could pay for much needed imports. Initially, Japan exported light industrial products, particularly textiles and consumer electronics. Then, as its economy grew and moved into heavy industry and higher technology, its exports began to include steel and, by the 1980s, automobiles, semiconductors, and computers. U.S. industries in various sectors were adversely affected and sometimes destroyed by competition from Japanese imports. Those industries and the geographical regions most threatened by this new source of competition naturally began to pursue their interests through pressure groups and Congress, thereby greatly expanding the actors shaping U.S. policy toward Japan.

By 1957, the United States had reached a bilateral agreement with Japan to limit the expansion of Japanese textile exports. As Japanese exports in other sectors increased, however, U.S. industry, labor unions, and regional politicians became heavily involved. In 1962 a Special Trade Representative office in the White House was established to take charge of trade policy, which had been handled by the U.S. State Department since the end of World War II. This transfer allowed politics to play a greater role in formulating trade policy. By 1967, for the first time, Japanese exports to the United States exceeded imports, and the trade imbalance would continue to grow. In 1971, in what would prove a crucial turning point, Congressman Wilbur Mills, head of the House Ways and Means Committee, almost succeeded in brokering a trade agreement with Japan. But in the end, it was President Nixon, pursuing a "southern strategy" for winning the 1972 election and well aware that U.S. textile manufacturing was based overwhelmingly in the South, who took a tough stand on textiles. The Japanese, learning from Mills's near success the importance of Congress in resolving the textile dispute, then expanded their contacts with Congress and sent more representatives to Washington, thus instigating a political battle between representatives of Japanese industry (and their allies, U.S. importers and retailers of Japanese goods) and representatives of U.S. industry.

The two "Nixon shocks" to Japan in 1971—the floating of the exchange rate and the decision to visit China without notifying Japan—reflected growing trade tensions. The yen appreciated after floating, temporarily slowing the increase in Japanese exports, but soon they rose again, and the affected U.S. industries mobilized political support. Over the long term, however, political support slowed but could not stop the flood of Japanese imports. By the 1970s and 1980s, fearing the rise of protectionism, those Japanese industries that sold to the U.S. market decided to build factories in the United States. They took advantage of opportunities in states interested in attracting industry, spreading their factories throughout the country. From this strong political base they hoped to counter the calls for protectionism stemming from U.S. industry and mediated through Washington.

In general, a combination of forces—Japanese interests and U.S. economists believing in free trade—discouraged U.S. protectionism. In particular, U.S. officials at the White House, the Department of State, and the DOD, who were concerned with national security, argued that in dealing with Japan, national security interests outweighed commercial interests. They therefore constrained protectionist pressures for fear of damaging U.S.-Japan security relations.

But in the 1970s and 1980s, as protectionist pressure grew stronger, automobile and semiconductor manufacturers, two powerful industries threatened by Japanese imports, mobilized support. As a result, the United States insisted on agreements with Japan that would protect these two sectors. The belief that Japan was "unfair" in keeping out foreign products while promoting its own exports helped U.S. industries mobilize against Japan to pressure it to open its markets and cut back exports in critical areas. Business leaders in these two industries also worked hard to improve quality control and increase production efficiency. Their success marked a turning point in U.S.-Japanese industrial competition. Until then, the Japanese had been gaining on the Americans in almost every sector they entered. When Japan's economic bubble burst and its economy stagnated in the early 1990s, U.S. businesses, especially in the high technology sector, surged ahead and interest in protectionism declined.

Although by the 1990s the U.S.-China trade imbalance was almost as large as the U.S.-Japan trade imbalance, political pressure against imports was never as strong toward China as toward Japan. In part this was because China was more open to imports than Japan had been at a comparable stage of development. But an even more important factor was that Japan was the pioneer exporter, and that many of China's exports to the United States were not at the expense of U.S. manufacturers. Because Chinese exports to the United States replaced exports from Japan and the four little dragons and did not directly clash with U.S. manufacturers, political battles with the United States over trade issues did not develop. Yet where Japan's military alliance with the United States helped keep other issues, including trade disputes, under control, the United States and China had no such alliance to contain the problems that arose after 1989. And Japan, as a democracy, was not a target for criticism by human rights groups.

Inside the Sausage Factory: U.S.-China Policy in the New Era

By the late 1980s, the diverse and contending interests at stake between the United States and China had become so extensive that the White House, even with an assertive president, could no longer fully manage China policy. Once U.S.-China relations deepened, the U.S. policymaking process became—and is likely to remain—an open system with many actors, a multiplicity of access points, and myriad ways of affecting outcomes.

THE GOVERNMENT AGENCIES

Each of the four dimensions of the U.S.-China relationship—strategic, economic, human rights, and Taiwan—falls within the jurisdiction of several different agencies in the executive branch and at least four different congressional committees. In such an institutional setting, problems of coordination and consistency are endemic. The strategic dimension is largely the responsibility of the National Security Council (NSC), the State Department, and DOD, with the Foreign Relations, Armed Services, and Appropriations committees in the Senate and the International Relations, International Security, and Appropriations committees in the House playing the major congressional roles. The economic dimension falls primarily to the White House National Economic Council, the United States Special Trade Representative, the Treasury Department, and the Commerce Department (with the involvement of DOD on matters of technology transfer), while the Senate Finance Committee, the House Ways and Means Committee, and the relevant appropriations subcommittees monitor the situation from a congressional perspective. The third dimension, human rights and governance, falls primarily in the domain of the State Department and the NSC; after the Tiananmen incident, a number of congressional members, including

Nancy Pelosi, Christopher Smith, Jesse Helms, and Benjamin Gilman, voiced special concern in this area. For the fourth, the Taiwan issue, the government has funded the legally private American Institute on Taiwan (AIT), which manages America's unofficial relations with the island. But the initiative resides to a considerable extent with the Congress through its vigilant monitoring of the executive branch's implementation of the Taiwan Relations Act of 1979 and through its members' more intimate contact with Taiwan, which top administration officials are permitted to enjoy. (Members of Congress can travel to Taiwan without restraint, whereas the executive branch is constrained by agreements between the U.S. government and Beijing made at the time of normalization and after.)

The congressional committees acquire leverage through their authority to draft and initiate laws, hold hearings, authorize expenditures, appropriate funds, and, in the case of the Senate, approve presidential appointments. Iron triangles operate in this setting. Government agencies in the executive branch must first secure authorization for their programs from the congressional committees that oversee their activities and then secure appropriations from an entirely different set of committees. Each government agency is beholden to four separate committees—two in the House and two in the Senate. Government agencies recognize that they cannot rely solely on the White House to do battle with the four committees on their behalf; these bureaucracies must therefore cultivate their own separate support within the committees that control their destiny. In this process it is often very helpful to enlist the support of think tanks and interest groups that have their own intimate connections with the committees. Members of Congress may be particularly responsive to a select number of these think tanks and lobbyists, on whom they depend for campaign financing and headline-producing policy initiatives. When interagency differences arise, it is because various parts of the bureaucracy are linked to different iron triangles.

Even within the same government agency, the policy process can be fragmented and contentious unless the head of the agency plays a strong role. In most instances, moreover, the leader of any agency faces choices in defining the leadership role he or she wishes to play. Within the NSC system, for example, the head of the NSC staff is at the same time the president's national security adviser, and can fulfill the responsibilities of these dual roles in various ways. He can give primary emphasis to his role as the president's personal foreign policy adviser, keeping the staff and even the departments somewhat at arm's length concerning the advice he offers. Under such circumstances, the president's adviser for national security affairs becomes somewhat secretive but quite powerful in those areas in which he enjoys the president's confidence. He becomes the agent through whom the president conveys and enforces his will, as was the case with Henry Kissinger. Or the national security adviser can instead give primary emphasis to his role as the head of the National Security Council, the interagency body through which national security policy is coordinated. Now he becomes a team player seeking to build consensus among the heads of the chief national security agencies (primarily State, Defense, Treasury, and the CIA). Interagency differences are taken to the president for resolution or, on those matters in which the president has a firm opinion, the adviser ensures that the president's team understands the policy. Brent Scowcroft envisioned his responsibilities in this fashion. Or, finally, the national security adviser can emphasize his role as a political adviser, focusing less on the foreign policy implications of his advice and more on its domestic political implications. Washington insiders observed that Sandy Berger, the security adviser during Clinton's second term, paid particular attention to the domestic political ramifications of the foreign policy choices confronting the president.

As in other government agencies, the NSC staff consists of an inner core, most of whose offices are in the White House, and about fifty assistants (the number varies from administration to administration and tends to grow throughout each administration), grouped into several regional and functional clusters, who work next door, in the Old Executive Office Building (Old EOB). China policy falls within the East Asian cluster, but other clusters that deal with, for example, intelligence, human rights, or defense also become involved in China policy. These clusters are supposed to assist the president and the national security adviser to initiate, coordinate, and implement policy throughout the executive branch. They represent the White House in interagency meetings and in drafting documents. Sometimes the national security adviser relies very heavily on his inner staff but does not keep the clusters in the Old EOB well informed. Or the adviser relies primarily on his functional specialists—for example, the human rights adviser—but does not consult his China assistant. Such was the case during much of the first Clinton administration, when the NSC staff person for China could not effectively fulfill his responsibility of bringing coherence to China policy. In 1993, for example, an inner staff person deeply concerned with human rights issues was intimately involved during the last stages of drafting a speech for National Security Advisor Anthony Lake, while the China staff person was not. Unfortunately, no one noticed that the speech, which placed China in the category of "rogue" states, was to be delivered the day before an important meeting between Lake and the Chinese ambassador intended to assure him of the administration's desire for a constructive relationship.

Similar situations exist throughout the executive branch. The officials responsible for bringing coherence to China policy in a particular department are usually located two to three levels below the top and must compete with the functional specialists and the inner aides of the secretary in order to achieve a coordinated view even within their own building. The Congress and the interested public hold the assistant secretary of the East Asian Bureau in the State Department and the deputy secretary for East Asian affairs within International Security Affairs at DOD responsible for China policy in their departments. In reality, they are engaged in continual battles to protect their turf. And within the Pentagon, of course, there are the complexities of relations between the Office of the Secretary of Defense (OSD) and the civilian agencies under him on the one hand, and on the other, the uniformed Joint Chiefs of Staff (JCS) and the three armed services under its command, each of which reports to OSD but also has its own channels to the congressional committees and the White House.

The various functional and regional agencies that formulate and implement policy toward China usually have responsibility for policy toward other countries as well. They do not evaluate the policy recommendations they make to their superiors or determine their behavior toward China in isolation from the U.S. posture in other parts of the world. The functional agencies, which focus on issues such as human rights, technology control, trade, and arms control, are reluctant to make exceptions for China out of concern that dangerous precedents could undermine broader global or regional policies. Similarly, when considering China policy, bureaus with regional responsibilities, such as the East Asia shops at the NSC, State, and DOD, are particularly sensitive to the reactions of their Japanese, South Korean, Taiwanese, and Southeast Asian counterparts. NSC, State, and DOD East Asian bureaus have a somewhat different set of counterpart agencies in the region, however, which partially explains their differing assessments of regional reactions to China policy initiatives.

THINK TANKS AND INTEREST GROUPS

As already noted, think tanks and interest groups have clustered around
each of the four dimensions of China policy. Law firms and public relations
firms have been hired to monitor and influence congressional and executive
branch activities. Of course, a Taiwan lobby has long been active on the
American scene, but even on the Taiwan side groups seeking to bring ideas
and money to bear have proliferated. Not only did Taiwan's ruling Kuomin-
tang expand its efforts, but after 1987, when the island began to permit opposition parties, a new opposition party, the Democrat Progressive Party
(DPP), also entered the fray. Supporters of the Dalai Lama and the Tibetan
government-in-exile have established a well-funded and well-connected operation in Washington. Meanwhile the business community, acting through
such long-established associations as the National Association of Manufacturers, the Business Roundtable, and the United States Chamber of Commerce and through more specialized associations such as the Business Software Alliance and the Motion Picture Association, has become quite active
on China issues. Christian fundamentalists, pro-life activists, and labor
unions have become assertive as well, and on China policy these interest
groups have the capacity to bring together members of Congress who rarely
cooperate on other issues.

Once an interest group or think tank takes root and identifies a reliable
constituency or base of support, it can become self-sustaining, adjusting its
cause to fit new situations. Thus, with the collapse of the Soviet Union and
the end of apartheid in South Africa, many human rights groups turned
their attention to China. Likewise, arms control groups and strategic think
tanks that had concentrated on the Soviet Union during the cold war found
in China a possible substitute. Their Washington-based employees know
how to perpetuate themselves through publicity, sophisticated appeals for
additional funds, and usefulness to the executive and congressional branches.
They can be important sources of information and policy innovation. They
can even acquire government funding directly or place their adherents on
congressional staffs or in government agencies. Radio Free Asia, the Voice of
America, and the National Endowment for Democracy, for example, are all
government-funded agencies that provide employment opportunities for
those interested in advancing human rights in China.

To some observers, interest group politics precludes the formation of
a foreign policy rooted in an overarching concept of American interests.

Inviting and encouraging foreign countries to participate in the Washington game while abiding by American laws—as Taiwan separatists, Tibetan exiles, Chinese dissidents, and Hong Kong democrats have done—subordinates American interests to foreign interests. But to other observers, interest group politics and the pluralism it embodies not only are central to the system and have been so since its inception, but also help to explain the strength of the United States. The open and intense clash of ideas and economic interests produces sounder, more innovative policy. Through the tortuous and time-consuming processes of consultation and negotiation, the executive and congressional branches of government, monitored by the judicial branch to ensure that the rules conform to the constitution, arbitrate and reconcile competing interests. As with sausage, the manufacturing process is not attractive, but the product generally has popular appeal. And those who find the output distasteful have ample opportunity to alter the outcome in the next round of the ongoing struggle.

THE MEDIA AND PUBLIC OPINION

The clash of interests and the competition among the White House and the iron triangles in shaping China policy occur against a background of incessant media coverage of China and U.S. China policy. The role of the media and media coverage have changed considerably since the early 1970s, when China was unknown territory and pre-Watergate media were not yet affected by the transformation in information technologies. The stationing of American journalists in China, the advent of investigative journalism, the arrival of CNN and the twenty-four-hour news cycle, and the proliferation of television news channels and Web-based news media have simultaneously improved and debased the quality and quantity of information that is available to the public. Interested publics enjoy a range of sources and a depth of reporting that was unimaginable only twenty years ago. But at the same time, rumors and distortions can spread unchecked with lightning speed and, once implanted in the popular mind, are difficult to eradicate.

The Chinese government incessantly complains that the American media have provided a biased and negative picture of China by focusing on human rights violations while neglecting the enormous progress of the past twenty years. Americans respond that the journalistic traditions of the United States emphasize problems to be remedied rather than accomplishments; the job of journalism is to serve as critic. Further, journalists based in Beijing tend to grow cynical and weary of the regime under the restrictions and surveillance to which they find themselves subjected. Indeed, it could be argued that the American media are more accurate in their portrayals of China and Sino-American relations than the Chinese media.

Two serious media deficiencies, however, do merit mention. One is the erosion in foreign news coverage in general and in China coverage in particular. None of the three major networks (CBS, ABC, and NBC) has retained a permanent bureau in Beijing, and their worldwide coverage has shrunk. The amount of time Dan Rather (CBS), Peter Jennings (ABC), and Tom Brokaw (NBC) devote to foreign news has steadily dropped. A comparison of the daily *London Financial Times* with the *New York Times*, or the weekly *Economist* with *Newsweek* or *Time* reveals the provincialism of even the leading American print media. To the extent that media coverage affects Washington, the lack of interest and sophistication can be attributed in part to the inadequate information the media provide.

At the same time, the media are also vulnerable to manipulation by the White House and the iron triangles. In 1998–99, the *Washington Times* and, to a lesser extent, the *New York Times* received misleading scoops on the progress of the House of Representatives Cox committee investigation into allegations of Chinese espionage in the United States. Clearly, sympathetic journalists at those papers were the beneficiaries or the victims (depending on one's perspective) of leaks from congressional staff members and the intelligence community. The contrast between the coverage of the story in the *Washington Post* and in the *Los Angeles Times* was striking. Hints of behind-the-scenes activities were revealed when the *New York Times* assigned another journalist to the story: the tone of the reporting immediately changed from one of wholehearted acceptance to one of skepticism about the more lurid dimensions of the Cox committee report.

There can be no doubt that the major networks, CNN, and the print media—the titles mentioned above plus the *Wall Street Journal*—play a major role in shaping the daily agenda of Washington bureaucrats. A story in any of these media prompts government press spokespersons to demand that officials from the relevant agency prepare answers to hypothetical questions that might be posed at the daily briefings. Top officials are sometimes influenced as much by media coverage of a particular development as by the internal reports they receive. Certainly media coverage of the events of 1989 was crucial in shaping government and public reactions.

Yet when it comes to shaping public opinion, it is not clear that media coverage of China—whether positive or negative, sophisticated or superficial—has much effect on the views of the average American. All the opinion polls reveal that the American public is uninterested in foreign affairs and rather ignorant about foreign policy. Although China policy is made inside the Beltway, the money that finances the iron triangles and the interest groups comes from the outside. The paradox is not easily explained.

PRESIDENTIAL ELECTIONS AND THE PRESIDENT'S FIRST TERM

China policy can become an issue in presidential elections: in 1952, for example, Republicans charged that the Democrats had lost China and blundered into a war with China in Korea; in the 1960 election, John Kennedy and Richard Nixon disagreed over U.S. defense of Quemoy and Matsu; in 1980, Ronald Reagan criticized Jimmy Carter for abandoning Taiwan; and in 1992, Bill Clinton condemned George Bush's alleged coddling of China's brutal leaders. As these examples reveal, turning China into an election issue is not a post-1972 phenomenon; it has occurred whenever a candidate thinks he can score a tactical advantage over his opponent. In all these instances, the candidate was using the issue to consolidate his political base and differentiate himself from his opponent.

Opportunism may prompt the initial tactical decision, but the consequences are long-standing. In each of the above instances, the winner's approach to China was constrained by his campaign legacy. Moreover, the candidate's foreign policy advisers frequently ended up in influential positions in the administration. Although the candidate may have accepted their foreign policy campaign recommendations on tactical grounds in consultation with his political advisers, the foreign policy advisers were usually true believers in the frequently erroneous advice they offered.

Once the successful candidate takes office, however, he must give greater weight to the operation of national policy. Because China is an important nation whose cooperation is necessary for resolving international issues, even if the candidate criticized the previous administration's handling of China and China itself, the newly elected president must moderate some of his views. Since he faces some of the same problems as his predecessor and many of the specialists in the government remain the same, it is likely that on some crucial issues his actions will be more like those of his predecessor than appeared likely during the campaign. Candidate Kennedy talked of not defending Quemoy and Matsu, but Taiwan did not need to yield on these islands after he came into office. Candidate Jimmy Carter talked of pulling troops out of Korea, but President Carter kept them there. Candidate Ronald Reagan talked of being much tougher with mainland China on the Taiwan issue, but President Reagan developed good relations with Deng Xiaoping. Candidate Clinton talked of being tough on the butchers of Beijing, but by May 1994, after sixteen months in office, he had already agreed to continue the Most Favored Nation treatment of Beijing and to delink that issue from human rights. In both the Reagan and the Clinton presidencies, however, it took almost two years to abandon the campaign rhetoric, make adjustments in the foreign policy team, and adopt a more practical approach. In both cases the lessons were costly.

The Structure of U.S. Policymaking Toward Japan

The U.S.-Japan relationship is even broader and deeper than the U.S.-China relationship, but the political issues are overwhelmingly economic. Within the United States, political support for the security relationship with Japan has generally been sufficient to allow bureaucrat specialists in the White House and in the Departments of Defense and State to manage security issues. Congressional committees are involved but play a lesser role. The relationship between Japanese and U.S. bureaucrats over defense issues is generally nonadversarial.

Because trade and investment issues have been highly controversial, Congress and the U.S. Special Trade Representative as well as bureaucrats dealing with trade issues—particularly those in the Departments of Commerce, Agriculture, and Transportation—tend to have adversarial relationships with their Japanese counterparts. In other fields, relationships between bureaucrats tend to be less adversarial. The many deep relationships between local government and local citizens' groups in the United States and their Japanese counterparts help to strengthen the overall relationship between the two countries even though they have little impact on daily policy issues.

Living with Complexity

The relationships between the United States and China and between the United States and Japan have become multidimensional and multilayered. Policymaking and policy implementation toward both countries are deeply immersed in the domestic political system, which is open but fragmented. At the international, regional, and national levels, the private sector can seek to influence government policies in various arenas, and disgruntled actors inside and outside the U.S. government have ample opportunity to voice their grievances to sympathetic audiences. The resulting policies lack coherence, consistency, and clarity. Only the president commands the resources to bring unity to U.S. policy toward China and Japan, but his ability to command public attention and support and to impose discipline upon the executive branch and the Congress is limited. In addition, before he attempts to undertake such a task, he must be confident in his purpose and in his expectation that foreign allies will support his efforts. When the president has difficulty providing this unifying purpose, initiatives are likely to remain enmeshed within the departments, their subordinate bureaus, and the iron triangles. This complex process, which emerged during the 1970s and 1980s as U.S. relations with both Japan and China expanded, continued into the 1990s. At the beginning of a new century, there is no indication that this process is likely to end soon.

CHAPTER TWO

Chinese Politics and Asia-Pacific Policy

Zhang Baijia

From the late 1960s to the early 1990s, China experienced a fundamental change, turning from being a closed country into being an open one. Although such a transformation can be examined from without or from within, here I will focus on the changing influence of China's domestic policy on its foreign policy during this historic transitional period.

This period of critical change encompasses three phases: (1) late 1960s–early 1970s, (2) late 1970s–early 1980s, and (3) late 1980s–early 1990s. All three are significant, whether viewed from the perspective of China's internal development or from that of its external, diplomatic development. This essay compares these three phases at two levels, the microlevel and the macrolevel. At the microlevel, I will consider the influence of domestic political and economic factors on foreign policy during each phase; at the macrolevel, I will discuss the mutual interactions between these domestic factors and foreign policy and between China and the altered external environment.

The Separation of Foreign Policy from Domestic Policy

From the late 1960s to the early 1970s, China's foreign policy underwent tremendous changes that were unanticipated by the Chinese as well as by other countries. The direct cause was external and led to a new foreign policy that was neither consistent with nor coordinated with the domestic policies of the time. In the early stages of the cultural revolution, which began in June 1966 and ended in October 1976, China attempted to carry forward a "world revolution," adopting slogans such as "Down with imperialists, revisionists, and reactionaries." This ultraleft approach to foreign policy fit well with the period's ultraleft domestic policy. These domestic policies led to internal chaos and disaster, yet they were not seriously challenged within China, where Mao Zedong's personal cult was at its height. But its ultraleft foreign policy isolated China diplomatically and was difficult to maintain. The Sino-Soviet border clash in 1969 and later, the Soviet nuclear threat, forced Chinese leaders to pay greater attention to national security. They came to view the Soviet Union not as a socialist country but as a socio-imperialist country and thus a highly dangerous enemy.

In 1968 Mao Zedong and Zhou Enlai began to make adjustments in China's foreign policy. Initially, since the cultural revolution had virtually suspended ordinary diplomatic relations, they focused on eliminating the more extreme aspects of Chinese diplomacy. The Sino-Soviet border conflict of 1969, however, forced a change in their perspective, and they enlarged the scope of this adjustment. Then, in a further development, an unexpected opportunity presented itself: the United States, in an attempt to revise its own policy toward China, introduced the possibility of more fundamental change. Following his election as president, Richard Nixon opened relations with China as a way to extricate the United States from its difficulties in resolving the Vietnam War and strengthen its strategic position in checking Soviet expansion.

To deal with their particular national security considerations, both China and the United States needed to bring their twenty-year confrontation to an end. In the spring of 1971, "Ping-pong diplomacy" launched the process of rapprochement. In July, after Henry Kissinger's preliminary visit to China, the two sides reached an agreement and announced President Nixon's forthcoming China trip. In February 1972, at the invitation of Zhou Enlai, Nixon visited Beijing. Later, the two sides published the Sino-American joint communiqué at Shanghai, laying the foundation for further improvement and development of relations between the two countries.

These dramatic changes in Sino-American relations set off a chain reaction. In October 1971, the Twenty-sixth Assembly of the United Nations passed a resolution restoring China's seat in the UN. China soon established diplomatic relations with more than forty Asian, African, and Latin American countries as well as all the major Western European countries. In varying degrees, relations between China and the Eastern European countries also improved. Shocked by the achievement of Sino-American reconciliation, Japan also reexamined its China policy. In 1972, Japanese premier Tanaka Kakuei decided to complete the normalization of Sino-Japanese diplomatic relations. At Premier Zhou Enlai's invitation, he visited China for ten days at the end of September, establishing official diplomatic relations between the two countries.

What role did domestic factors in China play in these fundamental foreign policy changes? Since the founding of the new China in 1949, Chinese leaders had repeatedly expressed their wish to establish normal diplomatic relations with the United States, other Western countries, and Japan. But before the cultural revolution, no such opportunity had ever presented itself, and during the cultural revolution, there were no political or economic issues that seemed likely to push such a major foreign policy change forward. Although rapprochement with the United States ultimately strengthened the authority and reputation of Mao Zedong within China, domestic politics did not require such a dramatic alteration in foreign policy. On the contrary, Mao was taking a political risk. There is evidence that neither his designated successor, Lin Biao, nor his wife, Jiang Qing, who was then at the peak of her power, was favorably disposed toward his policy changes, although they did not openly oppose them. At the same time, although changes in diplomatic relations were beyond their expectations, the masses and the cadres regarded them with relative calm. Most accepted the arguments offered by the Party Central Committee: Nixon's visit was another great victory for "Chairman Mao's diplomatic line" and a demonstration of "the failure of American policy to contain and isolate China." Only a few expressed doubts. They could not understand how China, which had believed so strongly in its duty to "fight against imperialism and revisionism," could reconcile itself with the leader of the imperialist camp. Yet everyone enjoyed the new, less threatening political atmosphere. After all, China now had one less enemy.

Economic considerations, meanwhile, were completely subordinated to politics. There is no evidence to suggest that Mao Zedong, who had held the banner of self-reliance high, sought to improve Sino-American relations in order to solve the serious economic problems caused by the cultural revolution. In May 1971, just before Kissinger's visit, as China's Politburo considered possible items to place on the Sino-American agenda, it decided not to raise trade issues unless the Americans did so. Politburo members concluded that such topics could be discussed only after the core issue, U.S. troop withdrawal from Taiwan, had been resolved.[1]

During this period, Mao Zedong's absolute authority and the highly centralized system of rule remained critical factors on the domestic scene. Seizing the opportunity offered by the changing international situation, Mao Zedong personally initiated the Sino-American normalization process. Although working with capitalists was absolutely contrary to the orientation of the cultural revolution, the unchallengeable authority of Mao Zedong, which had been heightened by the cultural revolution, and his highly centralized rule ensured a smooth foreign policy transition.

The sudden diplomatic policy shift of the early 1970s did not surprise the general public. Under a highly centralized system, the pressure of public opinion, whether stemming from the economic situation or from domestic political factors such as the opinions of leading groups, constituencies, and bureaucracies, is not decisive. The influence of economic and political factors is also mediated to a large degree by the subjective judgment and will of the preeminent leader, who can choose to make use of these factors to enforce his foreign policy or simply ignore them. During the cultural revolution, the Chinese people held strong anti-Soviet and anti-American sentiments. By strengthening anti-Soviet feeling and weakening anti-American feeling, Mao succeeded in achieving a peaceful transformation in China's foreign policy. But not all domestic factors are flexible and amenable, even to the will of the preeminent leader. On the question of territorial integrity and sovereignty, Chinese leaders have been resolute and cautious about showing any weakness. The talks between Mao Zedong, Nixon, and Kissinger in the early 1970s, which have recently been made public,[2] show that Sino-American reconciliation was achieved because of U.S. concessions on the Taiwan problem, although there were also tactical compromises on the Chinese side.

These foreign policy developments produced profound domestic consequences. By departing so dramatically from the ideology of the time, they undermined the unifying integrity underlying a broad range of policies.[3] Separating foreign policy from ideology set a precedent that opened the way for fundamental domestic policy changes. The radical line of the cultural revolution was first challenged by Mao Zedong's own foreign-policy formulations and then further weakened by the Lin Biao affair, which became public between 1971 and 1973. Although the leftist line dominated China until Mao Zedong's death, these changes rendered it increasingly ineffective, and after Mao's death it became even more vulnerable.

The successful rapprochement with the United States, a fundamental break in the pattern of Chinese foreign relations since 1949, propelled Chinese diplomacy into a period of great historical significance. But the initial stage of this new policy was achieved before the other, fundamental domestic political changes that would make deepening relations with other countries possible. Despite its limited trade and diplomatic contacts, with the non-aligned Third World in the 1950s and with the West before 1970, China was restricted to half of the world stage—the socialist half. Since the mid-1970s, however, Chinese diplomacy has been active on the entire international stage. More important, since that time, overall relations between China and the rest of the world have experienced a dramatic transformation. From a historical perspective, in the first half of the twentieth century the main task of Chinese diplomacy was to restore China's independence and territorial integrity; in the second half, it was to determine how to deal with the contemporary world as a fully independent state.

In the bipolar world of U.S.-Soviet confrontation that emerged after World War II, the path taken by the new, post-1949 China has been a tortuous one. In the early years, the People's Republic of China, like the Soviet Union, held that the socialist and capitalist systems could coexist for a period of time, but after a period of struggle, the socialist system would replace the capitalist system. Later, however, China fought against the Soviet Union and the United States, the two dominant powers, to challenge the existing world order. In the early 1970s, following the normalization of Sino-American relations, China began the process of merging into the modern world system. It became a member of the UN and established diplomatic relations with most of the world's countries; it also broadened its foreign economic relations, which produced dramatic increases in its external trade.[4] Had there been no fundamental change in China's relations with the rest of the world, its smooth and rapid pursuit of "reform and opening" would have been unimaginable, even after the end of the cultural revolution.

Adjustment of Diplomatic Policies to Promote "Reform and Opening"

During the period of "reform and opening," which started in the late 1970s, adjustments to China's foreign policy became obvious by 1982; they had actually begun in 1978 and were basically complete by 1985. In contrast to the foreign policy changes of the late 1960s and the early 1970s, this time domestic factors were the crucial considerations.

The cultural revolution ended in the autumn of 1976, after the death of Mao Zedong and the arrest of the Gang of Four. Over the next two years indications that significant political and economic changes were under consideration increased, but ideological and political differences had yet to be resolved. In July 1977, Deng Xiaoping reemerged on the political stage. Then, during the spring of 1978, there was widespread public discussion of the "criterion of truth" and questioning of the correctness of the decisions made by Mao in his last years, especially his launching of the cultural revolution. At the same time, the Communist Party announced that the strategic goals of the "four modernizations" should be extended in scope and the timetable speeded up. That summer the State Council convened a conference, which lasted for two months, to discuss ideological guidelines, in particular how to assist efforts to accelerate economic development. The first cries for reform and opening came from economic circles.

To realize this new goal of accelerated economic development, Chinese leaders went abroad in greater numbers and with greater urgency. Making contacts with the outside world and opening China up became the new fashion. In 1978 alone, twenty-one delegations, led by thirteen vice premiers and vice chairmen of the People's Congress, traveled abroad, visiting fifty-one countries. Deng Xiaoping himself visited eight countries.[5] It was said that this was the first high tide of China's "opening its eyes to look at the world." Once they had done so, Chinese leaders came to believe that China's economic development lagged at least fifteen to twenty years behind that of capitalist countries, but they also perceived a favorable opportunity for development. In the late 1970s many Western economies were experiencing "stagflation." The developed countries in the West not only wanted to expand trade with China, they also wanted to give concessional loans to China and even to invest in China. Chinese leaders, returning from their travels abroad, all emphasized that China should grab hold of these emerging opportunities, absorbing and making use of foreign technology, equipment, capital, and managerial experience to expedite its economic development.[6]

Pressure to speed up economic reconstruction and carry out a policy of reform and opening produced a new political line that supported the opening. After the cultural revolution, the Central Committee of the Chinese

Communist Party (CCP), headed by Hua Guofeng (1976–78), still upheld the political line, formulated by Mao Zedong, of "class struggle as the key link." But if such a political line were to continue, it would be almost impossible to gain wholehearted cooperation either from a cross-section of people at home (there were no real capitalists at that time) or from capitalists abroad, whose help was needed to achieve rapid economic progress. Thus, dropping "class struggle as the key link" and reorienting the party and the state to a socialist modernization program became China's core political task after 1978. Recent research indicates that key high-level leaders of the CCP undertook this policy revision between late September and early October 1978.[7] As is well known, it became official at the CCP Central Committee's Working Conference and at the Third Plenary Session of the Eleventh Central Committee in December.[8]

On the eve of these political and economic reforms, Deng Xiaoping made two important foreign policy decisions: to sign the Sino-Japanese Treaty of Peace and Friendship and to establish formal Sino-American relations. These two steps had in fact been approved as early as 1972, but their implementation was delayed due to domestic political uncertainties on the one hand, and to Japan's concerns about the treaty and U.S. concerns about the Taiwan issue on the other. It was not until 1978 that the time was ripe for a solution. In May, during a visit to China, Zbigniew Brzezinski conveyed to Deng Xiaoping the clear message that President Jimmy Carter had decided to accept China's three conditions for the establishment of diplomatic relations between the two countries: severing diplomatic relations with Taiwan, ending the U.S.-Taiwan defense treaty, and withdrawing American troops from Taiwan. In July, talks on the Sino-Japanese peace and friendship treaty, which had been suspended for over three years, resumed.

But some obstacles remained. Despite China's opposition, the United States insisted on continuing to sell weapons to Taiwan after the normalization of relations with China. The United States also sought to sign the SALT II Treaty with the Soviet Union, and Soviet leader Leonid Brezhnev was scheduled to visit Washington. If China and the United States could not reach an agreement, the establishment of diplomatic relations would once again be delayed. In addition, the dispute between China and Japan over the Diaoyu Islands had not yet been resolved, further complicating their treaty discussions.

Deng Xiaoping solved the problem by first signing the treaty with Japan. When the Japanese foreign minister visited China, Deng told him that the problem of the Diaoyu Islands could be shelved for twenty or thirty years, and that China would not take action before that time.[9] On the same day, both sides agreed to the Sino-Japanese Treaty of Peace and Friendship. Deng Xiaoping's visit to Japan in October 1978 to participate in the treaty ceremony marked the first time a high-level Chinese leader had visited Japan since World War II.

Negotiations between China and the United States on establishing diplomatic relations were delayed until the last moment because the issue of U.S. arms sales to Taiwan could not be resolved. At 4 P.M. on December 15, 1978, Deng Xiaoping received Ambassador Leonard Woodcock. The Central Working Conference had just ended, and only eighteen hours remained before the two nations were scheduled to announce the successful establishment of diplomatic relations. As Deng once again pointed out to the U.S. envoy, "After the establishment of diplomatic relations between China and America, it is hoped that the U.S. government will cautiously cope with the problem of Taiwan. In your relations, do not do anything that would affect the effort made by China to solve the Taiwan problem in the most reasonable way. If the United States continues to sell weapons to Taiwan, in the long run it will place obstacles in the way of a peaceful return of Taiwan to the motherland. America could exert some effort to realize the peaceful unification of China, and it should at least do nothing to oppose it."[10] Finally, Deng Xiaoping agreed to realize the normalization of relations between the two countries "as planned." Three days later, the Third Plenary Session of the Chinese Communist Party began. Fifteen days after that, official diplomatic relations between China and the United States were established.

The foreign policy decision-making process during this period represented a clear change from that of the Mao-Zhou era. Soon after he was restored to power, Deng Xiaoping took control of foreign affairs by playing the dual role of decision maker and implementer. Although he enjoyed high prestige within the Party, Deng did not have Mao's absolute authority. Not being Party chairman also placed restraints on him as he faced arguments from other senior comrades, and thus he had to take pains to persuade his colleagues to accept his proposals. Moreover, as paramount leader but without a brilliant assistant like Zhou Enlai, Deng also had to implement his own policies. He usually took part in key negotiations and rapped the gavel himself.

Deng Xiaoping decided to shelve the issue of the Diaoyu Islands and of arms sales to Taiwan out of consideration for domestic affairs as well as current and long-term foreign policy. Domestically, he wanted to ensure a smooth transition from "class struggle" to the "four modernizations" in the Party's political line and to provide a more stable and more favorable international environment for subsequent economic reform. During the Central Working Conference that ended in mid-December 1978, Deng explained to intimates that the establishment of Sino-American relations was intended to serve "the overall situation."[11] According to the major points of his talk, "overall situation" refers to the connection between the strategic considerations in the normalization of Sino-American relations and the fundamental shift in priorities within China. Nearly all important speeches, including those delivered at the Central Working Conference and the Third Plenum, had mentioned one important aspect of this external environment, namely, that "most countries in the world . . . would like to see a powerful China."[12] This conclusion, based on information provided by the Americans, was soon passed to high-level cadres to justify the party center's new political line and new policy. One Chinese scholar commenting on the history of this period sees the normalization of Sino-American relations as a "clever move" in "the big chess game" of China's political transformation.[13]

Along with the change in the party's political line and the introduction of economic "reform and opening" from the late 1970s to the mid-1980s, China also made overall adjustments in its diplomacy. After the establishment of Sino-American relations, China for a while strengthened its "one line" strategy of uniting with the United States to oppose the Soviet Union. But in 1982, abandoning this strategy, it began to keep a certain distance from the United States and to pursue a more balanced approach to foreign relations. Through a series of diplomatic initiatives, China improved relations with its neighbors, strengthening its political and economic cooperation with the countries of the Third World, gradually moving toward normalizing its relations with the Soviet Union, and steadily improving Sino-American relations. It also continued to develop political and economic relations with Western countries and Eastern European countries. Moreover, China actively promoted multilateral diplomacy, increasing its involvement with the

UN and participating in projects to encourage international economic development and to solve regional conflicts.

Underlying these policy shifts was a change in the guiding principles of Chinese foreign policy. China continued to take maintaining national independence and sovereignty, ensuring security, and preserving the socialist system as the main tasks of diplomacy. It continued to stress the importance of reunification of separated areas with the mainland. It still practiced non-alignment and fought against hegemony. But the major new principle, to support the task of national economic development, represented a profound change. To support its economic goals, China worked to create a peaceful international environment and establish good relations with potential economic partners. Furthermore, it dealt with various countries differently, according to specific needs, no longer using ideology as a criterion to distinguish friends from enemies, or to unite with some while attacking others.

China not only changed its guiding principles, it also gained a new perspective in identifying significant international problems and in analyzing its own relations with the world. First, considering the changes in the international situation in the early 1980s, especially the relaxation in U.S.-Soviet tensions, China gradually abandoned its earlier assumption that a large-scale world war was inevitable. Chinese leaders came to believe that the forces for peace exceeded those for war and that peace and development were now the major global trends. Second, China acknowledged that the existing world was diverse and complex, that countries had different political systems, historical-cultural backgrounds, religions, and types of economic development. This led to complex patterns of contradiction and mutual dependence in various parts of the world. Among some countries, especially the big powers, common interests played a part in a number of significant problems. Countries needed to cooperate, and it was possible for them to do so. Third, China clarified the scope of one continuing principle: "Independence does not mean isolation, self-reliance does not mean blind opposition to anything foreign."[14] China wanted the advanced science and technology and the managerial skills it encountered abroad, and it also wanted to expand its economic cooperation with all the countries of the world.

The diplomatic adjustments that began in the late 1970s were obviously promoted by domestic factors. They resulted not only from the practical need to adapt China's political and economic policies to changing conditions, but also from continuous reflection on historical experience. Although the policy changes during this period were not as dramatic or wide-ranging as the opening to the West in the early 1970s, they were, nevertheless, as fundamental. The change in the guiding principles of China's foreign policy and the new view of significant international questions and China's relations with the world indicated that China had bid a firm farewell to its past idealistic "revolutionary diplomacy" and was moving toward the existing international system. China recognized that to play an important role in international affairs and finally solve the problem of unification, the paramount task was "to do our own work well."[15]

Maintaining Foreign Policy Continuity in a Turbulent World

A well-known saying suggests that "the diplomacy of China changes every ten years."[16] According to this "rule," some drastic change should have taken place between the late 1980s and the early 1990s. This period saw both political and economic instability. After the June 4, 1989, incident (known in the West as the Tiananmen incident), the United States and other Western countries imposed sanctions on China. Dramatic changes in Eastern Europe and the dissolution of the Soviet Union brought about the greatest change in the international situation in nearly half a century, and the bipolar world ended abruptly. But this time, the rule of "change every ten years" did not apply; there were no major changes in China's foreign policy.

In the early 1990s, the Chinese government successfully adapted to domestic and international changes through gradual and consistent adjustment of its policies. China continued to follow the principles of actively developing friendly cooperation with all countries of the world in all fields, persisting in opposing hegemony, maintaining world peace, and promoting development around the world. China's purpose was to strive for a favorable external environment and to speed up its own development to achieve modernization. But first, the Chinese sought to do their own work well. Compared to the situation in the 1980s, this time basic principles and policy aims were better coordinated.

In response to changing circumstances, China made three limited adjustments in its foreign policy. First, it resolutely opposed the sanctions imposed on it by Western countries such as the United States and took the necessary steps to restore and stabilize relations with these countries. It also continued to strengthen friendly relations with neighboring countries, including Russia and the newly independent Central Asian countries. It worked to help establish a new international political and economic order after the cold war based on the five principles of peaceful coexistence. Second, on the question of Taiwan, Hong Kong, Tibet, and Macao, China struggled against any actions detrimental to its national sovereignty. In the 1980s it began to pave the way for the return of Hong Kong and Macao, which occurred in 1997 and 1999, respectively. Third, emphasizing a country's right to choose its own development model, China selected the measures, sectors, and speed of reform and opening it deemed appropriate to its own particular domestic situation. On the one hand, China wanted to stand firm against pressure from Western countries, rejecting any demands concerned with human rights and economic openness that might be potentially detrimental. On the other, China wanted to express a willingness to start a dialogue with Western countries on the issue of human rights and to expand economic cooperation.

The continuity of China's domestic political line ensures the continuity of China's foreign policy—continuing to pursue the policy of reform and opening through public support for this line. In treating the various contradictions that emerged inside China in 1989, the principal guidance offered by Deng Xiaoping was to maintain the stability of the state. In the spring of that year, he repeated on various occasions that the most important problem for China was to maintain stability. Without a stable environment, nothing could be achieved and what had been achieved could be lost. China must avoid disorder and work to prevent disorder.[17] After taking resolute action to suppress the turbulence, Deng immediately pointed out that the policy of reform and opening was still correct. China should continue to carry out the basic lines, principles, and policies already formulated.[18]

Following his election as general secretary at the Fourth Plenum of the Thirteenth Congress, Jiang Zemin commented that China's fundamental policies since the Third Plenum of the Eleventh Congress had not changed and should be carried out.[19] Although during the process of reform and opening inflation and corruption were important problems and led to political disturbances, the overwhelming majority of the Chinese people were beneficiaries. The damage done by the cultural revolution had not yet been fully eliminated, but people were leading better lives, and their dissatisfactions and worries were not so great as to cause grave disorder. The decisions of the high authorities and the mood of the public, pleased with progress and reluctant to return to chaos, enabled China to weather the political crisis caused by the Tiananmen incident.

During the political disturbances in China, Western public opinion doubtlessly added fuel to the flames. Because of the sanctions imposed by Western countries, such as the United States, after the Tiananmen incident, China's key foreign policy issue became the question of how to treat its relations with these countries. For Deng Xiaoping, the problem was composed of two parts: the first, how to deal with the attempts of Western countries to exert pressure on China; the second, how to handle relations with Western countries. Deng thought that Western countries were exerting pressure on China in an attempt to force it to abandon socialism and that China should stand up resolutely against such pressure. First, he said, "Never back down. The more you back down, the more they will pressure you." Second, "Remain calm, do not be agitated." He believed that in very unfavorable circumstances, "the only way to deal with the problem is for us to stand firm." China should not abandon socialism simply because of pressure from the West, and China should reject those measures for reform and opening stemming from such inappropriate pressure. As for the second part of the problem, how to deal with Western countries, Deng Xiaoping said, "No matter what has happened, we should still have friendly relations. We should go on making friends, but we should have a clear mind." The principle guiding foreign relations, he suggested, was "to observe calmly, hold our ground, and meet the challenge steadily." He further said, "Be calm and calm and calm, commit ourselves to our work."[20] During that difficult period in its relations with foreign countries, the great danger for China was returning to the old principle of class struggle. By thus adroitly dividing the question into two parts, Deng Xiaoping found intelligent answers and played a key role in steadying China's foreign policy.

The continuity of China's foreign policy had also been shaped by its ever-broadening integration with the world. Although the policy of reform and opening, practiced since the late 1970s, was the basis of China's domestic strategy, this policy demanded close coordination with China's foreign policy, without which it would be impracticable. After ten years of the new domestic policy, the political and economic links between China and the world had become so close, a return to isolation might have created problems more serious than those caused by the earlier reform and opening. To continue that policy, it was—and is—imperative that China not be hostile to the developed countries of the West. At the same time, Western countries such as the United States and China's neighbors have gained important economic and security benefits from China's present policies. Should China retreat from these policies, their interests would also suffer considerably. This realization has helped to limit these pressures.

From a macroperspective, the great importance of China's economic reform and opening policy lies in the fact that it initiated the process of integration into the world system. Along with the deepening of reform and opening, China became increasingly aware of the fact that the changes in the international system were not simply a struggle to replace the old with the new. To promote its own development, China would have to join the existing international system, enjoying its benefits while protecting China's interests within existing rules. At the same time, China also realized that the existing world order was not perfect, and that a new international political and economic order could only be achieved by joining the system, a gradual and complicated process.

The domestic benefits of China's integration into the world system from the late 1980s to the early 1990s were enormous. But contradictions and conflicts also developed. One interesting phenomenon was the goal of "aligning ourselves with international norms." This became a clearly defined aim that influenced China's domestic policy, including its continuing reform of the economic system. But in its contacts with foreign countries, China persistently held to the principle of independence and the ability to act without interference so that it could safeguard its own interests and maintain its own initiatives. During this period, domestic stability was a primary goal, and this was also true in foreign relations. Since 1989, the process of merging into the world system may have been slowed down temporarily, but it has never been interrupted. If domestic factors were once a significant influence on China's foreign policy, now with greater integration into the world system outside factors wield increasing influence in domestic policymaking.

CHAPTER THREE

Japanese Politics and Asia-Pacific Policy
Kamiya Matake

This essay investigates the ways in which domestic factors affected Japan's basic foreign policy toward the United States and China during the two decades following 1972. In the United States, major political change occurs almost every four years with the election of a new president. These changes were particularly marked in 1977 and 1981, when the presidency passed between the Republicans and the Democrats (from Ford to Carter and from Carter to Reagan). In China, after the deaths of Mao Zedong and Zhou Enlai in 1976 and a short period of political turmoil caused by the Gang of Four, the political posture of the Chinese Communist Party shifted drastically under the leadership of Deng Xiaoping, who introduced the new policies of economic "reform and opening" to the West. In Japanese politics over these two decades, however, no such clear change occurred. The one-party dominant system through which the Liberal Democratic Party (LDP) had ruled since 1955 continued until the summer of 1993, when internal splits allowed opposition parties to come to power.[1] The most salient characteristic of Japan's domestic politics during this period was the growing fluidity of domestic politics under LDP rule.

The Fluidity of LDP Rule

Until July 1972, when Prime Minister Sato Eisaku resigned after more than seven-and-a-half years in power, successive LDP administrations had been, for the most part, stable.[2] During the next twenty-one years, however, until the LDP's loss of power in August 1993, ten prime ministers held office in rapid succession: Tanaka Kakuei, Miki Takeo, Fukuda Takeo, Ohira Masayoshi, Suzuki Zenko, Nakasone Yasuhiro, Takeshita Noboru, Uno Sosuke, Kaifu Toshiki, and Miyazawa Kiichi. Excluding Nakasone, whose administration lasted for five years, and Uno, who, because of a sex scandal, was forced to resign after only two months, their average length of time in office was less than two years. Two major reasons for the frequent turnover are the intensified confrontation among LDP leaders and the decline of public trust in the party.

In the last years of the Sato administration, five factional leaders of the LDP—Tanaka, Fukuda, Ohira, Miki, and Nakasone—were recognized as potential future prime ministers. Sato wanted Fukuda to become his successor, but in the LDP presidential election of July 5, 1972, he was defeated by Tanaka, who was supported by Ohira, Miki, and Nakasone. The major factor in Tanaka's victory was growing public outcry for political change. There were increasing signs that Japan's economic growth rate, at a high since the early 1960s, was gradually slowing down. The public was also critical of the Sato administration for not foreseeing the two "Nixon shocks" of 1971, the United States opening to China and the ending of the fixed yen-dollar exchange rate. After the U.S.-China rapprochement, the Japanese public's demand for early normalization of relations with China increased, and Sato, whose relations with China were poor, seemed incapable of achieving it. Tanaka showed greater enthusiasm than Fukuda, and many also believed that Fukuda would not be successful because of his close connections with the pro-Taiwan group within the LDP. The public was thus attracted to Tanaka rather than to Sato's chosen successor.

The other major factor contributing to Tanaka's success was the enormous amount of money he spent on his presidential campaign. Defeated in an election that drew on unprecedented "money power," Fukuda later confessed that he had almost been fed up with the election and had even thought about withdrawing from the race.[3] The deep antagonism between Tanaka and Fukuda that ensued, sometimes called *on'nen no seiji,* the "politics of a deep-seated grudge," fueled a period of interfactional strife within the LDP.

The Tanaka administration, which began with a popular support rating of 62 percent,[4] achieved normalization of relations with China in September 1972. But Tanaka's initial popularity dropped rapidly as problems in the Japanese economy worsened. Following the second Nixon shock of August 1971, the Bank of Japan had purchased a huge quantity of dollars to avoid the devaluation of the yen, but this move resulted in excess liquidity, which, to-gether with Tanaka's expansive land and economic policy, dubbed the "Re-making of the Japanese Archipelago," set off steep inflation. The first oil cri-sis in October 1973 further intensified the inflation. When the monthly magazine *Bungei Shunju* published reports of Tanaka's financial scandals, the public had had enough. Tanaka resigned on November 26, 1973.

The LDP then faced a serious crisis. LDP leaders feared the loss of pub-lic support if they failed to clean up their money-tainted image. They also feared that if either of the two leading candidates for prime minister, Fukuda or Ohira, was selected, the other might split from the LDP and form a new political party. Seeking a way out of the crisis, the LDP selected Miki Takeo, an elder from a minor faction within the party, as its leader. Miki's one great attraction was that he was known for being financially "clean."

The Miki administration resolved the LDP's immediate need for a cleaner image, but Miki's power base within the LDP was weak. His gov-ernment was known for mending fences but for little else.[5] When the Lock-heed scandal was revealed in the early spring of 1976—Lockheed had given huge bribes to high-ranking Japanese politicians to ensure sales of its Airbus to Japan—Miki tried to gain popular support by thoroughly investigating the scandal. Although his efforts led to the arrest of former prime minister Tanaka on July 27, this attack on a senior LDP leader incurred strong re-sentment within the party. Many blamed Miki for lacking a deeper sense of responsibility to his colleagues. Members of the mainstream LDP factions launched a "remove Miki" movement, and he was forced to resign in De-cember 1976. Meanwhile, although Tanaka was a criminal defendant, he continued to head the largest LDP faction, becoming a "shadow shogun" who controlled the party behind the scenes.

The three largest factions within the LDP, those headed by Tanaka, Fukuda, and Ohira, managed to cooperate to select Fukuda as Miki's succes-sor. Fukuda's primary achievement as prime minister was the signing of the

Japan-China Treaty of Peace and Friendship in August 1978, normalizing relations between the two countries, which had been pending since the Tanaka administration. Fukuda, however, would spend less than two years in office. In November 1978, at the preliminary election of the LDP president by popular vote, Ohira, with the support of the Tanaka faction, won an overwhelming victory over Fukuda, despite the almost unanimous predictions of the press in Fukuda's favor.

The Ohira administration lasted only 554 days. After the LDP lost the general electionof 1979, the election of prime minister by the Diet members turned out to be an unprecedented one in which two LDP candidates, Ohira and Fukuda, contended for the position. Ohira edged out Fukuda in the race. In May 1980, however, a vote of no confidence in the cabinet submitted by the Socialist Party was approved in the House of Representatives because most of the anti-Ohira LDP members were absent from the voting. Ohira responded by dissolving the House of Representatives but died suddenly of a heart attack during the ensuing electoral campaign. In the "double elections" of the House of Representatives and the House of Councilors that took place only ten days after Ohira's death, the LDP received a large sympathy vote and won both contests by a landslide.

During the administrations of Miki, Fukuda, and Ohira, Japan's domestic politics was shaken by successive scandals and a continuing struggle for power by LDP factions. News of scandals among senior LDP politicians— the financial scandal of Tanaka in 1974, the Lockheed scandal and consequent arrest of Tanaka in 1976, and the Douglas-Grumman scandal in 1979—intensified public distrust of politics. In other mature democracies, a change of parties would have been inevitable, but in Japan, the impotence of the opposition allowed the LDP's continued rule. According to public opinion polls, from the end of the 1970s to the middle of the 1980s, the rate of support for the LDP almost always exceeded 50 percent.[6]

LDP members, weary of their leaders' struggles, now chose Suzuki Zenko, a dark horse who had inherited the Ohira faction, to be prime minister. Suzuki had never been considered as a prospective prime minister and was completely unknown outside Japan. Seasoned in domestic affairs, having served ten terms as the chair of the Executive Council of the LDP, he was an amateur in international matters. His only foreign affairs experience involved participating in fisheries negotiations with the Soviet Union. Journalists dubbed him a "typical leader of a Japanese village society" and a "leader who does not lead."[7] During the general meeting of LDP members of both houses at which he was elected the party president, Suzuki himself said, "I realize that I do not have the makings of a prime minister."[8] His administration was an interim one as the LDP sought to escape the crisis in its rule brought about by the political rancor between Tanaka and Fukuda. From the start, it was clear that Suzuki would not put a distinctive stamp on politics either "in his policies or in his political stance."[9]

In the autumn of 1982, although his reelection seemed almost certain, Suzuki surprised not only the party but the entire country by refusing to run again. Nakasone was chosen as his successor. Frustrated by a decade of weak leadership, the public and political leaders were willing to grant Nakasone considerable leeway in his exercise of power. Known for his strong convictions, he might not have been chosen were it not for the general dissatisfaction with the continuing political drift. And Nakasone did, in fact, exercise exceptionally strong leadership. He is always remembered as the prime minister who sought the "final settlement of postwar politics," the resolution of issues remaining from World War II, in both domestic and foreign affairs. Giving higher priority to foreign policy than the LDP prime ministers who preceded him, he attempted to transform Japan into an "international state." The public generally welcomed his strong leadership style, but he still felt hampered by factional politics within the LDP. His faction was the fourth largest, and he achieved office only with the support of the Tanaka faction.

The Tanaka faction remained the largest, but Tanaka himself, convicted in the Lockheed scandal trial in October 1983, was incapacitated by a stroke in February 1985 and thus no longer capable of carrying on his political activities. In addition, in January 1985, Takeshita Noboru established the "Sosei-kai," a proto-factional breakaway group (later transformed into the Takeshita faction) in which most Tanaka faction members participated. During his terms as prime minister, Nakasone saw his political freedom increase as Tanaka's political influence declined. This fact, together with the positive state of U.S.-Japan relations under the "Ron-Yasu relationship," helped keep Nakasone in office for five years.

Nakasone's popularity eventually waned when he attempted, unsuccessfully, to introduce a large-scale indirect tax system. By the time he resigned in November 1987, however, LDP rule had regained its vitality. The three major candidates for prime minister, referred to as the "new leaders," were Takeshita Noboru, Abe Shintaro, and Miyazawa Kiichi. This time there were no personal "grudges" to complicate the transition. To succeed Naka-sone, Takeshita, then the leader of the largest faction in the LDP, was selected. His administration was supported by the other two new leaders, Miyazawa as deputy prime minister and minister of finance, and Abe as the secretary general of the LDP. The booming Japanese economy (later known as the "bubble" economy) was then at its peak. Because of the appreciation of the yen after the Plaza Accord in 1985, the Japanese economy had become, at the then-current exchange rates, the largest in the world. Japan's per capita GNP exceeded that of the United States, and Japan became the globe's larg-est creditor nation. Most Japanese were overjoyed at their economic success. For the LDP, everything seemed to be going well. During the five years fol-lowing Nakasone's resignation, however, the LDP again became very weak, and its decline culminated in the end of its one-party dominance in the 1993 general elections. Between 1982 and 1992, Japan had four prime ministers: Takeshita Noboru (1987–89), Uno Sosuke (1989), Kaifu Toshiki (1989–91), and Miyazawa Kiichi (1991–93).

Takeshita attempted to implement the large-scale indirect tax system that the Nakasone administration had been unable to introduce successfully; the consumer tax bill passed the Diet in 1988. Just as this move was provok-ing a strong popular outcry, another political embarrassment, the Recruit scandal, broke. A number of senior LDP politicians and business executives had made huge profits by trading in a Recruit subsidiary's, Recruit Cosmos, prelisted shares, obtained as a special favor from the company. Miyazawa, Abe, Nakasone, and Takeshita were all implicated. Public distrust of the LDP surged, and in June 1989, Takeshita was forced to resign. Since all its leaders were tainted, the LDP chose two unknowns, Uno and Kaifu, as the next two prime ministers. The party's desperation was obvious: neither was the leader of an LDP faction, and neither had ever been regarded as a candi-date for the premiership. When Uno was forced to resign because of an ex-tramarital scandal after only two months in office, public disgust toward the LDP increased even further.

In November 1991, when Miyazawa became prime minister following the two "lightweights," the public welcomed him as a well-trained leader, and for a time he enjoyed high support. It was unfortunate for him and for the LDP that at the beginning of the 1990s the economic bubble burst. Furthermore, during Miyazawa's time in office, new political scandals involving LDP Diet members were revealed, and public criticism of LDP corruption mounted.

Miyazawa's leadership, which attempted to balance interests within the LDP, made it difficult for him to take the bold steps necessary to achieve political and economic reform.[10]

The debilitating LDP factional battles for the premiership between 1972 and 1992 were never a competition over policy but merely a struggle for power within the same political party. Japan's basic foreign policy posture changed very little, despite the frequent replacement of prime ministers.[11] Most of the prime ministers had only a weak power base in the LDP and thus could not exercise strong leadership. They tended to give higher priority to domestic politics than to diplomacy, and when they dealt with foreign policy issues, they often deferred the difficult ones out of fear that action would invite strong domestic opposition. These tendencies left foreign policy to the professional bureaucrats, ensuring a pattern of continuity rather than change.

Domestic Factors and Japan's Foreign Policy Toward the United States

JAPAN'S U.S. ALLIANCE POLICY

What is most noteworthy about Japan's foreign policy toward the United States in the two decades between 1972 and 1992 is that it changed so little, despite domestic political confusion. None of the ten Japanese prime ministers who held office during this period made any attempt to alter the basic policy framework: Japan depended on the U.S.-Japan alliance for its security and did not seek military autonomy. The alliance with the United States remained the basis of Japan's diplomacy during these two decades. On important international political issues, Japan generally followed the U.S. lead, thus maintaining its postwar foreign policy stance.

The decisions of these successive administrations, however, were by no means inevitable. By the early 1970s, Japan had become the second largest economy in the world, after the United States. As the history of international relations shows, once a country achieves economic power, it usually seeks to achieve military autonomy. According to "realist" explanations, in the highly anarchic international arena, a state must fend for itself in seeking security and prosperity, because there is no central global authority able to exert control over sovereign states; individual states are highly averse to becoming dependent on other states. Yet in reality, except for a small number of the strongest states, most have no choice but to rely on others, at least in some areas. As weaker states gain in strength, they are likely to throw off such reliance as quickly as possible and seek to become more independent.[12] Over the past three decades, many observers have predicted that Japan would prove to be no exception, and would strive to become a strong, autonomous military power. Some have even argued that Japan would acquire nuclear capability.[13] But Japan's actual choices contradict such "commonsense" interpretations.

Following the two Nixon shocks of 1971, there was even a period when Japan developed a distrust of the United States. At the time, even the most devoted supporters of U.S.-Japan relations were stunned by U.S. actions. Many Japanese regarded Washington's failure to consult Japan beforehand on its opening to China as a betrayal, and some feared that the United States might be shifting the main focus of its East Asian policy from Japan to China. Even in this climate, however, few in Japan advocated a reconsideration of the country's relationship with the United States, and almost no one suggested that Japan stop depending on the United States militarily and seek its own military autonomy. By the usual standards of international relations, these attitudes were extraordinary.

The primary factors that brought about such remarkable continuity in Japan's policy toward the United States during this period were domestic. The most decisive was the fact that among the Japanese public, so-called postwar pacifism remained strong.[14] From the end of World War II until the present, the Japanese people have been skeptical about the legitimacy and usefulness of military power and have viewed anything having even a remote connection to the military with a degree of wariness bordering on total rejection. There has been strong public abhorrence toward using any military-related measures as a tool of foreign policy, even the defense of Japan, because this is seen to contradict the ideal of peace embodied in Japan's Peace Constitution. Consequently, security has been one of the most sensitive issues in Japan's postwar domestic politics. The national consensus has held that Japan should not participate in international power politics unless forced to do so. This pacifism changed little between 1972 and 1992. Its remarkable strength and continuity were very clearly shown in Japan's response to the Gulf crisis (August 1990 to February 1991), which, because it involved only a monetary commitment, invited severe criticism from other countries.

Even after Japan's economy became one of the largest in the world in the 1960s, the vast majority of the Japanese still opposed policies that would make their country a major military power. Although the U.S.-China rapprochement and the normalization of relations between Japan and China removed the Chinese threat, Japan still faced the Soviet threat. But to maintain its security without changing its Peace Constitution and its traditional postwar military posture of "exclusively defense-oriented defense," Japan chose to continue its reliance on the U.S. alliance.

What can be called the "small-power mentality" of the Japanese people, or, to put it another way, their tendency to consider their country a small one, also contributed to the continuity of Japan's basic posture toward the United States. The Nixon shocks and the oil shocks of the 1970s planted the strong feeling that despite its remarkable economic growth and economic power, Japan was still only a small nation, poorly endowed with natural resources and vulnerable to changes in the international system. Even as late as the 1990s, many Japanese had not been able to free themselves of this traditional image. A book by the opposition Sakigake Party leader Takemura Masayoshi, entitled *Chiisakutomo Kirari to Hikaru Kuni, Nippon* (Small, but brilliant country, Japan), became a best seller in the mid-1990s.[15] In the words of Kuriyama Takakazu, former ambassador to the United States and administrative vice minister of foreign affairs, the basic goals of Japanese diplomacy remained the same: "to adapt themselves best to the existing [international] order" supported by the United States and "thereby to protect [Japan's] security and to preserve its economic interests," based on the recognition that "the international order is basically a given framework." As late as 1990, Kuriyama had to advocate that Japan increase its share of the burden: "Japan's diplomacy should transform itself from that of middle and small powers into that of a major power."[16]

During the 1970s and 1980s, the climate of public opinion in Japan moved in a more conservative direction. In spite of the two oil shocks and the rapid appreciation of the yen following the Plaza Accord of 1985, Japan's economy remained strong until the early 1990s. Enjoying affluence, the Japanese wanted to maintain the status quo. In the early 1990s, when the bubble economy burst, people started to criticize the government, but most Japanese had not yet noticed that the country was facing a serious crisis. In addition, any remaining illusions about the value of communist ideology still held by some intellectuals finally evaporated in the first half of the 1980s as the Japanese witnessed the Soviet invasion of Afghanistan and the Soviet military buildup in the Far East. The decline of leftist influence accelerated the shift toward conservatism.

Since 1952, when Japan recovered its independence, public opinion polls have indicated that more citizens support the U.S.-Japan security treaty system than oppose it.[17] Until the mid-1970s, however, the majority of intellectuals and journalists opposed the security treaty, and their views were influential because of Japan's strong pacifist tradition. But by the late 1970s, the climate had changed dramatically, and the vast majority of the Japanese then agreed that Japan should maintain the security treaty system with the United States.[18]

Within this basic policy framework a question remained: How far was Japan willing to go toward actual military cooperation with the United States? Tokyo's willingness was influenced by the views and personalities of its successive prime ministers. Miki, for example, who was said to belong to the "leftist wing" of the LDP, made a cabinet decision to set the ceiling of its 1976 defense budget at 1 percent of Japan's GNP, despite growing U.S. pressure on Japan to strengthen its defense efforts. U.S. officials were critical of the decision. On May 8, 1981, the joint communiqué issued after the summit meeting between Prime Minister Suzuki Zenko and President Ronald Reagan characterized the relationship between the two countries as an "alliance." It was the first time in the nearly four decades of U.S.-Japan security ties that the Japanese side agreed to use the term. Until then, Japanese leaders had avoided the word, fearing that its military connotations would arouse domestic opposition. On the day he signed the communiqué, however, Suzuki, who had originally been a member of the Socialist Party and acknowledged himself as a dove in the LDP, repeatedly told the Japanese journalists covering the meetings that the word "'alliance' does not have any military implications."[19] This statement was harshly criticized by the U.S. side. Washington was also irritated by Suzuki's reluctance to accede to its repeated requests for the principle that military technology could be transferred from Japan to the United States.

In contrast, Suzuki's successor, Nakasone Yasuhiro, assumed an exceptionally positive attitude toward military cooperation with the United States. Less than two months after he came into office, Nakasone decided to make possible the transfer of Japanese military technology to the United States.[20] Shortly thereafter, at his first summit meeting with President Reagan, Nakasone said that Japan and the United States formed a community with a single destiny. In the budget for fiscal year 1987, he abolished the 1 percent of GNP ceiling for the defense budget set by Miki.

JAPAN'S POSTURE TOWARD ECONOMIC FRICTION
WITH THE UNITED STATES

Between 1972 and the early 1990s, as Japan's exports continued to grow stronger, economic tension between Japan and the United States became more troublesome. According to one Japanese scholar, this economic friction follows a cyclical pattern. In the initial stage, the U.S. side protested and applied "external pressure" (*gaiatsu*) on Japan, demanding one of the following: (1) voluntary export restraints on certain products, (2) the opening of the Japanese market, (3) a decrease in Japan's trade surplus, or (4) structural reform of the Japanese economy. The Japanese government at first responded by brushing U.S. protests aside, avoiding the problem. Only after the U.S. side linked economic issues to maintaining a good relationship between the two countries did the Japanese government agree to enter into negotiations. Eventually it made some concessions, but only in small doses. The dissatisfactions on the U.S. side remained, and sooner or later the same issues came up again. The U.S. side then put further gaiatsu on Japan.[21]

Considering that Japan had ten prime ministers in only two decades, a question arises: Why did government attitudes toward economic friction with the United States change so little over time? Here, several domestic factors came into play. First, by and large, those ten prime ministers could exercise only weak leadership. Institutionally, on economic issues LDP prime ministers were weak and the bureaucracy strong. The office of the prime minister was itself politically weak, and the medium-size electoral district system, with several Diet members elected in each district, produced factions in the LDP with competing interests. By custom the cabinet was reshuffled almost annually to maintain the factional balance, and the bottom-up, decision-by-consensus system that developed in the 1960s made new initiatives difficult.[22] To retain power, moreover, successive LDP prime ministers during this period found that they had to expend a great deal of energy to maintain factional coalitions and were preoccupied with the continuing intraparty power struggle twenty-four hours a day, every day. While he was prime minister, according to one biographer, Ohira Masayoshi always said to himself when he came home: "How silly it is! Every day I am [engaging in intraparty power struggles]."[23]

For these reasons, most prime ministers during this period tended to give higher priority to avoiding domestic friction than to developing foreign policy. When dealing with foreign policy issues, they tended to defer those most likely to provoke a negative domestic reaction unless action seemed unavoidable. When they attended to economic friction, they tended to wait until gaiatsu became unbearable before facing issues; only then was it possible to obtain the necessary domestic support to take serious measures.

Another important factor reinforcing the prevailing image of "no moves by Japan without *gaiatsu*" was the absence of political parties that appealed to urban voters and represented consumers wanting more opportunities to buy imported goods. In Japan, in the division of the constituencies, rural areas traditionally had an advantage over urban areas, so that all political parties tended to represent the voices of farmers wanting protection against imported agricultural products. Consequently, differences among them in responding to gaiatsu were very small. On no other political issues except that of economic friction could the LDP and the opposition parties come together so easily.[24]

Finally, many ministries and agencies having their own varying interests were involved in economic issues, and the complexity tended to delay government reaction. Major actors on the question of U.S.-Japan economic tension included the Ministry of Foreign Affairs, the Ministry of International Trade and Industry, the Ministry of Finance, and the Ministry of Agriculture, Forestry, and Fisheries. Over time, other ministries, such as the Ministry of Construction and the Ministry of Posts and Telecommunications, were also gradually involved. Among these actors, the Ministry of Foreign Affairs gave top priority to maintaining good U.S.-Japan relations. This ministry, however, had only a small number of *zoku-giin* (Diet members who belong to a "tribe" or *zoku* that focuses on a particular policy area), and limited domestic political power, particularly compared to that of the Ministry of International Trade and Industry and the Ministry of Agriculture, Forestry, and Fisheries, both of which had many powerful zoku-giin protecting the interests of Japanese producers.

Domestic Factors and Japan's Foreign Policy Toward China

The most significant change in Japan's foreign policy toward China during this period was Prime Minister Tanaka's normalization of diplomatic relations with Beijing in September 1972. This change was brought about, however, by external rather than domestic factors. After World War II, when Japan recovered its independence, U.S. pressure forced it to establish diplomatic relations with Taipei rather than Beijing. Firmly incorporated within the United States' anticommunist global strategy, Japan found its China policy virtually prescribed by the U.S. policy of isolation toward China. Although Tokyo always felt uncomfortable about following Washington, and many Japanese desired to reestablish relations with the mainland, it was impossible for Japan to normalize its relations with the People's Republic of China as long as the Sino-U.S. confrontation persisted. Sino-U.S. rapprochement finally removed the most fundamental obstacle to normalization, and after the first Nixon shock of July 1971, it was in a sense an "expected fact"[25] and simply a matter of time before Tokyo restored relations with Beijing.

Although domestic factors did not bring about normalization, they strongly influenced its timing. Among LDP Diet members in the autumn of 1971, the pro-Taiwan group was still larger than the pro-China group.[26] In the Ministry of Foreign Affairs, those who advocated early normalization were in the minority.[27] It was thus by no means a foregone conclusion that a Japanese premier would travel to China only seven months after Nixon's February 1972 visit or that he would go a step further than the United States by granting political recognition to the PRC in place of Taiwan and establishing formal diplomatic relations. It was due largely to Prime Minister Tanaka's leadership and actions that normalization occurred at such an early stage.

The normalization of relations with China became the largest issue in the 1972 LDP presidential race between Tanaka and Fukuda. While Tanaka showed great enthusiasm for normalization, Fukuda, who was serving as foreign minister and whose faction included many pro-Taiwan Diet members, took a more cautious approach. This difference was the major factor that persuaded Ohira, Miki, and Nakasone to support Tanaka rather than Fukuda. The normalization issue "played a role as a litmus paper to distinguish between Tanaka supporters and Fukuda supporters."[28]

As soon as he assumed office in July, Prime Minister Tanaka made energetic moves toward normalizing relations with Beijing. Enjoying the strong support of the Komei Party and the Socialist Party, as well as that of the mass media and the public, he overcame demands on the part of the Ministry of Foreign Affairs and the pro-Taiwan group within the LDP for a more cautious approach and succeeded in establishing formal diplomatic relations with the mainland less than three months into his administration.

Once normalization was achieved, the conclusion of the Treaty of Peace and Friendship between the two countries was only a matter of time, a "natural and expected consequence."[29] Nonetheless, the negotiations, which were initially expected to be smooth and swift, took nearly six years. Why such a long time? The major reason was external rather than domestic: the negotiations deadlocked over the Chinese demand for the inclusion of the so-called antihegemony clause, which stated that neither side would seek hegemony in the Asia-Pacific region and that each would oppose efforts by any other country or group of countries to establish such hegemony. Japan resisted because of the apparent anti-Soviet implications of the proposed clause.

As in normalization, however, domestic factors again affected the timing of the resolution of the issue. A major reason the long and difficult negotiations came to a conclusion in August 1978 was that Fukuda was now prime minister. Even after normalization, a considerable number of pro-Taiwan Diet members in the LDP were reluctant to conclude the peace and friendship treaty with the PRC. A large percentage of the members of the Fukuda faction and other pro-Fukuda LDP Diet members were pro-Taiwan. No one but Fukuda could have persuaded them to consent to signing the treaty.

Even for Fukuda, this task was by no means easy. As his term as LDP president and prime minister neared its end, however, the objections of the Diet members who were both pro-Fukuda and pro-Taiwan waned. They realized that if the treaty was not signed during Fukuda's term, it would be counted as his failure and would work against his reelection.[30] After pro-Taiwan LDP Diet members consented to the conclusion of the treaty with Beijing in the summer of 1978, intraparty conflict between the pro-China and the pro-Taiwan groups almost disappeared.

Thus, in both the normalization of relations in 1972 and the conclusion of the Treaty of Peace and Friendship in 1978, the primary factors that produced a change in Japan's foreign policy posture toward China were external, but the major factors in the timing of the decisions were internal. Aside from these two cases, however, domestic factors supported continuity in Japan's China policy.

During the postwar period, including the two decades covered here, Japan's policy toward China was formulated within the limits set by U.S. China policy.[31] Between 1972 and 1992, Japan rarely, if ever, took any diplomatic posture toward China that was not compatible with U.S. policies and intentions. The normalization of relations with Beijing became possible only after the revolutionary change in the U.S. posture toward China in July 1971. Indeed, before his visit to China, Prime Minister Tanaka had gone to Honolulu to attend bilateral summit meetings with President Nixon on August 31 and September 1, 1972, during which he obtained Nixon's agreement on normalization. Later, President Carter's encouragement played a significant role when Prime Minister Fukuda decided to seek the early signing of the Treaty of Peace and Friendship. At a summit meeting in Washington in May 1978, Carter told Fukuda that he wished him success in concluding the treaty with Beijing.[32]

During the two decades following the normalization of relations between Japan and China, the influence of U.S. relations on Japan's China policy was rather limited. It would be wrong, however, to conclude that the United States was no longer a factor, given the strategic structure in Northeast Asia in which the United States, Japan, and China united to face the Soviet threat. Tokyo's handling of the Tiananmen Square incident in June 1989 confirmed a still strong American influence on Japanese decisions about China. After the Tiananmen incident, Japan was initially reluctant to apply sanctions of any kind, not wanting to isolate China: it feared that isolation might lead to the political and social destabilization of its giant neighbor. In addition, Japanese business circles wished to maintain economic exchanges with China. In a few weeks, however, Japan followed the lead of the United States and other Western countries and applied tough sanctions, including suspending the extension of the third yen-loan package, which was scheduled to start in 1990. Although Japan wished to resume economic cooperation with China as soon as possible, it was only after the visit of two American senior officials to Beijing in December 1989 and the visible improvement of Sino-U.S. relations that Japan took actual steps to do so.

The United States remained a dominant force in Japan's China diplomacy between 1972 and 1992, primarily because Japan did not seek military autonomy and thus remained heavily dependent on its security alliance with the United States. Why didn't Japan choose to become militarily autonomous once it had achieved a great-power economy at the end of the 1960s? The answer lies in Japan's postwar pacifism, and here the domestic factor in Japan's China policy again becomes important. A vast majority of the Japanese people wanted their country to maintain its traditional "exclusively defense-oriented defense" posture and otherwise to rely on its security alliance with the United States.

Another aspect of the remarkable continuity in Japan's postwar China policy can be found in its nonconfrontational, reactive approach, which also derived from domestic factors. As others have pointed out, Japan has experienced cycles of "China boom" and disappointment, which have coincided with, respectively, political progress and friction in Japan-China relations since normalization.[33] The nonconfrontational, reactive nature of Japan's China policy during this period was typically demonstrated in its responses to these political frictions. None of the political disputes of the time was started by the intentional actions of the Japanese government. In all cases, Japan reacted in a conciliatory manner to the events and policies of others.[34] In the cases of the "Hozan (Baoshan) shock" in 1981, when China unilaterally canceled its contract with New Japan Steel, and the Kokaryo problem in 1987, when China complained about the Osaka High Court ruling that ownership of a student dormitory named Kokaryo, which had been purchased by the Taiwanese government in 1952, still belonged to Taiwan even after the termination of diplomatic relations between Tokyo and Taipei, it was Beijing's actions that brought about Sino-Japanese tension. In the case of the textbook controversy in the summer of 1982, Beijing's erratic reaction to false reports in the Japanese mass media that Japan's Ministry of Education, through the official school textbook screening system, had ordered the publishers of school history textbooks to replace the term "aggression" (*shinryaku*) with the term "advance" (*shinshutsu*) to describe Japan's military actions in Asia before 1945, set off a chain reaction throughout East Asia. In the case of the stormy anti-Japanese demonstrations triggered in China by Prime Minister Nakasone's visit to Yasukuni Shrine on August 15, 1985, several factors were involved: growing ill-feeling in China about its rapidly expanding trade imbalance with Japan; the nationalistic Chinese political climate of the time; and China's official campaign on the fortieth anniversary of its victory over Japan, which called on the Chinese people never to forget the wartime struggle against Japan.

In all these cases, Japan's reaction followed a discernibly conciliatory pattern. The Japanese government consistently attempted to maintain and promote friendly relations with China. Whenever political disagreements arose, Tokyo attached the highest priority to avoiding serious confrontation, restraining itself from asserting its own position in front of China and making the concessions necessary to diffuse the crisis.

Japan's nonconfrontational posture toward China can be understood as a consequence of several domestic factors. The most basic is the fact that the Japanese people's view of China, with few exceptions, remained highly favorable. The results of the annual "Survey of Public Opinion on Foreign Affairs" conducted by the Office of the Prime Minister since 1978 showed that every year from 1978 until 1988, the percentage of respondents who answered that they held friendly sentiments toward China was remarkably high—between 62.1 and 78.6 percent. Although this percentage dropped after the Tiananmen incident in 1989, and the percentage of those who said they did not have positive sentiments toward China increased, until the mid-1990s at least 50 percent of respondents reported friendly sentiments toward China.[35] Another annual public opinion survey conducted since 1978 by *Yomiuri Shinbun*, Japan's largest national daily, asked respondents to "list five countries which you think especially reliable." Although the largest number of those surveyed between 1978 and 1992 listed the United States, the number of those who listed China was almost always high as well. Until 1988, China ranked from second to fifth in these polls. In 1989, because of the effect of the Tiananmen incident, China's ranking dropped to eleventh. In each year from 1990 to 1992, however, China ranked eighth.[36]

A second factor in Japan's conciliatory diplomacy was the belief of many Japanese that it was natural for their country to develop friendly relations with a neighbor with whom it shared a history of cultural and other ties stretching over more than two thousand years. Third, the Japanese believed that friendly relations with China were essential to Japan's economic interests. Fourth, the strong pacifist orientation among the postwar Japanese inspired a desire to avoid political or military confrontations with their giant neighbor. Fifth, a sense of guilt over Japan's prewar treatment of China fostered the belief that Japan had a moral responsibility to build friendly relations with China. Finally, the existence of strong leftist movements among intellectuals and journalists in postwar Japan also contributed to its nonconfrontational approach.

The reactive nature of Japan's China diplomacy from 1972 to 1989 can also be understood as a consequence of these domestic factors, particularly Japan's postwar pacifism and feelings of guilt toward China. Without autonomous military power, Japan's ability to conduct an active foreign policy in relation to the major powers, including China, was severely limited. For example, Japan was not capable of controlling the political and strategic atmosphere between China and Taiwan. Furthermore, Japan's widely shared sense of guilt and shame over its past actions toward China allowed the Chinese to assume the moral high ground in the relationship and thus gave China political leverage it would have lacked otherwise. The Japanese, meanwhile, have presumed little right to criticize China, and their attitude toward China has been far more passive than it might have been.

Nakasone's Leadership and Domestic Constraints

To clarify the continuity of Japan's foreign policy posture, this section analyzes Prime Minister Nakasone Yasuhiro's attempts to make changes in Japan's foreign policy from the early to the mid-1980s, focusing on his alliance diplomacy with the United States. Even Nakasone, by far the strongest and most independent leader of the period, was greatly constrained by some of the same domestic factors noted earlier, so that his diplomacy exhibits remarkable continuity with that of his predecessors and his successors.

Nakasone, who served as prime minister from November 1982 to November 1987, put a much higher priority on foreign policy than had LDP prime ministers before him and attempted to transform Japan into an "international state." In a personal memo shortly before he took office, he wrote that he would "attach great importance to foreign relations."[37] *Nakasone Naikaku-shi* (History of the Nakasone Cabinet), edited by the Institute for International Policy Studies, which Nakasone established after his retirement from the premiership, summarizes his diplomatic aim: "to search for the international political role proportionate to Japan's economic power." Nakasone "intended to change the style of Japanese diplomacy which had been carried on by the successive conservative administrations after World War II," or, to put it more concretely, he "tried to pull the rudder [of the Japanese external policy] from the self-restrained, passive diplomacy based on economism to a course for Japan to obtain political major power status."[38] On June 3, 1983, as he flew back to Japan from the Williamsburg summit, generally regarded as one of the major achievements of his diplomacy, Nakasone noted in his diary:

Departing from the traditional, opportunistic, wait-and-see, egoistic style [of Japanese diplomacy], I behaved broad-mindedly and led [the meeting] with my own strategy and with my goals of [promoting] the interests of the free world and Japan. I believe that I made the boldest diplomatic move in the postwar period next to Yoshida's peace settlement[in 1951]. [Japan] has not been, thus far, able to make good use of its capability as an economic major power from the standpoint of international politics. I made 100 percent use of it. It is the true value of politics. . . . This new emergence of Japan in international politics must be maintained, and this status must not be curtailed or abandoned. Such will be the single most important qualification for Japanese leaders from now on.[39]

One question remains: How and to what extent could Nakasone actually change Japanese foreign policy? Today, more than a decade after his resignation, Japan's diplomatic style has moved in only limited ways toward the bold international role Nakasone advocated. The late Kosaka Masataka, one of the most influential experts on international politics in postwar Japan, repeatedly criticized Japanese diplomacy in the 1990s for remaining a basically reactive "typical small-power diplomacy," a stance that was no longer appropriate for Japan.[40] Even now, at the start of the twenty-first century, similar voices criticizing and lamenting Japan's role are still frequently heard, both inside and outside Japan.

CHANGES IN NAKASONE'S U.S.-JAPAN
ALLIANCE DIPLOMACY

By the time Nakasone succeeded Suzuki on November 27, 1982, U.S.-Japan relations had seriously deteriorated, and economic tensions were rapidly becoming more serious. In 1982, the U.S. trade deficit with Japan amounted to $19 billion, or about half the total U.S. trade deficit. In the area of security, the United States was irritated by the lukewarm attitude of the Suzuki administration, which did not respond well to U.S. demands that Japan bear a greater share of the defense burden. On December 12, 1982, the U.S. Senate unanimously adopted a resolution calling for a rapid increase in Japan's defense spending, to between 1.4 and 2.0 percent of its GNP. But Japan did not change the Miki cabinet guideline of keeping military expenditures below 1 percent of GNP.

As soon as he took office, Nakasone surprised Washington and the Japanese public by exercising strong leadership in an attempt to strengthen U.S.-Japan security relations. First he decided to increase Japan's defense budget for fiscal year 1983 over fiscal year 1982 by 6.5 percent, despite a severe revenue shortfall and strong resistance by the Ministry of Finance. According to Nakasone's diary entry of December 30, 1982, when he ordered Yamaguchi Mitsuhide, the director general of the Budget Bureau of the Ministry of Finance, to institute the increase, Yamaguchi's face "twitched and became pale." Nakasone, however, "stuck to" his position.[41] Two weeks later, Nakasone responded positively to a U.S. request authorizing the transfer of Japanese military technology, a question that had been on the table for a year and half. He decided to make the transfer possible by not applying the "Three Principles on Arms Export" to the United States. Shortly thereafter, during his visit to Washington for the first summit meeting with President Reagan, Nakasone made a series of candid remarks, such as "Japan and the United States form . . . a community with a single destiny" and Japan would serve as an "unsinkable aircraft carrier" in the Pacific, about the alliance between the two countries. These statements clearly indicated to everyone that Japan was willing to undertake more defense efforts on its own initiative and to carry out its responsibilities as a U.S. ally. The Reagan administration enthusiastically welcomed Nakasone's active commitment to the U.S.-Japan alliance, and it was appreciated above all by President Reagan himself.

Throughout his tenure in office, Prime Minister Nakasone maintained his active commitment to the U.S.-Japan alliance. During the period when Japan tried to reduce its budget deficit by imposing a severe limit on almost all categories of national expenditures, he gave the defense budget special treatment, allowing an annual increase of between 5.2 and 6.9 percent every year. In December 1986, he decided to lift the 1 percent of GNP ceiling on defense expenditures and set the figure for fiscal year 1987 at a level of 1.004 percent of GNP. Throughout the Nakasone years, joint exercises between the Japanese Self-Defense Forces and U.S. forces increased in number and expanded in scope. Joint study on the defense of sea lanes of communication was also conducted. At the annual Group of Seven summit meetings, Nakasone took a strong pro-U.S. stance based on his personal, intimate friendship with President Reagan, the celebrated "Ron-Yasu" relationship, and emphasized the indivisibility of the security of the Group of Seven countries.

CONTINUITIES IN NAKASONE'S U.S.-JAPAN ALLIANCE DIPLOMACY

Despite these remarkable changes, considerable elements of continuity from the past are also discernible in Nakasone's U.S. alliance policies. First, even he did not attempt to change the traditional framework of Japan's U.S. alli-

ance policy. Under the Nakasone administration, as in the past, Japan
showed no sign of seeking military autonomy and continued to rely heavily
on the United States for its security. Nakasone's attempt to strengthen
the U.S.-Japan alliance did not go beyond the limits set by the Japanese
constitution.

A second, related point is that constitutional restraints on Japan's defense
and U.S. alliance policies also remained unchanged. Nakasone did not touch
the issue of Article 9 of the constitution or the self-imposed restraints on Japan's defense policies that are derived from it. According to the history of
the Nakasone cabinet published by his research institute,

> If we think seriously about the security issues [of Japan], in the end we will inevita-
> bly come up against the issue of the Constitution. . . . Nakasone is not an advocate
> of a hasty revision of the Constitution. He, however, believes strongly that now is
> the time for that issue to be discussed widely at the political scene as well as among
> the people. This represents the fundamental issue in the final settlement of postwar
> politics and the biggest taboo that must be broken. Nakasone, however, could not
> carry out this task after all.[42]

For example, in placing such a high priority on strengthening the U.S.-
Japan alliance, Nakasone was unwilling to reconsider the Japanese government's traditional constitutional interpretation of Japan's exercise of the
right of collective self-defense as unconstitutional. Nor during his administration could Nakasone dispatch the Self-Defense Forces abroad. In 1987,
when Washington asked its allies, including Japan, to consider sending
minesweepers to the Persian Gulf, he had to abandon his effort to dispatch
the Maritime Self-Defense Forces' ships in the face of strong objections
from Chief Cabinet Secretary Gotoda Masaharu.[43]

Third, the abolition of the 1 percent of GNP ceiling on defense expenditures was a symbolic act that did not in itself lead to a real change in the substance of Japan's defense posture. Since then, these expenditures have never
exceeded 1.013 percent of GNP, and in the 1990s, the figure again dropped below 1 percent. As Muroyama Yoshimasa demonstrates, excluding the cost of
stationing U.S. forces in Japan, the size of Japan's "genuine" defense expenditures in the postwar era has been remarkably stable, from 0.8 to 1 percent of its
GNP.[44] Even Nakasone's decision did not deviate much from that tradition.

Fourth, as for concrete measures to improve the effectiveness of the U.S.-
Japan alliance, Nakasone did not do much. His administration, for example,

could not remedy the lack of bilateral discussion on joint operations in the case of any contingency beyond Japan's territories in the Far East. In addition, the transfer of Japanese military technology to the United States proceeded very slowly.[45]

FACTORS AFFECTING CHANGE AND CONTINUITY

Several factors affected Japan's U.S. alliance policy under the Nakasone administration. First, the demand for change came mainly through external pressure (gaiatsu), that is, from the United States. During that time, the relative expansion of Japan's economic power and the poor performance of the American economy produced increasingly fierce economic friction between the two countries. Under these circumstances, U.S. demands that Japan bear a greater share of the defense burden intensified. Because Prime Minister Suzuki Zenko, whose strategic ability and capacity for leadership were both arguably weaker than those demonstrated by almost all other postwar prime ministers, failed to respond to such demands effectively, U.S.-Japan relations were at a nadir when Nakasone took office in November 1982. To remedy the situation, Nakasone issued a series of bold decisions during the first fifty days of his administration that dramatically eased American frustration. Here, Nakasone's personality was quite obviously a significant factor. It is also certainly true that some of the changes already taking place in Japanese society eased the way for Nakasone's actions. For example, from the late 1970s to the mid-1980s, the Japanese public had in general become much more conservative, with the important result that public support for the U.S.-Japan security treaty system had stabilized at a high level. In a further notable change, *Yomiuri Shinbun*, the national daily with the largest circulation, became remarkably progovernment and began to support the U.S.-Japan alliance and the constitutionality of the Self-Defense Forces.

At the same time, however, Nakasone was confronted with several domestic factors that hindered the achievement of dramatic changes in Japan's U.S. alliance policy. First and fundamentally, postwar pacifism remained strong. During the Nakasone years, despite the conservative shift in public opinion, the Japanese public continued to feel strong abhorrence toward the use of any military means in foreign policy, including defense policy. The national postwar consensus had been that Japan should not participate in international power politics unless forced to do so, and the majority of the Japanese people were still far from enthusiastic about the idea.

Thus, Nakasone's attempts to strengthen the U.S.-Japan alliance in his early days as prime minister were unpopular domestically. According to the public opinion poll conducted by *Yomiuri Shinbun* in February 1983, shortly after Nakasone had attended his first summit meeting with President Reagan in Washington and made statements favoring U.S.-Japanese relations, the approval rating for the Nakasone cabinet dropped 5.1 percent from that of the previous month.[46] Clearly the public did not like what Nakasone said in Washington. His bold moves to push Japan into a more active role in the U.S.-Japan alliance were severely criticized not only by the general public, the mass media, and the opposition parties but also from within the ruling Liberal Democratic Party. Nakasone had to make a public statement that his cabinet would thereafter "attach greater importance to domestic politics."[47] Nakasone had sought to compensate for his weakness in the LDP by cultivating a high level of popular support, but as long as the Japanese public was unsympathetic to a stronger U.S.-Japan alliance, Nakasone's freedom of action in that direction was limited.

Second, Nakasone, like the prime ministers who preceded him, also faced limitations in power and leadership under the long one-party dominance of the LDP. Third, even within the LDP, members disagreed over how and to what extent the U.S.-Japan alliance should be strengthened. Anti-American nationalists and pacifists severely criticized Nakasone's approach. For example, Gotoda Masaharu, one of the most powerful cabinet members throughout the Nakasone administration and a strong pacifist, strongly opposed sending Japanese minesweepers to the Persian Gulf in 1987. Such opposition also limited Nakasone's freedom of action.

Fourth, many Japanese felt that U.S. demands in both economic and security areas were often unreasonable, even outrageous. They reacted to the U.S. attitude toward Japan with a widely shared sense of revulsion. Nakasone himself also seemed to consider some U.S. economic demands unjust; in a personal memorandum (of December 1982 or January 1983), he wrote: "The laziness of America, how strange it is that an honor student is scolded!"[48] On security issues, however, Nakasone believed that Japan must meet U.S. demands immediately. In his first press conference as prime minister, he noted, "It cannot be said that Japan has made great defense efforts in the past."[49] Here again, however, Nakasone, who depended on popular support, could not ignore the reactions of a considerable proportion of the Japanese public.

To understand Japan's foreign policy toward the United States and China during the two decades following 1972, one must understand its domestic situation and the constraints such factors imposed, which may in many respects be more severe than those in other countries. Domestic factors promoted continuity in Japan's external posture. Even a strong leader like Nakasone, whose administration lasted for five years, more than twice the average of other administrations during this period, could not conduct diplomacy without taking domestic constraints into account.

Most of these domestic factors have changed little even today. Although the LDP's one-party rule came to an end in 1993, the LDP itself returned to power in less than a year and remains at the center of Japanese politics. Domestic politics, however, became more fluid in the 1990s. Since 1993, for example, Japan has had six prime ministers, whose brief administrations have undercut any attempt to exercise strong political leadership. Postwar pacifism also continues to play an influential role, as does the lack of an urban-based political party and the limited political power of the Ministry of Foreign Affairs. As the twenty-first century begins, the continuities in Japan's foreign policy toward the United States and China remain, and there are few signs, at least domestically, that Japan's foreign policy will soon undergo drastic change.

II

U.S.-China Relations

CHAPTER FOUR

U.S. Relations with China

Robert S. Ross

Between 1969 and 1972, the United States and China formed a de facto strategic partnership to oppose Soviet power in East Asia. In doing so, they did not put aside conflicts of interest but negotiated over these issues, especially U.S. policy toward Taiwan. From 1972 to 1989, these conflicts of interest contributed to periodic ups and downs, depending on each side's respective domestic politics and its assessment of each other's security circumstances. This essay examines the evolution of U.S.-China relations during this period of strategic partnership, focusing in particular on the international and domestic sources of their bilateral conflict and cooperation as they joined together against a common security threat, the Soviet Union. It also considers the impact of changing U.S.-China relations on Sino-Japanese relations.

The United States and China were not only great powers seeking to pursue their respective national interests while opposing the Soviet Union, they were also anchors in a regionwide coalition against Soviet power. During the 1970s and 1980s, China exercised considerable influence over Thailand and, with uneven results, Cambodia. The United States, for its part, influenced the foreign policies of its closest allies in the region, South Korea, Japan, and the Philippines. As the dominant players, China and the United States were in a position to shape the foreign policies of these respective strategic dependencies, especially in relation to the Soviet Union. But the state of U.S.-

China relations also influenced the bilateral relationships between each power and the subordinate states. U.S.-China relations, for example, affected both Sino-Thai relations and Sino-Japanese relations.

After Shanghai: China Policy Under Nixon and Ford

The cold war conditions that shaped U.S. policy toward China from 1969 to 1972 were also the primary policy determinants during the remaining years of the Nixon administration and throughout the Ford administration, in which Henry Kissinger, as national security adviser and secretary of state, provided continuity between the two periods. Under both Richard Nixon and Gerald Ford, the United States focused on protecting its security in the post-Vietnam era as the Soviet Union expanded its defense budget, its hardware deployments, and its efforts in the Third World.

Throughout these years, China remained a strategic U.S. partner. In laying out his post-Vietnam regional security policy in the "Guam Doctrine" in 1969, President Nixon observed that the United States could no longer contain Soviet power throughout the world by itself and that it would now have to work closely with regional partners who shared this goal. By ending Sino-American hostility and managing the Taiwan issue, he said, Washington could reduce the need to prepare for war against China and maintain deployments in Indochina. It could retrench in East Asia and manage its regional commitments without necessarily ceding ground to Soviet power. U.S.-China rapprochement also enabled Beijing to focus on resisting Soviet encirclement rather than on dividing its resources to prepare for war on two fronts—against both the United States and the Soviet Union. China could therefore try to prevent the Soviet Union from capitalizing on the U.S. defeat in Vietnam by filling the "vacuum" and bringing all of Indochina and Thailand into its strategic orbit. Equally important, Sino-American rapprochement sent a strong signal to the region that cooperation with China was preferable to accommodation to Soviet power. Hence Thailand, for example, by developing relations with China, could resist expanded Vietnamese power in Indochina and, by extension, expanded Soviet influence on its borders. Malaysia and the Philippines also adjusted their China policies accordingly.

Nixon's opening to China in 1971–72 set in motion America's new security policy for East Asia. The U.S.-China security relationship, however, required continuing action. It was premised on a U.S. commitment to normal-

izing relations with the People's Republic of China and breaking off diplomatic relations with the Republic of China. Failure to fulfill this commitment could lead to renewed U.S.-China friction, with obvious implications
for U.S. security in Asia. Equally important, U.S.-China friction might em-
bolden the Soviet Union to take advantage of America's post-Vietnam passivity, further undermining U.S. security. Following President Nixon's visit
to China in February 1972, U.S. security policy required that the White
House further consolidate U.S.-China cooperation by normalizing relations,
yet its ability to do so was increasingly hampered by domestic politics. The
Watergate affair, beginning in 1974, and its aftermath, and the politics of
the 1976 presidential campaign seriously undermined Washington's position
in the cold war as well as its ability to realize its objectives for U.S.-China
relations.

The Last Success: Establishing Liaison Offices

After Nixon's 1972 visit to China, conducting diplomacy and normalization
negotiations through diplomats in Paris was no longer adequate. Since October of the previous year, the United States had been proposing that the
two sides establish liaison offices in each other's capitals, but China had consistently rejected the proposal. Mao Zedong and other Chinese leaders pre-
sumably believed that until China could be confident about U.S. intentions
and the direction of the relationship, posting officials was premature. Then,
in preparation for the 1972 summit, China's Politburo authorized acceptance
of the liaison office proposal if the summit proved successful. When Kissinger repeated the proposal during his February 1973 visit to China, Zhou
Enlai accepted.[1]

Kissinger's visit accomplished a number of other objectives beyond simply enhancing communication. For the United States, the liaison office
agreement was a visible step toward improved political cooperation between
the two countries. Within Kissinger's grand strategy, the agreement cautioned the Soviet Union against challenging U.S. interests in Europe and
elsewhere by raising the prospect of a common U.S.-China strategic response. The establishment of liaison offices also suggested that U.S.-China
momentum had not ebbed, and that greater cooperation was possible, inclu-
idng normalization of relations. This possibility offered a further incentive
to the Soviet Union to cooperate in arms control, rather than escalating the
nuclear arms race and thus exacerbating U.S.-Soviet conflict. Finally, Nixon

and Kissinger may have believed that establishing a liaison office in Beijing would help mitigate later political reaction to normalization at home. As a halfway measure, the liaison office would prepare the American public and members of Congress for the final step—U.S. recognition of Beijing and the breaking off of diplomatic relations with Taipei.

The establishment of liaison offices also served a number of important Chinese interests. Like the United States, China used U.S.-China relations as a way to caution the Soviet Union against challenging its interests. Although China had weathered the storm of the 1969 Sino-Soviet border conflict and thinly veiled Soviet nuclear threats, the Soviet military presence on China's border remained a serious concern, and Chinese leaders feared that U.S.-Soviet détente might free Moscow to focus its attention on China rather than on Europe. As Chinese leaders explained to government and party officials, China needed to consolidate U.S.-China relations to manage the Soviet threat.[2] In this strategic context, improved relations in the form of liaison offices would bolster Chinese security by raising the prospect of U.S. cooperation against a possible Soviet attack on Chinese territory.

China also accepted Kissinger's proposal because, like the United States, it saw liaison offices as an intermediate step in the normalization process. But whereas for the United States establishment of liaison offices contributed to U.S. security without any downside, for China it was a compromise that did not achieve its ultimate goal, a clear U.S. decision to normalize relations. Earlier, Nixon and Kissinger had assured Chinese leaders that the United States would act on normalization during Nixon's second term. Kissinger repeated these assurances during his February 1973 visit, reportedly reassuring Chinese leaders that Nixon accepted China's condition that the United States break off relations with Taiwan and was prepared to do so in the final two years of his term.[3] China's decision to open liaison offices reflected its confidence in the Nixon administration's commitment.

The positive trend in U.S.-China cooperation opened the way for improved Sino-Japanese relations by transforming Chinese attitudes toward the U.S.-Japan alliance and U.S. attitudes toward improved Sino-Japanese relations. Because the United States was no longer an adversary, Chinese leaders no longer aimed to weaken U.S. influence in Asia. On the contrary, now that China could avail itself of American power to offset the Soviet threat, it was to China's advantage to be a tacit member of the U.S. coalition in East Asia, which posed the strongest possible challenge to Soviet power.

In Chinese eyes, the U.S.-Japan alliance was not U.S. "imperialism" in the service of a resurgent Japanese "militarism" but an asset in China's effort to oppose Soviet power in Asia.

In 1971, Zhou Enlai had frequently complained to Kissinger about the revival of Japanese militarism and Japan's desire to acquire nuclear weapons. He also complained about the role of the U.S.-Japan alliance in promoting Japanese militarism. Throughout that year, the Chinese media characterized Japan as China's second most worrisome security problem. But following the 1972 U.S.-China Beijing summit, Chinese leaders assured Japanese leaders that they did not consider the U.S.-Japan security treaty a problem. During Kissinger's 1973 visit to Beijing, Chinese leaders indicated that Japan was an "incipient ally" of China in its continuing effort to resist Soviet and Indian pressure, and that the U.S.-Japan security treaty in fact contributed to Japanese resistance to Soviet pressure.[4]

The impact of U.S.-China rapprochement on Japan's China policy was even more dramatic. Japan had long struggled with U.S. demands for constraint in its China policy. Although it had never been passive and, within the parameters of U.S. policy, had developed its own policy toward China, especially in economic relations, on political issues Japan had usually deferred to the United States.[5] A large sector of the Japanese public and opposition politicians, however, had long argued that Japan should establish diplomatic relations with China and conduct normal trade relations. But as a dependent ally of the United States, Japanese leaders felt compelled to take U.S. policy toward China into account. Thus, many Japanese, particularly Prime Minister Sato Eisaku, felt betrayed when Nixon "shocked" them by suddenly changing course on China without consulting Japan beforehand. Sato had wanted to improve relations with China and had signaled Beijing of his interest in normalization, but he held back for fear of alienating the United States.[6] Many Japanese suspected that the United States had kept its China policy secret to give U.S. firms a head start over Japanese firms in penetrating the Chinese economy or to punish Sato for his failure to restrain Japanese textile exports.

But even after Nixon's visit to Beijing in 1972, Prime Minister Tanaka Kakuei, Sato's successor, continued to defer to Washington on political matters. Although Kissinger's and Nixon's visits to China and the signing of the Shanghai Communiqué signaled Japan that the United States could open relations with Beijing, Tokyo sought further assurances of support for normalization from Nixon and Secretary of State William P. Rogers.[7] Only when it was confident of U.S. support did Tokyo take the initiative. Shortly after Tanaka assumed office in July 1972 with the help of the campaign slogan "Don't miss the boat to China," he traveled to Beijing. Zhou Enlai reassured him that China no longer opposed the U.S.-Japan security treaty and would not seek war reparations once Tokyo had normalized relations with Beijing. In an implicit acknowledgment that U.S.-China cooperation against the Soviet Union provided a foundation for Sino-Japanese rapprochement, Tanaka and Zhou also pledged not to seek hegemony in Asia and to oppose the hegemony of others.[8]

During the cold war, developing U.S.-China-Japan cooperation was possible, but always within the context of the U.S.-China security relationship. First, relations between the United States and China constrained their respective policies toward third parties. China was thus prepared to cooperate with Japan, an American ally, following the development of U.S.-China security cooperation. Second, as the two dominant powers in the tacit anti-Soviet coalition in East Asia, China and the United States established the foreign policy parameters of their security partners. Japan thus followed the U.S. lead and revised its policy toward China, a pattern that would endure through the end of the cold war.

The Impasse: Watergate and the Ford Administration

Although Kissinger had told Chinese leaders in 1973 that Nixon intended to normalize relations with China in the last two years of his presidency, Nixon's second term lasted less than two years. Gerald Ford finished out his term and immediately faced a reelection campaign, which complicated any attempt to fulfill Nixon's commitment to China. Washington's inability to take up the normalization issue introduced a degree of tension into U.S.-China relations.

Following the liaison offices breakthrough of 1973, Kissinger remained convinced of the strategic utility of U.S.-China cooperation. The next step, normalization of relations, would signal that Sino-American conflict had ended, that the Taiwan issue was no longer an obstacle, and that future cooperation might entail coordination of security policies. Normalization would also compensate for U.S. retrenchment in Asia and further caution the Soviet Union against taking advantage of U.S. isolationism. Indeed, U.S.-China cooperation had assumed greater significance in U.S. security policy after Kissinger's February 1973 visit to Beijing. Then came the revelations of the Watergate scandal, which first weakened and then destroyed the Nixon presidency. His successor, Gerald Ford, the first U.S. president who had not been elected, soon found his legitimacy in question. Moreover, the Congress elected in 1974 was isolationist, resisting both defense spending and active U.S. opposition to Soviet strategic initiatives in Europe and the Third World. Then, in April 1975, America watched as Cambodia and then Vietnam fell to communist armies, thus finalizing the U.S. defeat in Indochina.

As Nixon and Ford faced increasingly difficult domestic circumstances, Kissinger's role in policymaking assumed greater importance. In August 1973, Nixon appointed Kissinger secretary of state but allowed him to retain his position as national security adviser. Ford came to depend on Kissinger for advice on all foreign policy issues. His presence brought continuity to foreign policy during a period of domestic upheaval. Convinced of the need to shore up alliances in Asia, Kissinger wanted to move ahead on normalizing relations with China. During his November 1973 visit to Beijing, he assured his Chinese hosts that he had come "to speed up progress toward normalization" and that the United States wanted to complete the normalization process "as rapidly as possible."[9] The United States moved to resolve the claims-assets issue, which concerned Chinese and American seizure of each other's assets following the establishment of the People's Republic in 1949.

But as American domestic politics unfolded, Kissinger's strategy shifted. By April 1974, four months before Nixon's resignation, Kissinger had begun to temporize, explaining to Deng Xiaoping that Washington needed to give further study to resolving the "one-China" problem. In August, Ford wrote to Mao to say that he had no higher priority than "accelerating normalization." But by November, as Chinese leaders observed, it was clear that Kissinger was only interested in "gaining time." Raising new obstacles to a normalization agreement, he offered a proposal that was less accommodating than Japan's formula for normalization. He expected a statement from China of its plans for peaceful unification and suggested that after normalization, Taiwan should have a liaison office in Washington. Deng Xiaoping noted, quite accurately, that Kissinger's suggestions were a retreat from previous U.S. proposals.[10]

Kissinger was stalling for time, but he was not content to allow relations with China to stagnate. His strategy for dealing with Soviet power from a position of weakness after the failure in Vietnam required additional U.S.-China cooperation. Faced with domestic constraints and Soviet opportunism, Kissinger sought at least an illusion of progress in U.S.-China cooperation, both to appease Chinese impatience and to enhance U.S. efforts to caution the Soviet Union against risk-taking in Asia. Kissinger therefore suggested to Chinese leaders that the two countries agree to intermediary steps. He wanted President Ford to visit China, hoping that a U.S.-China summit would produce a joint statement suggesting enhanced U.S.-China cooperation. Kissinger likewise significantly reduced the U.S. troop presence on Taiwan, a necessary prelude to normalizing diplomatic relations with the PRC, and sanctioned the sale of British Rolls-Royce aircraft engines to China without the approval of the Coordinating Committee for Multilateral Export Controls, suggesting nascent U.S.-China military cooperation.

But while the United States sought the illusion of progress, China wanted real progress and was unwilling to allow itself to be used as a pawn in U.S. security policy. It resisted Kissinger's gestures, creating tension in relations between the two countries. During his visits to China, Kissinger was subjected to snubs and to persistent, and often harsh, criticism. China implied that without normalization, there should not be a summit. In response to Kissinger's proposed joint statement, Foreign Minister Qiao Guanhua suggested issuing one that would sharply delineate U.S.-China differences, in effect exposing U.S.-China tensions to Moscow and undermining Kissinger's strategic objective. When Kissinger rejected Qiao's proposal, Qiao responded that perhaps there should not be any statement. Indeed, Beijing refused to set a date for Ford's visit until just before the summit, implying that it might not occur. Although China finally received President Ford in November 1975, it refused to play the role assigned to it in Kissinger's diplomatic maneuvering: there was no joint statement and no suggestion of enhanced U.S.-China cooperation.[11]

Not only had Kissinger been unable to normalize relations with China, he could not conceal growing U.S.-China friction. Washington cut short President Ford's visit when it became clear that Beijing would not provide the appropriate grand welcome. The American media, aware that something was amiss, pressed Kissinger for an explanation, thus putting the U.S. policy failure on public display.

The new impasse in U.S. policy toward China also slowed progress in Sino-Japanese cooperation. The apparent obstacle was Japan's reluctance to undertake expanded Sino-Japanese security cooperation while U.S.-China relations stagnated. Although China and Japan had established diplomatic relations in 1972, legally they were still at war: Tokyo and Beijing had yet to sign a peace treaty concluding their hostilities in World War II. Peace treaty negotiations began in late 1974, when Vice Foreign Minister Togo Fumihiko of Japan met with Vice Foreign Minister Han Nianlong of China in Tokyo.[12] After a series of meetings, the two sides agreed to a basic peace treaty framework, and Japanese leaders were optimistic that the two sides would soon reach agreement. But agreement was held up by a late Chinese demand that the peace treaty include a statement from the Sino-Japanese normalization agreement committing China and Japan to oppose the efforts of any country to establish hegemony in Asia.

China was attempting to use the peace treaty to strengthen its security vis-à-vis the Soviet Union. Japanese leaders rejected China's demand, and negotiations quickly reached an impasse. Japan had originally accepted the antihegemony clause during normalization negotiations because it was a near replica of the antihegemony clause in the 1972 U.S.-China summit communiqué. Now, however, the United States and China were unable to expand cooperation, so that reaffirming Sino-Japanese security cooperation against the Soviet Union would place Japan ahead of the United States, just as Moscow was pressuring Tokyo to resist Beijing's designs to lure Japan into an anti-Soviet alliance. Indeed, there were even suggestions that Washington might not be pleased should Japan reach an early agreement with China. These uncertain diplomatic circumstances, combined with domestic ambivalence toward the antihegemony clause, persuaded Japanese leaders to refuse to compromise. Tokyo and Beijing failed to reach agreement.

In the years following the normalization of relations, Japan and China focused on the relatively less sensitive issue of economic cooperation. During this period as during most of the post–World War II era, Japan enjoyed greater policy autonomy from the United States in its economic than in its political relations with China. Moreover, because Japan had already established diplomatic relations with China, it could, unlike the United States, negotiate legal state-to-state agreements governing economic relations. In January 1974 the two governments signed a trade agreement. Later that year they concluded agreements on civil aviation and maritime transport and, in

August 1975, a fisheries agreement delimiting the areas for each side's fishing activities. These four agreements provided a foundation for expanded economic relations.[13]

But following the pattern established in 1971–73, on the issue of political cooperation with China, Japanese policy was affected by U.S. policy. Japan was reluctant to be out in front of the United States. On the other hand, China did not want to retreat from cooperation with Japan. On the contrary, once the new structure of the anti-Soviet coalition had been established and China was confident that the United States would not use its alliances in Asia to undermine Chinese security, China's policy toward Japan took a further turn. In the new triangular relationship, while U.S.-China relations were at an impasse, China planned to expand its relations with Japan. China's insistence on including the antihegemony clause in the peace treaty reflected Beijing's interest in expanded security cooperation with Tokyo. When China first presented this demand to Japan, in February 1975, U.S.-China relations were at a stalemate. Improved Sino-Japanese relations might pressure Washington to accelerate the U.S.-China normalization process and would partially substitute for the setback U.S. temporizing had created in Beijing's anti-Soviet strategy.

But China's effort to use Japan to offset its problems with the United States failed. Japan was wary of antagonizing the Soviet Union, but perhaps even more important, it depended on the United States for security and could not depart in any significant way from established U.S. policy toward China. Progress in Sino-Japanese cooperation would wait until the United States was prepared to expand its cooperation with China.

The Carter Administration and China: Normalization of Relations

The Ford administration had been eager to consolidate U.S. relations with China to manage Soviet power but was deterred by domestic political considerations. The Carter administration, however, although unencumbered by domestic politics, did not share either the Ford administration's preoccupation with Soviet power or its sense of urgency about normalizing diplomatic relations with China. For the first eighteen months of the Carter administration, the United States continued to temporize. Only when President Carter was persuaded that cooperation with China was a necessary strategic response to Soviet foreign policy did his administration actively seek normalization. During the Carter administration as during the

Nixon and Ford administrations, Sino-Japanese relations reflected developments in U.S.-China relations. In the context of U.S.-China friction over normalization, Beijing sought improved relations with Japan. But Tokyo hesitated until the United States encouraged Japan to accept PRC conditions for the peace treaty.

DEFERRING NORMALIZATION

Nixon, Ford, and Kissinger had all based U.S. policy toward China on the premise that American domestic politics created opportunities for Soviet opportunism and prevented the United States from being able to manage Soviet power unilaterally. President Jimmy Carter differed from his predecessors in his belief that the Soviet Union was not resolutely opportunistic but was amenable to mutually beneficial arms control agreements that would constrain Soviet power. Ford had banished the word *détente* from his presidential campaign, but Carter embraced it. His Soviet policy was exemplified by his decision to cancel production of the B-1 bomber, end production of the Minuteman III intercontinental ballistic missile (ICBM), and delay the production of a mobile ICBM. The Carter administration also proposed a far-reaching arms control agreement calling for a disproportionate Soviet reduction of ICBMs.

Because of its active interest in détente, the Carter administration deferred normalization of relations with China. When Secretary of State Cyrus Vance visited Beijing in August 1977, he announced that the United States was prepared to normalize relations with China but would need to maintain an official presence in Taiwan through either a consulate or a liaison office. Beijing had rejected a similar Kissinger proposal in 1974, and the Ford administration had subsequently abandoned this position. Clearly, Vance's proposal was a "nonstarter." Even its proponents in the State Department understood that China was likely to reject it.[14] Nonetheless, since Vance and Carter were in no hurry on normalization, the proposal did not challenge U.S. policy objectives. They also hoped that delay would promote U.S.-Soviet détente by minimizing Soviet suspicions about U.S. intentions toward China.

But Chinese leaders were clearly dismayed. They had indicated their strong interest in rapid normalization, yet Vance's proposal was not only unacceptable, it also meant further delay. Deng Xiaoping told Vance that this U.S. position was a "step backward." China continued to undermine

U.S. efforts to achieve the appearance of progress in U.S.-China relations. When the White House reported that the Chinese had been flexible on the terms of normalization and Carter praised Vance for having achieved a "major step forward," Deng Xiaoping publicly countered that Vance's visit had been a setback to relations and that the Carter administration had retreated from the position of its predecessors. Deng's public rebuke not only protected him from domestic charges of weakness during a critical period in the post-Mao succession, it also undermined U.S. efforts to use China to strengthen its position vis-à-vis the Soviet Union while refusing concessions to China on normalization.

After Vance returned to Washington, where the White House was preoccupied with the Senate ratification of the Panama Canal treaty, normalization remained a low priority. Vance also preferred that U.S.-China cooperation remain dormant until he had achieved success in U.S.-Soviet relations. Indeed, the State Department had yet to decide to open substantive negotiations on the issue with Beijing. When Ambassador Leonard Woodcock demanded negotiating instructions regarding normalization before returning to Beijing, he encountered State Department resistance. When he finally received his instructions and returned in February 1978, he was permitted to report to Chinese leaders that Washington no longer sought an official presence in Taiwan after normalization, but he was not authorized to resume actual negotiations.

It was clear to Beijing that Washington was still not interested in rapid normalization. Deng complained that the momentum had slowed, and Li Xiannian, a key member of the Politburo, told reporters that he was "quite unhappy" with Carter's unwillingness to part with his "old friend" Taiwan. In this atmosphere, China was unwilling to reach any preliminary agreements with Washington. In 1977 Vance had hoped to complete negotiations on the claims-assets issue, but Beijing again resisted, just as it had during the Nixon and Ford administrations. As long as the Carter administration was content to maintain unofficial relations with China, Beijing was content to allow Sino-U.S. relations to remain at a standstill.

Inaction in U.S.-China relations continued to set the parameters of Sino-Japanese relations. On the one hand, trade relations between Japan and China continued to develop during the late Ford and early Carter years. In 1977 two-way trade increased by nearly 15 percent over the previous year, and in 1978 Tokyo and Beijing reached a five-year, $20 billion agreement calling for Japanese imports of Chinese oil and coal and Chinese imports of Japanese industrial plants and technology, construction machinery, and equipment. On the other hand, despite PRC efforts, developments in Sino-Japanese political relations continued to await the signing of a peace treaty.

Despite the coolness in U.S.-China relations, Beijing continued to pressure Japan to sign a peace treaty containing the antihegemony language of the 1972 normalization agreement. But Tokyo searched for compromise solutions to avoid the diplomatic consolidation of Sino-Japanese cooperation against the Soviet Union. It insisted that China agree to include a statement saying the treaty was not directed against any "third party." In January 1977, Fukuda Takeo, Japan's new prime minister, expressed strong support for a treaty and suggested that he could accept China's antihegemony terms. In May, Deng Xiaoping told members of the Japanese Diet that a peace treaty could be concluded quickly if Fukuda had indeed made up his mind. Nonetheless, Fukuda did not initiate substantive negotiations. Japanese policy did not change following the tensions arising from the Senkaku (Diaoyu) islands incident of April 1978, in which armed Chinese fishing boats approached the islands and challenged Japanese territorial waters. Japanese domestic politics, in the context of U.S.-Soviet détente and the associated temporizing in U.S. policy toward normalization of relations with China, persuaded Tokyo to resist Beijing's demands for a peace agreement on anti-Soviet terms.

The triangular connections established in the aftermath of Nixon's 1972 visit to Beijing continued to prevail during the Carter administration. Confident that U.S. alliances in East Asia were no longer directed at China, Chinese leaders did not view U.S.-China tensions as an obstacle to cooperation with Japan. On the contrary, China's inability to advance normalization with the United States seemed to encourage Beijing to try to improve political ties with Tokyo. No matter how persistent, however, Beijing lacked the leverage to persuade Japan to adopt a China policy fundamentally different from that of the United States.

THE SOVIET CHALLENGE AND U.S.-CHINA RELATIONS

Initially, the Carter administration was not prepared to follow its predecessors and use cooperation with China to manage Soviet power. Before long, however, it came to accept its predecessors' view of the Soviet Union and adopted its predecessors' China policy. Greater concern about Soviet power alleviated any concern about normalizing relations with China. Indeed, the growing importance of China as a key element in security policy actually expedited normalization and subsequent cooperation.

The primary reason for the Carter administration's reevaluation of U.S.-Soviet détente was Soviet policy. In 1977, the Soviet Union benefited from a Communist coup in Ethiopia and subsequently sent Cuban troops in support of Ethiopia's efforts to defeat Somalia in the conflict over the Ogaden region. Then, in April 1978, a pro-Soviet coup occurred in Afghanistan; in May, Soviet-backed rebels based in Angola occupied a part of Zaire; and in June Cuban-backed South Yemeni troops assumed control of Yemen and executed the president of South Yemen. Whereas in the past Carter had been prepared to separate Third World conflicts from superpower relations, this succession of events persuaded him to adopt a more critical view of Soviet intentions. Soviet military policy also affected the president's strategic perspective. While Carter had promoted arms control negotiations, in late 1977 the Soviet Union began deploying SS-20s and Backfire bombers in Europe and in early 1978 continued testing its next generation of ICBMs.[15]

In these changing circumstances, Carter adopted both a harder line toward the Soviet Union and a more active China policy. He gradually lost confidence in Secretary of State Vance's argument that normalization of U.S.-China relations should be delayed until U.S.-Soviet détente was secure and ultimately accepted National Security Advisor Zbigniew Brzezinski's argument that normalization of relations should be achieved as soon as possible. Over Vance's objections, the president decided that Brzezinski should visit Beijing in May 1978 to advance the normalization process. Brzezinski reported to Deng Xiaoping that Carter had "made up his mind" to break with Taiwan and establish diplomatic relations with Beijing. By the end of November, the United States had accepted China's three conditions: it would break diplomatic relations with Taiwan, remove all troops from Taiwan, and end the U.S. mutual defense treaty with Taiwan. Furthermore, it did not demand a Chinese statement about peaceful unification, but merely that China not contradict the U.S. statement about peaceful resolution of the Taiwan issue. Nonetheless, on one matter Carter was insistent: China must understand that the United States would continue to sell defensive weapons to Taiwan, leaving it to Deng Xiaoping to decide whether or not this was a deal-breaker. Ultimately, Deng decided to accept the U.S. offer, and on December 15 Washington and Beijing announced that China and the United States would establish diplomatic relations on January 1, 1979.

After normalization, Soviet foreign policy continued to drive U.S. policy toward China. The issue for the Carter administration was whether or not to develop defense ties with China. Once again, Vance opposed greater cooperation with China while Brzezinski and Secretary of Defense Harold Brown were in favor. First Carter sided with Brown and Brzezinski that Brown should visit China. But then the issue became whether or not Brown could offer China access to U.S. military-use hardware the Soviet Union could not buy. On December 17, 1979, the president sided with Vance, opposing the development of an arms sales relationship with China. Shortly thereafter, however, the Soviet Union invaded Afghanistan. In January, the day before Brown left for China, he received permission from Carter to offer China access to nonlethal U.S. military equipment and over-the-horizon hardware. The security relationship expanded further in December 1980, when CIA director Stansfield Turner secretly visited Beijing. Deng Xiaoping agreed to the installation of U.S. intelligence equipment in western China to enable the United States to monitor Soviet nuclear tests and compliance with arms control agreements.[16]

In the late summer of 1978, as U.S.-China cooperation gained momentum, Sino-Japanese cooperation also began to develop. Soviet policy was the spur to greater U.S.-China cooperation, and enhanced U.S. cooperation with China allowed for greater Sino-Japanese cooperation. Japan was now prepared to accept Chinese conditions for a peace treaty. In early May, Carter, just then deciding to expedite normalization negotiations with China, met with Prime Minister Fukuda in Washington and expressed strong support for Fukuda's plans to reopen treaty negotiations with China. Assistant Secretary of State Richard Holbrook also encouraged Tokyo to coordinate an anti-Soviet strategy with Beijing and Washington. In late May, when Deng Xiaoping complained to Brzezinski that Japan's position on the antihegemony clause was holding up the treaty negotiations, Brzezinski responded that he would encourage Fukuda to sign the treaty. From Beijing Brzezinski traveled to Tokyo, where he urged Fukuda and Foreign Minister Sonoda Sunao to accept China's demand that the antihegemony clause be included in the peace treaty and to sign the treaty.[17]

China's anti-Soviet policy encouraged Carter and Brzezinski to give Japan the green light on improving its relations with China. But equally important was Brzezinski's briefing of Japanese leaders on his China visit. Japanese leaders understood that Washington was now moving ahead on normalization of relations with China. Washington had encouraged Japan to improve its relations with China, with the reminder that, should Tokyo move too slowly, it would once again face a diplomatic setback similar to the "Nixon shock." On August 12, 1978, Japan and China reached agreement on the Sino-Japanese Treaty of Peace and Friendship. Both sides had compromised. As China had insisted, the treaty stated Sino-Japanese opposition to "hegemony." Although Japan succeeded in including a statement that the treaty was not directed against a third party, this statement was contained in an article separate from the antihegemony article. More important, as Chinese leaders had expected, the treaty was widely interpreted as bolstering China's anti-Soviet diplomacy.[18]

In the aftermath of the signing, Deng Xiaoping traveled to Tokyo twice. In October, he went to exchange the instruments of ratification and used the occasion to suggest Sino-Japanese cooperation against the Soviet Union and Vietnam (global and regional "hegemons") in Indochina. In February 1979, Deng again visited Tokyo, this time on his way back to China from the United States. Vietnam had invaded Cambodia the previous December, and Deng used his visit, a prelude to China's punitive mid-February attack on Vietnam, to suggest, as he had in the United States, expanding cooperation against Soviet-Vietnamese cooperation in Indochina. As much as Tokyo might have expressed dismay at Deng's provocative diplomacy, in May 1979, after Soviet naval vessels entered Vietnam's Cam Ranh Bay for the first time, Japanese Defense Agency (JDA) director Yamashita Ganri visited Beijing, inaugurating Sino-Japanese military ties. Yamashita and Chinese defense minister Su Yu expressed common concern over the expanded Soviet military presence in East Asia, including Vietnam. By the end of the year, the two countries had initiated reciprocal exchanges of military officials.[19]

China, which had sought to advance security cooperation with Japan since 1973, had finally achieved its objective, overcoming stiff Japanese resistance. Japan's initial resistance was based on its assessment of Washington's China policy. If at first Japan had been reluctant to be out ahead of the United States, its later concern was not to be left behind.

The Reagan Presidency: Consolidation of U.S.-China Security Ties

REAGAN, TAIWAN, AND U.S.-CHINA CONFLICT

Much like Carter, President Ronald Reagan entered office intent on developing a less conciliatory China policy than that of his predecessor. Reagan acknowledged official U.S. relations with China, but he was also intent on proving his loyalty to Taiwan by enhancing U.S.-Taiwan military relations. Before long, however, Reagan adopted his predecessor's China policy. After eighteen months of U.S.-China conflict, the Reagan administration acknowledged the strategic importance of U.S.-China relations, accommodated itself to the 1979 normalization agreement, and acquiesced to China's demands that the United States limit its arms sales to Taiwan. Moreover, once the Reagan administration had accepted the limits of U.S. policy toward Taiwan, its own preoccupation with Soviet power led it to develop military ties with China that were even closer than those of the Carter administration.

Reagan's reputation as an ideological opponent of Chinese communism and a friend of Taiwan preceded him. His administration aroused PRC suspicions even before he assumed office, when representatives from Taiwan were initially invited to participate in his inauguration ceremonies as government officials. Once in the White House, Reagan faced conflict with China over U.S. arms sales to Taiwan. Beijing had never accepted such sales but had agreed to normalize relations with the United States while leaving the issue unresolved. In 1980 the Carter administration had given permission to Northrop and General Dynamics to discuss the sale of an advanced military aircraft, dubbed the FX, with Taiwan. China protested the decision and when Reagan succeeded Carter, moved the issue to the top of the agenda. Chinese officials threatened to downgrade U.S.-China relations unless Washington made a significant concession—to end all arms sales to Taiwan.[20]

The Reagan administration was ill-prepared to resist PRC pressure. The president and his secretary of state, Alexander Haig, were convinced that the Soviet Union had made important advances that threatened U.S. security and that the United States had yet to begin to reverse its downward path. The U.S. economy remained mired in "stagflation" and, they believed, the defense budget was woefully inadequate to deal with recent and projected Soviet military acquisitions. Moreover, Haig did not share the president's misgivings about U.S.-China cooperation. On the contrary, he believed that Soviet opportunism required continuing expansion of cooperation with China. Ironically, just as President Reagan seemed intent on challenging the understandings enabling U.S.-China cooperation, the value of that cooperation to U.S. security had become all the more important. Chinese leaders had chosen an opportune time not only to resist Reagan's more provocative policies but also to seek additional U.S. concessions on Taiwan.

When Premier Zhao Ziyang met with President Reagan in Cancun in October 1981, he insisted that the United States agree to end arms sales to Taiwan within a specified period of time. The next week, in Washington, Foreign Minister Huang Hua reiterated this demand to Haig and warned that unless Washington complied, China would downgrade U.S.-China cooperation. Haig was alarmed. U.S.-China cooperation was the cornerstone of his strategy for contending with Soviet power. He quickly moved to assuage Chinese concerns. He asked the Pentagon to determine whether Taiwan's security required the acquisition of the FX, and was told that under the terms of the 1979 Taiwan Relations Act, Taiwan could maintain its security with additional F-5Es, the aircraft it had been receiving from the United States since the 1960s. Assistant Secretary of State John Holdridge then traveled to Beijing to convey the good news. But Chinese leaders were not satisfied. China had demanded an end to all U.S. arms sales to Taiwan within a specified period, and Washington had yet to agree.

Haig was now more alarmed than ever. It was clear that another U.S.-China communiqué was necessary to resolve the issue. After extensive negotiations over the language of the document, Haig was convinced that the only way to avoid a crisis that might end the strategically vital anti-Soviet coalition was for the United States to compromise with China and commit to end arms sales to Taiwan over an undetermined period. But Reagan balked at making this commitment. He insisted that the final U.S. offer merely commit the United States to the ambiguous language that it would "reduce gradually its arms sales to Taiwan, leading over a period of time to a final resolution." Faced with Washington's take-it-or-leave-it ultimatum, Beijing accepted Reagan's final offer, and the two sides issued the joint communiqué of August 17, 1982.

Reagan's policy toward China had a major impact on Sino-Japanese relations. In the context of heightened tension between the United States and China, China tried to promote Sino-Japanese cooperation, seeking to minimize its isolation as it contended with Washington. But Japan was caught in the middle. It had no stake in the Taiwan issue and derived real benefits from Sino-Japanese cooperation, but U.S. mismanagement could well embroil it in the U.S.-China conflict and compel it to take sides. But because Washington was actually trying to enhance U.S.-China cooperation to promote a broad front against the Soviet Union, Japan could continue to cooperate with China without fear of antagonizing the United States.

Just as U.S.-China relations encountered intensified conflict over U.S. arms sales to Taiwan, Sino-Japanese relations entered a period of economic friction. In 1980, recognizing that the ambitious 1978 development program drawn up under Hua Guofeng was based on faulty planning, inadequate resources, and unrealistic expectations, Beijing announced a major economic retrenchment, and Chinese contracts with Japan bore the brunt. In early 1981 Beijing canceled major joint ventures at Baoshan, Nanjing, and Dongfang. In 1982, two-way trade declined by over 14 percent from the previous year, the first such downturn since 1976. Nonetheless, Beijing tried to minimize the effect of its economic adjustment on Sino-Japanese relations. To Japanese officials and business leaders it reconfirmed its commitment to Sino-Japanese cooperation and tried to maintain Japanese interest in the Chinese economy. By the end of 1981, Beijing had secured Japanese loans, and work on the projects had resumed.[21]

China's interest in separating Sino-Japanese cooperation from U.S.-China conflict over U.S. arms sales to Taiwan was evident during Premier Zhao Ziyang's visit to Japan in late May–early June 1982. Zhao was clearly interested in minimizing the impact of China's economic retrenchment on Japanese investment in China and in promoting greater political cooperation. He did not press Japan on any bilateral conflicts and in fact went out of his way to stress that Sino-Japanese relations should "be lasting and impervious to international storms" and would "not be influenced by the current 'excitement' in the international situation," clear references to U.S.-China tensions. Hu Yaobang, the general secretary of the CCP, visited Japan in 1983 with the same objective. Despite ongoing U.S.-China conflict over Taiwan, Hu actively promoted closer Sino-Japanese relations, including expanded cultural ties, and made progress on an agreement for resettlement in Japan of Japanese "war orphans" still remaining in China.[22]

Japan reciprocated China's efforts. In addition to agreeing to a new loan package for China in late 1981, it increased its aid program to China, and in

June 1982 agreed to provide the capital, researchers and specialists, and technological assistance for the China-Japan Friendship Hospital. Cultural ties
also continued to expand. In 1982, over 150,000 Chinese and Japanese were
involved in cultural exchanges. Finally, in commemoration of the tenth anniversary of the normalization of Sino-Japanese relations, Tokyo staged major
events throughout Japan and agreed to finance the construction of the Sino-
Japanese Friendship Hall.[23] Between 1981 and 1982, U.S.-China tension
seemed to promote Sino-Japanese cooperation.

The one setback in the relationship occurred in June 1982, after Zhao Ziyang had returned to Beijing from Japan. China took issue when the Japanese Ministry of Education considered revising the treatment of the Japanese war in China in its school textbooks.[24] China, along with Korea,
Singapore, and other countries, charged Japan with rewriting history by sof-
tening the language used to describe its invasion of other Asian countries.
There then ensued a six-week Chinese diplomatic and media campaign
against Japanese textbook policy and the potential for the revival of Japanese
"militarism." The conflict finally ended in early September, when Tokyo
said it would review the language and make corrections.

Explanations for this event in Sino-Japanese relations include political
conflict among Chinese leaders and China's assessment of the international
environment. What is clear, however, is that the episode was an aberration
during this period of improving Sino-Japanese relations. In the context of
U.S.-China friction, China sought to maintain cooperation with Japan and
Japan worked to satisfy Chinese demands. Only in 1985 would the textbook
controversy and other issues present a serious challenge to Sino-Japanese
cooperation.

RESUMPTION OF U.S.-CHINA COOPERATION AND
THE WANING OF THE COLD WAR

Once the United States and China had resolved their conflict over Taiwan,
the two countries increased cooperation in all areas, including military cooperation. Bilateral stability was grounded in China's recognition, by 1983, that
the United States had improved its strategic circumstances and no longer
needed to accommodate Chinese pressure. Once Beijing understood this
new reality, it no longer focused on conflict with Washington but sought the
benefits of cooperation.

China's new attitude was clearly reflected in its response to U.S. policy toward Taiwan. Although the Reagan administration had agreed to reduce arms sales to Taiwan, the August 1982 communiqué had not specified the rate of reduction. Beijing spent the next year protesting American policy and insisting that the annual reduction be a significant one. Chinese leaders complained that the United States was in violation of the communiqué. Even after Washington liberalized restrictions on technology exports to China, Beijing continued to hold U.S.-China cooperation hostage to U.S. policy toward Taiwan. Premier Zhao refused to accept President Reagan's invitation to visit Washington, insisting that China was not satisfied with the relationship. But the administration refused to accommodate Chinese demands. On the one hand, the White House strictly abided by the terms of the communiqué; on the other hand, it refused to make additional concessions regarding the rate of reductions in arms sales to Taiwan. The Reagan administration was equally inflexible on the issue of Taiwan's membership in the Asian Development Bank (ADB). Beijing insisted that Taiwan be expelled, because only sovereign states could be members. Washington disagreed, threatening to withdraw its funding should the other members of the bank comply with Beijing's demand.[25]

The United States demonstrated its resolve in several other confrontations. One involved the first asylum request from a mainland Chinese, Hu Na, a professional tennis player. She applied for political asylum in the United States on the advice of a pro-Taiwan lawyer. Beijing, however, insisted that her request was illegitimate and that she should be sent back to China. The White House refused. In another case, Americans seeking PRC payment on Chinese government bonds issued in 1911, the last year of the Qing dynasty, brought suit against the Chinese government, which insisted that the White House intervene. Again the White House rejected Beijing's demands, insisting that China would have to make its case in the courts. Finally, when Beijing threatened to deny Northwest Airlines access to China as a punishment for the company's ongoing operations in Taiwan, the White House countered with a threat to retaliate against China's national airline.

By the end of 1983, China had come to terms with Washington's new policy. In January 1984 Premier Zhao visited Washington and stressed the bright prospects of U.S.-China cooperation. He had come to the United States, he said, to "stabilize" U.S.-China relations. In April, Beijing gave President Reagan a warm welcome as the first president to visit China following normalization. During Reagan's visit, Zhao explained that the Taiwan issue "might cause a setback" in relations if it was mishandled. China's new attitude was best reflected in its accommodation to U.S. technology transfers to Taiwan. Although the 1982 communiqué restricted arms sales to Taiwan, it did not restrict technology transfers. To upgrade Taiwan's rapidly deteriorating air force, the Reagan administration decided to permit technology transfers to enable Taiwan to build its own aircraft. Beijing was clearly unhappy with this manipulation of a loophole in the 1982 agreement, but it offered only muted protest. Instead, it welcomed U.S. interest in U.S.-China strategic cooperation. Over the next few years, Beijing and Washington developed a close strategic relationship characterized by U.S. arms sales to China, intelligence sharing, and cooperation with the Soviet Union's policy in the Third World. Equally important, stable U.S.-China relations facilitated Chinese access to Western markets, and to the investment capital and advanced technology China required to modernize its economy and military.

The change in U.S. policy and China's accommodation to it reflect more than simple U.S. toughness or shifts in White House personnel. George Shultz, Haig's successor as secretary of state, did not share Haig's preoccupation with U.S.-China cooperation and placed greater emphasis on cooperation with Japan. But the change in U.S. and Chinese policies showed both sides' appreciation for the changing U.S.-Soviet balance.[26] By late 1983, two things were apparent. First, significant change occurred in the United States. The U.S. economy had recovered from the stagflation of the Carter years, and U.S. defense policy was no longer inflicted with post-Vietnam isolationism. The economy was growing, and the defense budget included funding for many new strategic weapons programs. After much turmoil, Washington and its NATO allies agreed to the deployment of Pershing II missiles and cruise missiles in Western Europe. With popular domestic support, U.S. forces occupied the island of Grenada in the Caribbean to remove the Soviet and Cuban presence there. By April 1984, Reagan boasted, "American leadership is back."[27]

Second, it was increasingly clear that the Soviet Union had encountered significant foreign policy problems and that its economy was in serious trouble. It faced difficulties in maintaining stability in Eastern Europe and it had been unable to subdue the anti-Soviet military forces in Afghanistan.

Meanwhile, its economy was in decline and the burden of superpower competition was becoming unmanageable. As one leading Chinese commentator observed in late 1983, the Soviet Union had sunk into a "passive situation" and was "gasping for breath."[28]

The evolution of the U.S.-Soviet balance marked a new stage in the cold war: Washington was now able to reassert its leverage in U.S.-China negotiations. But this evolution also marked the early emergence of the post–cold war era. As Soviet power declined, Washington reevaluated the value of cooperation with China, and China reevaluated the value of cooperation with Japan. In the process, Sino-Japanese relations were transformed.

As the Reagan administration committed itself to U.S.-China cooperation and the Soviet Union began its steady descent, China adopted a far more belligerent Japan policy. The demise of Soviet power in the 1980s had reduced China's strategic dependence on Sino-Japanese cooperation. China no longer needed to ignore other concerns in order to achieve maximum containment of Soviet power. Thus, on the eve of the post–cold war era, China gradually shifted its attention from Japan's contribution to Chinese security to Japan's potential to challenge Chinese security, stressing the prospect of renewed Japanese "militarism." Japan was now on the defensive. Just as relations between China and the United States were improving, Chinese policy offered Tokyo a different choice: either conciliating China or facing heightened Sino-Japanese tensions. Not surprisingly, Tokyo chose the conciliatory option, seeking to reduce PRC pressure.

In 1985 China began pestering Japan on a wide range of seemingly minor issues.[29] The first was the 1985 visit of Nakasone Yasuhiro in his official capacity as prime minister to the Yasukini Shrine in Tokyo, the memorial to the Japanese war dead. Chinese leaders insisted that this visit reflected an unrepentant Japanese attitude toward Japanese atrocities. Throughout China, nationalistic students demonstrated against Japan's alleged attempts to sanitize its history. Concerned by the incident's potential to destabilize Sino-Japanese relations, Nakasone canceled his next planned visit to the shrine and acknowledged Chinese sensitivity on the issue. In June 1986, on the heels of this incident, Chinese officials and the Chinese media protested Japan's ongoing revision of its high school textbooks. Nakasone assured Beijing that portions of the textbooks "should be reexamined," and Japanese officials said that Japan would issue revised textbook guidelines in early July.

The revised guidelines, which had been reviewed by the Foreign Ministry according to Nakasone's instructions, did not significantly alter the earlier treatment of the war in China.

The following year, China criticized a Japanese court ruling confirming that Taiwan retained ownership of a student dormitory in Kyoto following the ending of diplomatic relations between Taiwan and Japan in 1972. Although the Japanese government refused to intervene in court deliberations, Japanese leaders frequently assured China that Tokyo did not have a "two-China" policy. To calm the heightened polemics, Nakasone removed a Foreign Ministry official from office. Finally, in 1987 and 1988, the issue was "militarism." China launched a media campaign denouncing Japan's increase in defense spending above 1 percent of its GNP, the ceiling set in 1976 by Prime Minister Miki Takeo, which had come to symbolize Japan's rejection of militarism.

For the first time since U.S.-China rapprochement, China took the diplomatic offensive against Japanese slights to its nationalism and security interests, disregarding the potential damage its actions might do to Sino-Japanese cooperation. Beijing focused on Japanese political cooperation with Taiwan rather than on the strategic benefits of the U.S.-Japan alliance and Sino-Japanese cooperation. Although Japan did not completely appease China's demands, it accommodated them whenever possible. As long as the United States was determined to expand cooperation with China, Tokyo balked at becoming embroiled in conflict with Beijing. Thus, despite Beijing's hostile posture, Sino-Japanese cooperation increased. In May 1986, Yang Dezhi, head of the general staff of the People's Liberation Army (PLA), visited Tokyo, and in May 1987, Kurihara Yuko, director of the Japanese Defense Agency (JDA), visited Beijing. Despite Beijing's criticism of Tokyo's defense policy, Tokyo contributed to PLA efforts to learn from the JDA. In economic relations, in 1986 Tokyo more than doubled its grant aid to China. Its overall development aid to China increased by 28 percent, and in late 1988, Tokyo reached agreement with Beijing on a third yen loan program, which called for Japan to loan Beijing ¥810 billion over five years.[30]

Tiananmen and the Transformation of U.S.-China-Japan Relations

In 1989 the Warsaw Pact collapsed and the Berlin Wall came down, ending the strategic essence of the cold war—U.S.-Soviet confrontation in Europe and global superpower competition. That same year, the Sino-Soviet conflict also came to an end. By the early spring of 1989 it was clear that Mikhail Gorbachev had made significant efforts to meet China's three conditions for normalization of Sino-Soviet relations: ending Soviet support for Vietnam's war in Cambodia, ending the Soviet military threat along the Sino-Soviet border, and withdrawing Soviet forces from Afghanistan. Gorbachev's visit to Beijing in May 1989 signified China's victory in the Sino-Soviet conflict just as the end of the Berlin Wall signified the United States' victory in the cold war.

These twin victories diminished the urgency of Sino-American cooperation. The anti-Soviet foundations of U.S.-China rapprochement in the early 1970s, and of subsequent cooperation through the 1980s, had ended. In the best of circumstances, this strategic environment would make it difficult for the White House to sustain U.S.-China cooperation, since Chinese and American leaders had less incentive to compromise. Enduring conflicts in each country's areas of interest assumed greater salience. But the reduced imperative for cooperation also created opportunities for opposition politicians in the United States and in China; no longer fearing criticism for irresponsibly endangering national security, they could seek to obstruct their respective leadership's bilateral policy. In this context, the Chinese government's violent suppression of the Chinese student movement in June 1989 unleashed significant domestic opposition in both countries.

In China, Deng Xiaoping bore the responsibility for weakened Party power.[31] Rather than accommodate the demands of conservative leaders that he combat "spiritual pollution" and "bourgeois liberalization," he had persisted in an open door policy that had exposed Chinese society to political values that fostered demands for political reform. Thus, for two years after the Tiananmen incident, China's conservative octogenarians, including Chen Yun and Wang Zhen, dominated the ideological debate and resisted efforts to continue China's pre-Tiananmen reform policies. They also opposed cooperation with the United States, which they regarded as a threat to the security of the Chinese Communist Party. These developments undermined Deng's foreign policy flexibility. Conciliatory gestures toward the United States further weakened his position and threatened his ability to regain control over China's political, economic, and foreign policy agendas before his death. In October 1989 he told Richard Nixon that the United States should take the initiative because it had "harmed" China, but also that the "United States is the one that can adopt positive actions. China cannot take the initiative. This is because the strong one is the United States and the weak one is China."[32]

Meanwhile, in the United States, congressional leaders called for extensive retaliation against the Chinese leadership.[33] Members of Congress charged that advocates of continued U.S.-China cooperation were indifferent to the fate of China's democratic activists and were motivated by profits or by outdated cold war concepts, such as China's strategic importance in opposing Soviet expansionism and the strategic triangle. The focus of their criticism was President George Bush, who insisted that opposing China's violent repression of the student movement did not necessitate severing cooperation with this great power. The president's critics charged that he preferred to "coddle" the dictators of Beijing rather than stand up in support of democracy activists. Thus on June 5, the day after the massacre, the White House suspended all sales to China of items on the munitions control list, the fulfillment of existing agreements for U.S. arms transfers to China, and all exchanges between U.S. and Chinese military officials. Then, as repression in China continued and congressional pressure on President Bush remained unyielding, on June 20 the administration announced additional sanctions: it suspended diplomatic exchanges with China at and above the level of assistant secretary as well as government economic assistance to U.S. companies doing business in China, and it declared its opposition to financial assistance to China from the World Bank and the Asian Development Bank, which affected over $1 billion in new loans to China. In addition, the planned visit to China of Secretary of Commerce Robert Mosbacher was canceled.[34]

Despite Beijing's inflexibility—including its unwillingness to allow the democracy activist and physicist Fang Lizhi to leave China—and domestic opposition in the United States to U.S.-China cooperation, President Bush believed in the importance of the Sino-American relationship and sought to restore U.S.-China cooperation. In early July 1989, he secretly sent National Security Advisor Brent Scowcroft and Under Secretary of State Lawrence Eagleburger to Beijing. In July, Secretary of State Howard Baker held meetings with the Chinese foreign minister, Qian Qichen, in Paris and again in October at the United Nations. The administration also approved preliminary licenses for the Chinese to launch U.S. satellites, allowed Chinese to return to work on a military technology transfer program in the United States, and held discussions with China over Chinese accession to the General

Agreement on Tariffs and Trade (GATT). Then, in late November, the president vetoed the Pelosi Bill, which would have enabled Chinese students to remain in the United States after their visas expired, despite a 403 to 0 vote in support of the bill in the House of Representatives. After extensive politicking and a promise to issue an executive order allowing the students to remain, the president upheld his veto in the Senate by a mere four votes. Congressional Democrats criticized the veto as "servile" and a "kowtow" to the Chinese leadership.[35] After Deng Xiaoping asked Nixon and Kissinger to tell President Bush that China was prepared to restore cooperation if America took the "initiative,"[36] the president again subjected himself to widespread criticism by sending Scowcroft and Eagleburger to Beijing in December. Laboring to restore a mere working relationship with China, President Bush received little assistance from China and faced active opposition from Congress. The one source of support and assistance was Japan.

Chinese leaders had identified the United States as China's political and ideological adversary, but they did not identify Tokyo as Washington's partner in crime. On the contrary, during its post-Tiananmen isolation from the United States and other advanced industrial democracies, China quickly moved to reduce conflict with other countries and turned first to Japan. Within days of the Tiananmen massacre, Chinese scholars and journalists were cautioned against writing or publishing anything negative about Japan.[37] The PRC muted its criticism of Japanese militarism, including the level of Japan's defense spending, its five-year defense program buildup launched in 1990, and Prime Minister Kaifu Toshiki's efforts to provide assistance to U.S. forces in 1991, during the Gulf War. Beijing also avoided controversy when a right-wing Japanese group occupied the Senkaku islands in September 1990.

Japan was as eager as China to avoid heightened tension.[38] In the past it had been careful to follow the U.S. lead on China policy, but after June 1989 it actively maintained cooperation with China. Shortly after the massacre, Prime Minister Sosuke Uno explained that because of the Japanese invasion of China, Japan could not punish China and that "Sino-Japanese relations differ from those of the United States." Tokyo's sanctions policy was the most restrained among those of the advanced industrial countries in the Group of Seven (G7). Its response reflected its efforts to maintain a balance between its relations with China and its perennial concern to avoid alienating the United States. Ongoing projects continued without interruption, but it suspended implementation of the most recent yen loan agreement on June 20 and cabinet-level exchanges with China on June 29. These steps reflected Japan's understanding that its restraint had isolated it from all the other advanced industrial countries, including the United States. But unlike the United States, Japan imposed no further economic, technological, or diplomatic sanctions.

China and Japan were successful in limiting the damage to their relationship from the Tiananmen incident. In a reversal of the previous cold war pattern, in which U.S.-China cooperation enabled the United States to promote Sino-Japanese cooperation, the post–cold war, post-Tiananmen cooperation between China and Japan enabled Japan to help the United States restore cooperation with China. Nonetheless, as in the past, it worked within the parameters of U.S. policy toward China, awaiting U.S. support before cooperating with China.[39]

President Bush and his staff understood that if Japan took the lead in cooperating with China, the United States would find it easier to do so. At the G7 summit in July 1989, Bush worked with Kaifu to soften the language referring to China in the summit communiqué.[40] In Beijing in December, National Security Advisor Scowcroft assured Chinese leaders that once Fang Lizhi, the democracy activist, left China, Washington would see to it that Japan resumed its yen loan program.[41] After the December 1989 Scowcroft visit to Beijing, Japan began planning resumption of the yen loan program and received Zou Jiahua, the head of China's economic planning agency and a ministerial-level official. In late May 1990, after President Bush decided to extend Most Favored Nation treatment to China for another year, Japanese leaders decided that Tokyo could now end its sanctions against China. After Fang Lizhi was released, and as Japan prepared for the July 1990 G7 summit in Houston, President Bush supported Japan's effort to ease Western sanctions and Japan's decision to implement the third yen loan program for China.

By 1991, long before the United States had done so, Japan had begun to restore full cooperation with China. In January, it reciprocated Zou Jiahua's visit of the previous year by sending its finance minister to Beijing, the first such visit by a cabinet-level official since June 1989. Throughout that year, economic relations flourished and political ties resumed. In August Prime Minister Kaifu visited Beijing, the first G7 leader to visit China since

Tiananmen. In October 1992, Emperor Akihito traveled to China, the first time a Japanese royal figure had ever visited.

The positive direction of post-Tiananmen Sino-Japanese cooperation, however, would be short-lived. It was an effort to restore the old cold war relationship just as the cold war was ending. When Tokyo realized that post-cold war U.S.-China relations would be characterized by fundamental political conflict, it became much less conciliatory to China on weapons proliferation, nuclear testing, and territorial issues. Similarly, when Beijing saw that Japan would cooperate with the American "containment" of China, the leadership and the media resumed their criticism of Japan's defense policy and its treatment of various historical issues.[42] What remained a constant in Sino-Japanese relations was both China's attention to the influence of the United States, and thus of U.S.-Japan relations, on Chinese security, and Japan's attention to U.S. policy toward China when making its China policy.

U.S.-China Cooperation and Conflict and Sino-Japanese Relations

From 1972 to 1989 the United States and China developed a complex relationship of cooperation and conflict. During periods of greater cooperation—in the late Carter and late Reagan administrations, for example—significant conflicts, capable of undermining cooperation at any time, remained. On the other hand, at the height of conflict—during the immediate aftermath of the 1989 Tiananmen massacre, for example—it was very difficult for both countries to maintain cooperation. Thus, throughout these years, China and the United States carried out continuous negotiations over the price each country would have to pay to maintain cooperative relations. During the cold war the most difficult issue was U.S. policy toward Taiwan. As the dissatisfied power, China looked for opportunities to pressure the United States into changing its policy; as the satisfied power, the United States resisted Chinese pressure. Conflict over human rights after 1989 further complicated relations and contributed to even greater bilateral tension. Despite frequent periods of relatively greater tension and reduced cooperation, neither China nor the United States allowed conflicting interests to destroy the foundations of cooperation. What they haggled over instead was the price of cooperation.

The ups and downs of U.S.-China relations had a pronounced effect on Sino-Japanese relations. Once it became clear that the United States was committed to cooperation with China, China changed its Japan policy, welcoming the U.S.-Japan alliance and Japanese defense spending as useful additions to the anti-Soviet coalition. Moreover, Beijing valued the contribution of Sino-Japanese cooperation in containing Soviet power, and it not only normalized relations with Tokyo, it actively pursued a Sino-Japanese peace treaty as an instrument of its own Soviet policy.

But even within the overall context of U.S.-China-Japan cooperation, changes in U.S.-China relations affected China's Japan policy. Chinese leaders seemed more eager to expand security cooperation with Japan when U.S.-China relations stagnated, as in 1975, or when U.S.-China tension increased, as in 1981–83 and 1989–92. In 1975 China sought to compensate for U.S. strategic passivity. In the latter two periods of U.S.-China conflict, China sought greater Sino-Japanese cooperation to minimize its isolation and its vulnerability to both Soviet and American power. But for Japan, U.S. policy, not Chinese pressure, was the most important factor in its China policy. This was the case from 1972 to 1989, it is the case now, and it is likely to continue to be the case well into the twenty-first century.

CHAPTER FIVE

Chinese Relations with the United States

Jia Qingguo

The history of Sino-American relations since 1972 has been characterized by repeated shifts between limited cooperation and limited confrontation. These interactions are limited because despite the emotional intensity evoked at different phases of their relationship, China and the United States have never forged a formal military alliance during friendly times nor have they ever opposed each other in a full-scale war. They have been unable to achieve a higher level of cooperation because they have too many differences between them. They have not engaged in an all-out war because they have too many important overlapping interests that they must protect.[1]

The evolution of Sino-American relations between 1972 and 1992 provides an excellent opportunity to examine the boundaries of their relationship. During the early 1970s, although strategic considerations compelled the two countries to seek reconciliation, their vast differences kept their cooperation within certain strict limits. During the early 1990s, when conflicts over values and priorities dominated the relationship, common interests made it necessary for the two countries to keep the relationship from further deterioration.

As the two countries enter the twenty-first century, both have much to reflect upon. Since at any given time they share both interests and differences, they must decide whether they want to emphasize the interests they share and enhance cooperation or stress their differences and let the relationship drift into conflict. Because both countries have extraordinary influence in world affairs, how they resolve this question will have a significant impact on the welfare of the international community.

The Road Toward Rapprochement

History, it is said, is full of accidents. However, when President Richard Nixon arrived in Beijing in February 1972, it was by no means a historical accident. Rather, it was the result of a series of calculated moves on the part of the Chinese and American governments to come to terms with each other in their attempt to cope with their commonly perceived threat: the Soviet Union.

On the surface, it appeared to be an unlikely time for rapprochement. China was in the middle of the cultural revolution, when "Down with American imperialism" was a prominent slogan and anti-American demonstrations frequently filled the streets of Chinese cities. Many Americans regarded China as a "rogue state" more dangerous than the Soviet Union, and were strongly opposed to any kind of Sino-American relations. Furthermore, both nations had sent troops to Vietnam, where they fought against each other in the jungles.

Beneath the surface, however, several developments made it increasingly necessary for the two countries to seek each other out. The first development was the change in the strategic balance between the United States and the Soviet Union. Since the early 1960s, the Soviet Union had been trying to build up its nuclear and conventional arsenal to counter U.S. military superiority. By the late 1960s it appeared to be having some success. In 1966 the United States had 904 intercontinental ballistic missiles (ICBMs), 592 submarine-launched ballistic missiles (SLBMs), and 630 long-range bombers, whereas the Soviet Union had 292 ICBMs, 107 SLBMs, and 155 long-range bombers. By 1970, the United States had 1,054 ICBMs, 656 SLBMs, and 550 long-range bombers, and the Soviet Union had 1,299 ICBMs, 304 SLBMs, and 145 long-range-bombers.[2] One unintended consequence of the nuclear parity between the United States and the Soviet Union was China's increasing weight in the strategic balance, despite the gap in military capabilities between China and either of the other two powers. China's strategic location allowed it to turn the balance in favor of whichever side it chose to join.

The second development was the intensification of the antiwar movement in the United States. By the late 1960s it was clear to many Americans that the United States was not winning the war in Vietnam. Moreover, an increasing number of U.S. citizens began to see involvement in Vietnam as something immoral, unnecessary, and costly: immoral, because it was clear that what the United States was trying to defend, against the interests of the Vietnamese people, was a corrupt and authoritarian regime; unnecessary, because it was clearly not in the U.S. national interest to fight a war in Vietnam; and costly, because the war was claiming the lives of an increasing number of U.S. soldiers as well as an unacceptable amount of resources, without a glimpse of victory. As a result, antiwar sentiment was strong, and American society was deeply divided. Most people realized that the United States must end the war, and this included politicians such as presidential hopeful Richard Nixon.[3] The U.S. government, however, felt that it could only accept an end to the Vietnam War in an "honorable" way, that is, through a negotiated withdrawal of U.S. troops without the appearance of defeat. Since the Vietnamese communists were backed by China and the Soviet Union, the United States needed tacit Chinese and Soviet cooperation to attain this objective. For the United States, the only way to attain their cooperation was to improve relations with them.

The third development was the U.S. realization by the late 1960s that China and the Soviet Union had little chance of reconciliation. Earlier, some had felt that the two former ideological allies could still patch up their differences, but Sino-Soviet military clashes over Zhenbao Island in March 1969 dispelled such optimism.[4] The bloody confrontation was significant for both China and the United States. China had just witnessed the Soviet invasion of Czechoslovakia the year before and had seen the Soviet Union justifying its invasion with the infamous Brezhnev Doctrine, which asserted that the sovereignty of socialist countries was limited. China had also watched with apprehension as the Soviet Union massed roughly one million troops on the Sino-Soviet and Sino-Mongolian border. The border clash could only convince the Chinese that a full-scale Soviet military invasion was a real possibility.[5] As far as China was concerned, the Soviet threat could not have come at a worse time. The cultural revolution had just paralyzed China's government as well as its economy. And since China had parted company with the Soviet Union, it had no powerful friends to come to its aid in case of a Soviet invasion.[6]

It was against such an unpleasant backdrop that in 1969 Mao Zedong asked four Chinese marshals (Chen Yi, Ye Jianying, Xu Xiangqian, and Nie Rongzhen) to undertake a study of the international situation. After considerable research and deliberation, these advisers, with the encouragement of Zhou Enlai, submitted their report. The differences between the United States and the Soviet Union, they argued, were greater than those between China and the United States. Therefore, it was possible for China to improve relations with the United States.[7] After careful thought, Mao decided that China should not be at odds with both the Soviet Union and the United States simultaneously and should try to seek better relations with one of them. Since the Soviet Union was believed to be more threatening to China and the Nixon administration had signaled its willingness to improve relations with China, Mao turned toward the United States.[8]

As far as the United States was concerned, the border clash between its two ideological foes had created both serious challenges and real opportunities. On the one hand, it suggested that the Soviet Union might launch a military attack against China. A successful Soviet takeover of China would immensely enhance the Soviet position. Even the failure of such an attempt would greatly disturb the existing global balance of power. Both scenarios would have serious negative implications for U.S. national interests.[9] On the other hand, the border clash also presented "an unprecedented opportunity" for the United States, which could make use of China's fear of a Soviet invasion to seek rapprochement with China.[10]

A Sino-American rapprochement would gain the United States at least three advantages. First, by bringing the "world's most populous nation" to the U.S. side, it would help tip the balance of power between the United States and the Soviet Union. Second, it would provide incentives for the Soviet Union to accept détente with the United States to reduce the danger of a nuclear war.[11] Third, it could help encourage the Vietnamese communists to reach a peace agreement with the United States and in the process permit U.S. withdrawal from Vietnam without concessions that were politically unacceptable at home. Thus, by the end of the 1960s, both Chinese and American leaders wanted to reach out to each other because of their respective strategic considerations. And as long as their shared perception of a Soviet threat existed, they would have no difficulty in searching for and justifying continued cooperation.

To be sure, twenty years of hostility and mutual suspicion made it difficult for China and the United States to reach accommodation. In both countries opposition to accommodation was strong. Between their leaders there was little understanding or trust. The ambassadorial talks between the two nations in Warsaw had become bogged down with many practical differences that made it impossible to reach a strategic understanding. According to Henry Kissinger, these differences could only be resolved as "a consequence of Sino-American rapprochement, not chart the path toward it."[12] The two sides began to explore other possibilities, making public gestures and sending private messages. On the public level, the United States issued a statement saying that it no longer wanted to have an adversarial relationship with China. It began to use the term "People's Republic of China" in place of "Red China" or "Communist China." It ended naval patrols of the Taiwan Strait and suspended reconnaissance flights over the Chinese mainland. In addition, it made known its opposition to Soviet efforts to isolate China by building a collective security arrangement in Asia. Moreover, in response to the likelihood of a Soviet military attack against China, the United States publicly announced that it would not tolerate China's defeat in a war between China and the Soviet Union. Finally, both at the ambassadorial talks in Warsaw and through the public media the United States informed the Chinese that it wanted to expand contacts with China in order to improve relations.[13]

China responded in kind. On October 1, 1970, Mao met the American journalist Edgar Snow on the Tiananmen rostrum. Soon after, Mao met with Snow again and told him that he welcomed Nixon's election as president. He asked Snow to convey the message that if Nixon wanted to visit Beijing, Beijing would accommodate him. China and the United States should talk to each other and should not allow the current relationship to remain stuck.[14] In April 1971 China invited an American table tennis team to visit China.

At the private level, Nixon asked the Pakistani president, who was visiting the United States, to inform Chinese leaders that he was planning to send a senior emissary for talks. Nixon also asked the visiting Romanian president to convey his willingness to establish dialogue between the two countries. Eventually, the Pakistani channel proved to be more effective.[15]

To his relief as well as delight, Nixon found Chinese leaders receptive to his ideas. On April 21, 1971, China passed a message through the Pakistani channel expressing its willingness to receive an American special envoy, such as Henry Kissinger or the secretary of state or even Nixon himself, in Beijing.[16] This offer accelerated the secret contacts between the two sides. In late May, with approval from Mao, Zhou Enlai passed another message to

Nixon to the effect that Chairman Mao invited President Nixon to visit China and expected to talk with him directly. Premier Zhou Enlai invited Kissinger to visit China to prepare for President Nixon's visit. This message in principle settled Kissinger's visit to China.[17]

The two Kissinger visits to China in July and October 1971 in preparation for President Nixon's visit were successful largely because the two sides gave priority to strategic interests. Ever since the 1950s the Taiwan question had been the most difficult problem they faced. And since the Taiwan Strait crisis in 1958, China had insisted that the Taiwan problem be solved before dealing with other practical issues.[18] Each side, however, had very different ideas as to how the Taiwan question should be resolved. China demanded that the United States withdraw its troops from Taiwan and the Taiwan Strait. The United States wanted China to renounce the use of force in its efforts to recover Taiwan. The two countries could not find any common ground, and this to a large extent explained the deadlock of the Warsaw talks, which before 1971 had served as the formal Sino-American channel.[19]

By the time Kissinger went to China, however, both sides had decided that they could not let the Taiwan issue block their efforts to advance other, more important interests. For China, the perceived imminent threat of a Soviet military attack necessitated cooperation with the United States. For the United States, the perceived necessity to shift the global balance of power, reconstitute U.S. relations with the Soviet Union, and extricate itself from Vietnam required cooperation with China. As Mao remarked, "The small issue is Taiwan; the big issue is the world."[20] "We can do without them [Taiwan] for the time being, and let it come after 100 years."[21] Nixon and Kissinger, for their part, were determined not to let existing issues overshadow the larger geopolitical ones in defining the Sino-American relationship.[22]

Accordingly, when Kissinger came to Beijing, he found that he could not have encountered a group of interlocutors "more receptive to Nixon's style of diplomacy than the Chinese leaders."[23] Chinese leaders were more interested in building confidence than in "fine drafting points." The United States got Mao's assurance that China would not use force against Taiwan, and Mao did not ask for reciprocity from the United States. Zhou Enlai too was more accommodating to the United States than Kissinger had expected. "While drafting the Shanghai Communiqué with Zhou Enlai," Kissinger later recalled, "I at one point offered to trade an offensive phrase in the Chinese draft for something in the American version to which Zhou might object. 'We will never get anywhere this way,' he replied. 'If you can convince me why our phrase is offensive, I will give it to you.'"[24]

Chinese leaders probably found their American guests similarly accommodating. On the Soviet Union, Nixon assured them that the United States was interested in maintaining the balance of power; that it would restrain the Soviet Union if American interests were involved; that it would try to reduce tensions with the Soviet Union but would make no concessions with the Soviets that it did not also offer to China; and that it would keep China informed of any deal made with the Soviet Union. On India, Nixon told Chinese leaders that the United States would coordinate its policies toward India with China. On Japan, Nixon tried to stress the common interests shared by the United States and China, that is, to prevent Japan from pursuing its own path militarily by maintaining U.S. forces in that country. Nixon referred to Taiwan as an "irritant" and told his Chinese hosts that the United States would recognize one China with Taiwan as part of China; that the United States would not support Taiwanese independence; and that it favored a peaceful resolution of the Taiwan issue. Finally, on Sino-American relations, Nixon expressed his desire for normalization of relations between the two countries.[25]

The Shanghai Communiqué concluded during Nixon's visit embodied this spirit of accommodation on the basis of a shared strategic conceptualization of world affairs. After listing their respective views on international politics, the two countries acknowledged "the essential differences between China and the United States in their social systems and foreign policies." The two sides agreed, however, that countries, "regardless of their social systems, should conduct their relations on the principles of respect for the sovereignty and territorial integrity of all states, non-aggression against other states, non-interference in the international affairs of other states, equality and mutual benefit, and peaceful coexistence. International disputes should be settled on this basis, without resorting to the use or threat of force. The United States and People's Republic of China are prepared to apply these principles to their mutual relations." The two countries also agreed that it was in their interests to normalize their relations and that they would oppose collusion between any major countries as well as efforts to seek international hegemony. Finally, on the question of Taiwan, the United States "acknowledges that all Chinese on either side of the Taiwan Strait maintain there is but one China and that Taiwan is part of China." The United States "does not challenge that position" but "reaffirms its interest in a peaceful settlement of the Taiwan question by the Chinese themselves." The United States "affirms the ultimate objective of the withdrawal of all U.S. forces and military installations from Taiwan" with that prospect in mind. In the meantime, it "will progressively reduce its forces and military installations on Taiwan as the tension in the area diminishes."[26]

President Nixon's visit to China indeed "changed the world," at least in terms of the nature of Sino-American relations.[27] The relationship entered a new phase in which China and the United States were to make their strategic cooperation a priority and put aside other issues, including that of Taiwan. Of course, as stated in the Shanghai Communiqué, neither side was to abandon its principles. Yet despite the two nations' cooperation, these principles were very different and were to impose strict limits on their relationship. What is surprising, however, is the degree to which these two countries suppressed their differences for the sake of strategic imperatives throughout the 1970s and the better part of the 1980s.

The Road to Normalization

In the Shanghai Communiqué, China and the United States expressed their desire to normalize their relations, although this did not happen until eight years later. On both sides the desire was genuine. Following Nixon's visit to China, the CCP Central Committee issued a circular on March 7, 1972, to its high-level party organizations. The circular justified Mao's invitation to Nixon and China's handling of the negotiations. Although it acknowledged that whether the agreements between the two sides could be put into practice depended on the United States, it stressed that China should be careful not to let its enemies sabotage the agreements. In particular, China should muffle its propaganda on this matter and avoid giving any impression that the Shanghai Communiqué represented a unilateral victory for China.[28]

Moreover, Mao took the unusual step of personally meeting with Kissinger when he visited Beijing in mid-February 1973. During their meeting, Mao expressed the view that since the Soviet threat to peace was on the rise, the Soviet Union should be isolated. Mao told Kissinger that he had been talking about developing a kind of united front linking the United States, Japan, China, Pakistan, Iran, and Europe to oppose international hegemony.[29]

The United States also made efforts to maintain the momentum of the communiqué. During his earlier visit to Beijing, in February 1972, Kissinger had told Chinese leaders that the United States was considering normalizing relations between the two countries. This might require two stages. During the first stage, the first two years of Nixon's second term in office, the United States would reduce U.S. forces in Taiwan and each country would establish a liaison office in the other's capital. During the second stage, the last two years of the second term, the two countries would realize normalization according to the Sino-Japanese formula, that is, the United States would establish diplomatic relations with China while maintaining unofficial relations with Taiwan.[30] With this understanding, the two countries set up liaison offices in Washington and Beijing. Both appointed senior officials to head the offices. By 1974 China and the United States had regular semiofficial channels for communicating with each other, and the normalization process was proceeding smoothly.

However, four developments impeded the process of normalization during the mid-1970s. One was the unraveling of the Watergate affair, which undermined the Nixon administration's political ability to take new initiatives in improving relations with China. By illegally spying on his opponents, Nixon not only jeopardized his political career but also contributed to the postponement of the normalization process he helped to initiate.

A second development was the widening difference between Chinese and American leaders over how to deal with the Soviet Union. Although both were concerned about the perceived Soviet threat, they disagreed on the appropriate strategy for dealing with it. Chinese leaders wanted the two countries to adopt a tit-for-tat strategy; American leaders, concerned that China's confrontational approach might draw the United States into direct conflict with the Soviet Union, believed that seeking détente with the Soviet Union was the best course. Hence, the harder the Chinese tried to persuade the Americans to accept their approach, the more suspicious the Americans became. Kissinger, for example, felt that the United States should not permit China "to manipulate us into unnecessary showdowns" with Moscow.[31] When the United States ignored China's advice and continued its efforts to achieve détente with the Soviet Union, China felt betrayed. From the Chinese point of view, U.S. policy allowed the Soviet Union to transfer more of its resources from the west to the east, where they could be used against China. Moreover, the Chinese felt that the United States had used China as a card in its effort to woo the Soviet Union. Chinese dissatisfaction and American suspicions grew over time and fed on each other. Their relationship stagnated.

The third development was the radicalization of China's domestic politics. Beginning in mid-1973, Mao became increasingly concerned over the policies pursued by pragmatic leaders headed by Zhou Enlai and later, by Deng Xiaoping. He believed that such policies were undermining his idea of egalitarianism and would bring about capitalism in China. He therefore started a campaign of criticism of Lin Biao and Confucius in an attempt to arrest the direction of these changes. Members of the radical left took advantage of this situation, advancing their interests by attacking existing policies, including foreign policy. At a Politburo meeting in November 1973 they condemned China's foreign policy as one of "rightist capitulationism." In later Politburo meetings held toward the end of 1973, they criticized Zhou Enlai for committing the error of capitulation in his talks with Kissinger.[32] Later they also repeatedly challenged the more liberal foreign economic policies of Zhou Enlai and Deng Xiaoping.[33] Since the leftist radicals had Mao's acquiescence, if not his complete support, the moderates could not do much to pursue further cooperation with the United States.

The fourth development was the two countries' widening perceptual gap on Taiwan. In his conversations with Chinese leaders, Kissinger received the impression that China was flexible on the Taiwan question and would accept both a renunciation of force in resolving it and a U.S. liaison office in Taipei. The United States therefore insisted on China's renunciation of force on the Taiwan question and its acceptance of an official or semi-official U.S. presence in Taiwan after normalization.[34] Meanwhile, Chinese leaders received the impression that the United States was prepared to adopt the Japanese formula in realizing normalization and assumed that Washington would sever all official relations with Taiwan before normalization.[35] China accordingly demanded that the United States withdraw all military forces from Taiwan, abrogate the U.S.-Taiwan mutual defense treaty, and sever diplomatic relations with Taipei. China had no intention of renouncing the right to use force on the Taiwan question. Both sides were disappointed when they found out the other's position.[36]

These four developments left little room for moving the relationship forward. When Gerald Ford came into office, there was little he could do to change the situation. Although he did manage to visit China, he came home empty-handed. The trip proved to be a failure that disappointed both sides. It confirmed the view of Chinese leaders that Ford was too weak to further the relationship. It also provided ammunition to the administration's critics, who charged that Ford was paying too much attention to China while neglecting more urgent problems at home.[37] Under the circumstances, the relationship dragged on without much progress.

Stagnation, however, did not mean retrogression. China and the United States maintained their liaison offices as well as other contacts, despite the fact that Chinese ideological radicalism reached the height of absurdity and the fact that pro-Taiwan rightists in the United States increased their opposition to sacrificing diplomatic relations with Taiwan. The anti-Soviet logic prevailed over ideological considerations and prevented the relationship from reverting back to prerapprochement days.

By 1977 the situation began to change. In both countries new leaders oversaw foreign policy. Having got rid of the ideological radicals, new Chinese leaders now had more room to maneuver in negotiating with their American counterparts. Jimmy Carter, the new U.S. leader, also had a political mandate to do more to improve relations with China. At the beginning, however, both sides gave priority to improving relations with the Soviet Union. China wanted to lower tensions between it and its neighbor, while the United States wanted to revive détente. Although President Carter sent Cyrus Vance, the secretary of state, to China in August 1977 to evaluate the possibility of normalizing relations on U.S. terms, the visit proved to be counterproductive. At the time, neither side was willing to compromise.[38]

Ironically, it was the uncompromising position of the Soviet Union that eventually gave both China and the United States more incentive to normalize relations. In response to Chinese overtures to improve relations, the Soviet Union remained uncompromising and showed no intention of reducing its troops along the Sino-Soviet border. Meanwhile, the Soviet Union stepped up its support for Vietnam, which sought to increase its influence in Indochina by annexing Cambodia and took an increasingly hostile position toward China. The Soviet Union did not reciprocate U.S. overtures to move toward a second phase of détente. It refused to incorporate deep cuts in strategic weapons into a SALT agreement and also stepped up activity in Africa.

Confronting an inflexible Soviet Union and an increasingly active pro-Soviet Vietnam in Indochina, China believed normalization of its relations with the United States was the best way to put pressure on the Soviet Union and cope with the Vietnam problem. The United States, in turn, believed that normalization would keep China from moving closer to the Soviet Union and put pressure on the Soviet Union to accept its terms for détente. Strategic considerations once again prompted the two countries to make serious efforts to move the relationship forward. Through intense negotiations, they eventually worked out a deal. The United States was to accept China's three conditions for normalization, namely, to withdraw its troops from Taiwan, to abrogate its mutual security treaty with Taiwan, and to cut its official ties with Taiwan. In addition, the United States would refrain from selling weapons to Taiwan during the first year of normalization. China was to allow one year for the U.S.-Taiwan mutual security treaty to terminate, to refrain from protesting the United States' unilateral statement that it would continue to be concerned about the Taiwan question and expect its peaceful resolution, and, for the time being, not to insist on discontinuation of America's weapons sales to Taiwan after its security treaty with Taiwan was terminated.[39] On December 16, 1978, China and the United States announced their agreement on normalization.[40] On January 1, 1979, the two countries formally established diplomatic relations.

Testing the Limits of Cooperation

The announcement of the normalization agreement between China and the United States was well received in both countries but not in the U.S. Congress, where it provoked strong opposition. A significant number in the Congress were Taiwan's "old" friends, who had supported Taiwan in part for ideological reasons and in part because the Taiwan authorities had treated them like kings, offering them many material and nonmaterial benefits. Second, many in Congress could not accept the fact that throughout the negotiation process, the administration had not consulted with them and felt that they had nothing to do with the agreement. Third, many believed that the agreement had failed to secure any significant concessions from China, especially on the security of Taiwan; it offered no guarantee that Beijing would not take over Taiwan by force.[41]

On January 28, 1979, Deng Xiaoping began a historic visit to the United States. During his visit, he tried to underscore the importance China attached to cooperative Sino-American relations. In addition to meeting with administration leaders, Deng Xiaoping also spent one day on Capitol Hill.

He had lunch with 85 senators, including all the members of the Senate Foreign Relations Committee, and tea with more than 40 House members including all the members of the House Foreign Affairs Committee. He also
met individually with the leaders of the Senate and the House. Deng Xiaoping told them that China had given up using the word "liberation" to refer
to the resolution of the Taiwan question and that as long as the Taiwan authorities acknowledged that Taiwan was part of China, Taiwan could maintain its current political and economic system and a separate military force
indefinitely.[42]

Deng's U.S. tour generated much goodwill among the American people
and helped moderate some of the emotional opposition in the Congress to
the terms of normalization. However, congressional efforts to protect
American interests in Taiwan and ensure Taiwan's security continued. Influential congressmen pushed for a Taiwan relations act and eventually got
their way. The Taiwan Relations Act emphasized the U.S. intention to
maintain and promote U.S.-Taiwan relations at the civilian level and stated
U.S. policy regarding Taiwan: (1) "to declare that peace and stability in the
area [the Western Pacific] are in the political, security, and economic interests of the United States, and are matters of international concern"; (2) "to
make clear that the United States' decision to establish diplomatic relations
with the People's Republic of China rests upon the expectation that the future of Taiwan will be determined by peaceful means"; (3) "to consider any
efforts to determine the future of Taiwan by other than peaceful means, including by boycotts or embargoes, a threat to the peace and security of the
Western Pacific area and of grave concern to the United States"; (4) "to provide Taiwan with arms of a defensive character"; and (5) "to maintain the capacity of the United States to resist any resort to force or other forms of co-
ercion that would jeopardize the security, or the social or economic system,
of the people on Taiwan."[43] Under strong pressure from Congress, President Carter signed the act on April 10, 1979.

The passage of the Taiwan Relations Act angered the Chinese and cast a
dark shadow on Sino-American relations. In his meeting with an American
congressional delegation, Deng Xiaoping urged Washington to note that the
act had already brought the relationship between the two countries to a halt
and even to the brink of complete retrogression. He warned that China
would watch U.S. actions on Taiwan closely. Official Chinese newspapers
also published harsh criticism of the passage of the act.[44]

However, Beijing also realized that it could not afford to break off its relationship with the United States. China had just waged a border war against Vietnam, and it was not clear whether the Soviet Union would use the issue to heighten tensions along the Sino-Soviet border. By this time, moreover, the Chinese leadership had already decided to concentrate its attention on China's economic development. To expedite economic progress, China adopted a policy of openness as well as reform, in part to maximize utilization of resources abroad. Under the circumstances, maintaining relations with the United States became especially important. Beijing was also aware that the Carter administration had tried to moderate the effect of the Taiwan Relations Act and had taken actions to make sure that U.S. relations with Taiwan remained unofficial.[45] Beijing decided to set the issue aside for the time being.

The election of Ronald Reagan to the White House in 1980 dealt a blow to the development of Sino-American relations over the next two years. Reagan was an old friend of Taiwan with a strong ideological bent but little understanding of international relations in general and China in particular. During the presidential campaign, he strongly attacked Carter for his betrayal of Taiwan and vowed that he would follow the Taiwan Relations Act and also restore official relations with Taiwan.[46] After assuming office, he attempted not only to resume relations but also to increase U.S. weapon sales to Taiwan.

Reagan's campaign rhetoric aroused great concern on the part of Chinese leaders and also drew criticism from the Carter administration.[47] Under pressure, Reagan began to moderate his plan to revive official relations with Taiwan and eventually gave up the idea. However, his persistence in selling arms to Taiwan led to an intense controversy between the United States and China. The Chinese government insisted that U.S. arms sales to Taiwan constituted a violation of China's national sovereignty; they would hamper China's reunification process and therefore must be stopped.[48] The Reagan administration, in contrast, believed that arms sales to Taiwan provided the most important guarantee of Taiwan's security and insisted on this policy as long as China refused to renounce force in realizing reunification.[49] As the two sides held to their respective positions, Sino-American relations entered a state of crisis.

However, despite their determination to uphold their respective principles, neither China nor the United States believed that it was in its interest to allow the relationship to unravel over the issue. The Reagan administration was predisposed to take a tough position against the Soviet Union and did not wish to push China toward its adversary. China was embarking on an ambitious modernization program and wanted to cultivate a favorable international environment. Eventually, both sides made concessions and in 1982 reached an agreement that became known in China as the August 17th Communiqué. Essentially, the United States stated that it did not "seek to carry out a long-term policy of arms sales to Taiwan" and that its arms sales to the island would not "exceed, either in qualitative or quantitative terms, the level of those supplied in recent years since the establishment of diplomatic relations between the United States and China." The United States also stated that it intended "to reduce gradually its arms sales to Taiwan, leading over a period of time to a final resolution." China for its part dropped its demand that a specific date be set for terminating sales.[50]

The Changing Basis of the Relationship

The August 17 Communiqué prevented a breakdown in the relationship but failed to prevent the Taiwan issue from continuing to irritate it. Even before the announcement of the communiqué, the Reagan administration attempted to appease Taiwan authorities with the so-called Six Points, promising that it was not going to end arms sales to Taiwan and would not mediate between Taipei and Beijing or exert any pressure on Taipei to enter into negotiations with Beijing. To appease domestic critics, the Reagan administration clarified its policy on arms sales to Taiwan. On the question of quantity, it introduced an inflation factor in determining the level of sales, thus justifying an annual increase. This increase was to be determined in relative terms, that is, the United States would sell weapons that were not the most advanced or those the United States had stopped producing. Finally, and most important, the United States would transfer advanced weapon manufacturing technologies to Taiwan, since the communiqué did not impose any restrictions in this regard.[51]

Watching U.S. behavior, the Chinese leaders were very disappointed. They concluded that the United States was not sincere in seeking genuine cooperation with China but was only interested in exploiting China's strategic cooperation to its own advantage. About the same time, Soviet leaders began to send out feelers exploring the possible improvement of relations with China. In a speech in Tashkent on March 24, 1982, President Leonid

Brezhnev admitted that China was still a socialist country and reaffirmed Soviet recognition of China's sovereignty over Taiwan. He also expressed willingness to hold negotiations with China over the border problem and to discuss measures to improve relations.[52] In Chinese eyes the contrast in the way the Soviet Union and the United States handled the Taiwan question could not have been greater.

By this time, China's perception of the international situation had also begun to change. Previously, the Chinese had seen the Soviet Union as aggressive, and Soviet expansionist activities as the principal threat to world peace. Now Chinese leaders discovered that the Soviet Union's previous expansionist thrust had lost its steam as it became bogged down in Afghanistan and that the United States, on the offensive, was doing the saber rattling. Under the circumstances, the Chinese leaders no longer felt the need to ally with the United States to deter the perceived Soviet threat. Coupled with their bitter experience in dealing with the Americans, this perception led them to make a fundamental adjustment in their international strategy. China would practice an independent policy rather than seek an alliance with any superpower.[53]

In the context of U.S.-Soviet confrontation, China's strategic reposturing opened new possibilities for improved relations with both the United States and the Soviet Union. On the one hand, in his attempt to deal with the so-called evil empire, Reagan saw China as a potential ally or at least an important country the United States could not afford to alienate. On the other hand, in its attempt to confront increasing U.S. pressure, the Soviet Union believed it necessary to improve relations with China in order to prevent China from allying with the United States. Consequently, China's relations with both the United States and the Soviet Union witnessed simultaneous improvement.

The year 1983 saw a significant improvement in relations between China and the United States. In May, Commerce Secretary Malcolm Baldrige informed Chinese leaders of the U.S. decision to move China's export status from the P category to the V category, which included most of America's friends and allies. This meant that China was eligible to import more sophisticated American technology and, more important, that the United States regarded China as a friend instead of a potential enemy.[54] In August, after several months of negotiations, the two countries reached an agreement on textiles. China also made progress in resolving the issue of the Huguang railway bond claims through the American legal system. On a visit to China, Defense Secretary Caspar Weinberger concluded agreements with China on U.S. arms sales to China and on the resumption of military exchanges between the two countries, which had been suspended in 1981 over U.S. arms sales to Taiwan. The relationship received a further boost from Premier Zhao Ziyang's visit to the United States in January 1984 and President Ronald Reagan's visit to China three months later.

By the mid-1980s, relations between the two countries were back on course, despite some irritants. The Taiwan question began to subside as China chose to emphasize peaceful exchanges with Taiwan to facilitate reunification and as the United States refrained from measures China would view as provocative. Meanwhile, trade between the two countries experienced rapid growth. American investment in China began to expand. Bilateral education and cultural contacts exploded. Within both countries a consensus favoring efforts to improve the Sino-American relationship developed. U.S.-China relations had never before enjoyed such extensive contacts and popular support.[55]

Against this backdrop, officials of both countries began to view the relationship in largely positive terms. In his speech at the welcoming dinner for Secretary of State George Shultz, the Chinese foreign minister Wu Xueqian said that the significance of Sino-American relations was being appreciated by more and more people, efforts to promote the relationship were receiving increasingly extensive support, and forces in favor of the improvement of the relationship were becoming stronger day by day.[56] In a report to Congress on U.S. security strategy, President Reagan stated that the United States was seeking a close, friendly, and cooperative relationship with China.[57] In his April 22, 1987, speech to the Brookings Institution on Sino-American relations, Gaston Sigur, the assistant secretary of state for East Asian and Pacific affairs, described the U.S.-China relationship as "mature." The two countries might have differences, he stated, but they had learned to discuss these differences without letting them hamper improved relations.[58]

Sliding Toward Confrontation

The euphoria proved to be short-lived. In the late 1980s important changes were taking place in the Soviet Union and other East European countries, and they in turn changed the international strategic environment in fundamental ways. Moreover, with very different historical, political, economic, social, and cultural backgrounds, the more the United States and China interacted with each other, the more aware of their differences they became and the more difficult it was to contain them. Then, in the spring of 1989, under mounting pressure from both international and domestic forces, social and political tension within China erupted into massive popular unrest. The government's belated but forceful response to the situation on June 4 furnished the occasion for a sharp downturn in the Sino-American relationship.

In the Soviet Union, the rise of Mikhail Gorbachev to the position of general secretary of the Communist Party in March 1985 had initially appeared to be just another reshuffle of the top leadership. To the surprise of the world, however, the new Soviet leader initiated a process that was to bring dramatic change to the strategic contour of the world and the nature of Sino-American relations. Upon assuming office, Gorbachev began a series of major moves to improve relations with both China and the United States. In a meeting with Vice Premier Li Peng in Moscow, he said that Soviet leaders believed it very important to improve relations between the Soviet Union and China. In a speech in Vladivostok on July 28, 1986, he announced that the Soviet Union would withdraw its military forces from Afghanistan and Mongolia, that it would use the middle line of the main navigational channel to determine the river border between it and China, and that it was prepared to discuss measures to establish good neighborly relations with China at any time and at any level.[59] The Soviet Union subsequently began to withdraw its troops from Mongolia, Siberia, and Afghanistan and to hold border talks with China. The improvement in Sino-Soviet relations culminated in May 1989, when President Gorbachev paid an official visit to China and he and Deng Xiaoping announced the normalization of relations between the two countries.[60]

Meanwhile, the Soviet leadership also made significant moves to improve relations with the United States. Realizing that the Soviet Union had little to gain through Soviet-American military rivalry and that the Soviet Union badly needed a relaxed international environment in order to concentrate its resources on domestic development, Gorbachev made repeated overtures to the United States, despite the Reagan administration's hawkish anti-Soviet policy. Eventually he managed to gain Reagan's goodwill in Soviet-American talks by offering major concessions eliminating mid-range missiles and making drastic cuts in strategic forces. As the two leaders developed rapport, relations between the two countries improved substantially.

By the end of 1988, both Reagan and Gorbachev claimed that Soviet-American relations were entering a new age.[61]

Although these changes were welcome news for Sino-Soviet and Soviet-American relations as well as for world peace, they undermined the most important basis of the Sino-American relationship: each country's anti-Soviet strategic considerations. Such considerations were the underpinnings of the Sino-American rapprochement of the early 1970s and had provided a strong argument in favor of a better relationship. Previously, when problems arose they could always be ignored or downplayed so that they would not stand in the way of strategic cooperation. Now that the Soviet threat was diminishing, this strategic rationale for cooperation also evaporated.

In response to this new reality, both China and the United States initially pointed to other aspects of the relationship, such as increasing economic ties, furthering cultural and educational exchanges, and improving social networks. They argued that after many years of contact, the relationship between the two countries had become stronger and more mature primarily because it had gone far beyond its narrow 1970s base in strategic necessity. Yet, to the unease of many on both sides of the Pacific, as their respective relations with the Soviet Union improved, China and the United States found that their underlying political relationship was encountering increasing obstacles.

First, there was the abortion issue. During the 1950s and 1960s, China's population explosion posed a serious threat to socioeconomic development. To cope with this problem, the Chinese government embarked on an ambitious population planning program in the 1970s with the aim of limiting families to one child. Owing to difficulties resulting from the scale of the program and the poor quality of implementation in certain areas, however, abuses, including forced abortion, occurred. Also during this time, American society was being ripped apart by prolife and prochoice political battles. Seizing on this question, some Americans began to take issue with the Chinese government, condemning China's population policy and demanding that the U.S. government put pressure on China. The Reagan administration, supporting the prolife position, suspended U.S. aid to the UN Fund for Population Activities in 1984 on the grounds that it was funding China's population program.[62]

Related to the abortion controversy was a second issue, the conflict over the Tibet question. In June 1987, members of the House of Representatives took advantage of the House deliberation on the State Department authorization act to propose an amendment related to China's human rights situation and another one on China's human rights violations in Tibet. These two amendments used much unsubstantiated information to discredit China. The amendment on Tibet claimed that China's Tibetan policy had resulted in the deaths of over one million Tibetans and stated that the United States should support the struggle for freedom and justice in China. Despite China's protests, the House passed the two amendments on June 18. In deliberations on the act, the Senate also included an amendment condemning China's policy in Tibet with similar allegations. This amendment was approved by the Senate on October 8. On December 15 and 16, the act passed both the House and the Senate, and on December 22, President Reagan signed it into law.[63]

Meanwhile, a third issue, China's international arms sales, was becoming controversial. China had previously refrained from selling weapons abroad, although it had provided military assistance in some instances. In the early 1980s, China began to emphasize economic development and kept its military spending at a low level. To compensate the military, China allowed it to run its own businesses and use the earnings to supplement its income. Some military enterprises began to reach out to other countries and sold some weapons, including missiles and materials that might be used for nuclear weapons.[64] Initially, the United States did not pay much attention to China's arms sales. By 1987, however, with an increase in U.S. military exercises in the Persian Gulf, the existence of China's Silkworm missile technology began to attract U.S. attention. Fearing that the missiles would be used to target U.S. military facilities, the United States began to put pressure on China to stop such sales. China's planned sale of C-SS-2 intermediate-range ballistic missiles to Saudi Arabia also upset the United States, which feared its potential implications for the balance of power in the Middle East. Reports of China's negotiation of the sale of medium-range M-9 missiles to Syria and Pakistan also alarmed the United States. The arms sales issue was partially settled through negotiations, but it cast a further shadow over Sino-American relations.[65]

Finally, the issue of trade began to cause increased friction between the two countries. After Nixon's visit to China in 1972, and especially after China's adoption of the policy of "reform and openness" in 1978, economic relations between the two nations developed rapidly. At first the total scale of trade was small, and when there were problems they attracted little attention. But from the mid-1980s, as China's exports created an increasing U.S. trade surplus and as U.S. protectionist forces gained strength, the United States began to pressure China to limit the growth of its textile exports and to complain about China's restrictions on imports, such as tariffs, foreign exchange controls, quotas, and licenses. Increasingly, the United States also criticized China for its failure to protect American intellectual property rights. China likewise complained about various forms of American protectionism, such as tariffs, antidumping measures, and voluntary export restraint quotas. China's poor investment environment also led to many complaints from American businesses.[66]

Once the earlier strategic rationale for cooperation had been reduced, these and other problems became increasingly troubling. Until the Tiananmen incident in 1989, however, supporters in both countries could point to the development of other aspects of the relationship as the basis for a more mature and stable bond. On December 15, 1988, speaking at an academic conference to mark the tenth anniversary of U.S.-China normalization, Winston Lord, the U.S. ambassador to China, remarked that the increasing maturity of Sino-American relations had made a fundamental change of course or a dramatic breakthrough in the relationship unlikely.[67] On the same occasion, Li Shenzhi, vice president of the Chinese Academy of Social Sciences, spoke in a similar way, commenting that if common security requirements had been the main consideration bringing the two countries together in the old days, now many more factors favored the development of the relationship. Chinese modernization required American cooperation. The United States also increasingly needed China's cooperation in resolving global issues. In this more interdependent world, both China and the United States felt that they could no longer be enemies; instead, they had to be partners.[68]

No one in China or the United States expected that a disaster was just around the corner. In China in the spring of 1989, under the cross-pressures of domestic and international forces, student demonstrations soon erupted into massive, uncontrollable protests. Fearing that the country was going to descend into chaos, the Chinese government used force to restore order on June 4, 1989, known as the June Fourth or Tiananmen incident. The U.S. government reacted strongly against the suppression, and immediately the already fragile relationship between the two countries was on the verge of a breakdown.[69]

Sino-American Relations in Disarray

The impact of the Tiananmen incident on Sino-American relations cannot be exaggerated. Almost overnight, the U.S. perception of China became completely negative. As television images of the Chinese suppression reached into millions of American households, China became the world's greatest disappointment and worst nightmare in the eyes of the American public, a reaction that was emotional and widespread. Many Americans began to ask themselves how their government had put up with this China for so long. Seizing on this opportunity, American politicians began to exploit the issue for their own political advantage. Criticizing the Bush administration for appeasing the so-called Chinese dictatorship, they pressured the government to take a tough position. Under the circumstances, President Bush announced a series of punitive measures against China on June 5 and introduced a further set of sanctions on June 20.[70] The Chinese government felt cornered and angry. As it sought to stabilize its domestic situation, it condemned U.S. attempts to interfere in China's internal affairs and ignored U.S. pressure.[71] China also canceled Foreign Minister Qian Qichen's visit to the United States, expelled two "Voice of America" (VOA) correspondents, and jammed VOA's frequencies.

Yet both the Chinese and the American government shared the belief that it was in their respective national interests to keep the relationship from collapse. While protesting U.S. sanctions against China, the Chinese government expressed hope that the Bush administration would refrain from taking actions that would harm the long-term interests of the two countries.[72] On June 9, in a talk to senior military officers in Beijing, Deng Xiaoping stated that despite the current storms, China would continue to pursue its policy of reform and openness.[73] On October 2, in an address to the New York Council on Foreign Relations, Foreign Minister Qian Qichen proposed four ideas for improving relations.[74] During their meeting on October 31, Deng Xiaoping told former president Nixon that the United States should be realistic about China and take the initiative to improve relations.[75]

For its part, despite the politically and emotionally charged anti-China atmosphere, the Bush administration also made efforts at amelioration. In remarks on the Chinese situation on June 8, President Bush said that U.S.-China relations were very important to the United States and, instead of following advice to break ties, he wished to maintain them by seeking an appropriate balancing point.[76] On June 27, Bush observed at a press conference that China had made positive changes over the years and that maintaining a good relationship with China was in the national interests of the United States.[77] In July, Bush sent National Security Advisor Brent Scowcroft to China to convey American concern over events in China and expressed his desire to prevent the relationship from breaking down.[78] In December, Bush again sent Scowcroft to China to explore possible ways of improving relations. Through Scowcroft, Bush reportedly conveyed a message to Deng Xiaoping that he still regarded Deng as a personal friend and that the United States still wished to improve relations.[79] Deng Xiaoping, in return, told Scowcroft to convey his personal appeal to Bush, urging him to take measures to mend the situation. He said that despite the problems between them, China and the United States must improve their relationship, because world peace and stability demanded it.[80]

Subsequently both sides made persistent efforts at stabilization. The Bush administration tried to block congressional efforts to suspend China's Most Favored Nation status. China moderated its anti-U.S. rhetoric, released most of the detained people directly involved in the Tiananmen protests, and agreed to let Fang Lizhi, one of the most outspoken critics of the Chinese government who had sought political asylum in the U.S. embassy in the wake of the Tiananmen incident, leave China for the United States.

Eventually, it was the war in the Persian Gulf that provided the occasion for the two countries to begin to renormalize their relationship. In its attempt to obtain the UN Security Council's authorization to fight against Iraq for invading Kuwait, the United States needed China's support, since the latter had veto power. In exchange, the U.S. government agreed to invite Foreign Minister Qian Qichen to visit Washington, breaking a ban on high-level contacts instituted in the wake of the Tiananmen incident. From that point on, relations between the two nations began to improve as the United States gradually lifted other sanctions against China.

By 1992 relations between the two countries had stabilized but remained cool. The old strategic logic for cooperation was behind them. The June 4 images were still very much alive in the minds of Americans, and anti-China rhetoric saturated American discussion of U.S.-China policy. Bill Clinton, the American president-elect, had little sympathy with China. Three conflicts—human rights, arms sales, and trade—overshadowed the relationship, which seemed headed for an uncertain future.

Over the nearly two decades between 1972 and 1989, the Sino-American relationship experienced repeated shifts between increased cooperation and increased confrontation. There were, however, constraints that prevented it from going to extremes. Although it never became a smoothly functioning, full-scale alliance at the best of times, even at the worst of times the two sides were able to continue to work together on issues of important and overlapping interest.

III

U.S.-Japan Relations

CHAPTER SIX

U.S. Relations with Japan

Gerald L. Curtis

The two decades under review in this chapter, 1972–89, form a discrete period in the history of U.S. relations with Japan. This period opens with the "end of the postwar years" symbolized by the reversion of Okinawa to Japanese sovereignty on May 15, 1972, the end of an international monetary regime of fixed exchange rates, the beginning of a new and bitter politicization of U.S.-Japan bilateral trade disputes, and the U.S. opening to China. It closes with the disintegration of the Soviet Union and the termination of the cold war, the start of a U.S. economic revival, and the bursting of Japan's economic bubble.

Five U.S. presidents—Nixon, Ford, Carter, Reagan, and Bush—held office between 1972 and 1989. Although all but Carter were Republicans, the continuities and the changes that characterized U.S. policy toward Japan during this period were not significantly affected by the president's political party affiliation. With respect to both political/security and economic matters, for example, there were far more commonalities in U.S. Japan policy between Republican Nixon and Democrat Carter than between Nixon and fellow Republican Reagan.

Many important issues involving U.S. relations with Japan came across the desks of senior American policymakers during this time. In setting this period apart from the preceding years of postwar U.S.-Japan relations, however, and establishing the patterns of diplomatic approach and policy substance that have continued to influence U.S. dealings with Japan to the present day, two issues stand out: U.S. relations with Japan as they involve and affect China and bilateral U.S.-Japan trade conflicts. These two issues are the focus of the analysis offered here.

The New Beginning

It is important to begin with a consideration of the Japan policy pursued by President Nixon and his national security adviser, Henry Kissinger. Nixon and Kissinger established patterns in process and in policy substance that marked a sharp departure from the earlier postwar U.S. policy toward Japan and had a profound influence on subsequent administrations.

Much of what we now consider the characteristic pattern of U.S. policy toward Japan originated in the Nixon presidency. One of its features was the decision not to inform Japan about developments in U.S. policy toward China or even to consult with Japan over China. This practice got off to a dramatic start with the Nixon administration's "China shock" in 1971, when the United States did not inform Japan beforehand about the dramatic changes ahead in its China policy. Gerald Ford, as well as Jimmy Carter and his national security adviser Zbigniew Brzezinski, also bypassed Japan in their dealings with China. Although this pattern was moderated somewhat under Reagan and Bush, it was once again in evidence during the Clinton administration.

The Nixon presidency also initiated a new era in U.S.-Japan relations in the areas of bilateral trade and economic interaction. Recurring confrontation, intense congressional pressure to "get tough" with Japan, and Japan's grudging concessions to administration demands have characterized U.S.-Japan trade relations since the celebrated textile dispute of the Nixon presidency. Every subsequent administration has thrashed about in an effort to define an effective approach for dealing with Japan on trade issues. U.S. policy has introduced import surcharges, antidumping sanctions, voluntary export restraints, market-oriented specific sector negotiations (the MOSS talks), a structural impediments initiative (the SII negotiations), and various other measures to secure guaranteed market share for American and other foreign businesses in Japan. This last culminated in the Clinton administration's spectacularly unsuccessful effort to establish a "results-oriented" trade policy toward Japan.

If tactical improvisation on trade issues has characterized U.S. policy toward Japan since Nixon, there has also been a strong determination to maintain a high firewall between trade conflicts and security relations. However heated trade and economic disputes have been, no president has sought to breach this firewall in order to extract trade concessions by threatening to withdraw from the U.S. security commitment to Japan. To some extent, this separation of economic and security issues may have been a matter of luck. Neither Nixon and Kissinger nor Carter and Brzezinski were particularly interested in, or knowledgeable about, trade and international economic matters, and none of them factored trade policy into foreign policy strategies. There was no linkage because these key foreign policymakers did not think beyond the security/economy divide.

But it was not only luck. Nixon surely must have been sorely tempted to hold back on the Okinawa reversion in order to extract concessions from Japan on textiles, and he was furious when his expectation that Prime Minister Sato Eisaku would deliver important concessions on textiles was betrayed. But neither Nixon nor any of his successors was about to hold the U.S.-Japan security relationship hostage to a satisfactory resolution of economic differences. Every post–World War II president has recognized that maintaining a strong security alliance with Japan is vital to the national interests of the United States. Even the Clinton administration, which went further than any previous administration in emphasizing the importance of economic factors in foreign policy, in the end maintained the firewall between the trade and security dimensions of the relationship.

Nixon and Kissinger also shifted control over political relations with Japan from the State Department to the White House National Security Council, a move that accelerated the fragmentation of overall Japan policy. As Nixon's national security adviser, Kissinger was determined to wrest control of foreign policy from the State Department and into his own hands, a goal that Nixon, who also preferred secrecy, supported unreservedly. The process by which they engineered the opening to China is the most conspicuous example of this approach.

The State Department's loss of control over Japan policy was the inevitable consequence of the new bureaucratic politics that developed in deepening and broadening the U.S.-Japan relationship and the growing importance of trade and monetary issues. These issues gave the Commerce and Treasury departments an important stake in Japan policy, brought the White House's economic advisers into the picture along with the members of the National Security Council, and made congressional pressure a much more potent force in policy formulation. Until well into the 1960s, the State Department, represented by the assistant secretary of state for East Asia and the chief of the Japan desk, dominated Japan policy within the U.S. government. After Nixon, however, it became impossible to speak of a "single" (in the sense of a coherent, comprehensive, or bureaucratically well-coordinated) Japan policy.

Another characteristic of U.S. policymaking during these two decades, one closely identified with Henry Kissinger, Treasury Secretary John Connally, and other key players in the Nixon administration, is the widespread acceptance of the idea that Japan is somehow unique, that its economic institutions, if not its basic cultural characteristics, make it an outlier among trading nations, and that this uniqueness requires and justifies tailor-made approaches and policies. This belief in Japan's uniqueness grew stronger over time, eventually taking the form of "revisionist" thinking about Japan and U.S. policy toward Japan. Such thinking influenced the Bush administration in its last year in office and became the ideational basis for the Clinton administration's trade policy toward Japan, at least during Clinton's first term, although it is rooted in the attitudes of Nixon administration Japan policymakers.

The China Issue

It is rather fashionable these days to speak of a U.S.-Japan-China "triangle," but the notion that these three countries are involved in some kind of triangular relationship has less analytical utility or historical relevance than the constant invocation of the metaphor might lead one to suspect. It is indeed true that the three countries have relationships and that the policies of one toward another will be of concern to the third. But it is misleading if implicit in the "triangle" idea is the assumption that each country formulates its own policies toward one of the two others only after carefully considering their impact on its relations with the third.

Until Richard Nixon initiated the opening to China in 1971, the singular goal of postwar American East Asian policy was to balance Soviet power and contain communist influence. Japan was incorporated into the U.S. military alliance structure as a junior partner whose role as provided for under the U.S.-Japan security treaty was to facilitate the projection of American power into East Asia. China was regarded as a member of a unified communist bloc, and it continued to be so regarded through the 1960s, despite evidence of a serious Sino-Soviet split. U.S. policymakers saw the world in bipolar, not multipolar terms. In this worldview there was no room for a U.S.-Japan-China triangle; indeed, the United States firmly rejected Japan's efforts to break out of the rigid bipolar mold and develop its own policy toward China.

Yoshida Shigeru, the Japanese architect of the postwar peace settlement Japan made with the United States and most of the Allied powers, viewed China quite differently from John Foster Dulles, the American architect of the settlement. Yoshida believed that nationalism in China was stronger than communism and assumed that access to the Chinese market would have to be an important element in Japan's economic recovery. Yoshida was eager to recognize the government of the new People's Republic in Beijing, quickly resume trade relations with the mainland, and possibly gain some diplomatic maneuvering room in relation to the United States by developing ties with China. He was dissuaded from pursuing this course only by the threat, issued by key U.S. senators at Dulles's request, that Japan's failure to recognize Chiang Kai-shek's government on Taiwan as the legitimate government of all China might cause the Senate to fail to ratify the San Francisco Peace Treaty. Until the Nixon administration's "China shock" freed Japan from U.S.-imposed constraints on its China policy, the Japanese government had pursued a "separation of politics and economics" (seikei bunri) policy by officially supporting the U.S. policy of diplomatically isolating China while developing low-level trade relations with mainland China through private and semiofficial channels.

President Nixon's decision to send Henry Kissinger on his famed secret mission to Beijing in July 1971 involved a triangular relationship, but the triangle was a U.S.-China-Soviet one. The United States hoped to use its new relationship with China to nudge Moscow toward accepting the concept of détente, and China hoped to use its new relationship with the United States to strengthen its power and position in relation to its communist camp adversary.

That the U.S. decision to end China's isolation had everything to do with the Soviet Union and nothing to do with Japan was made all too obvious to the Japanese by the manner in which it was accomplished. It may have been unrealistic to expect that Kissinger would consult Japan about a shift in China policy—Kissinger, after all, did not even consult Nixon's own secretary of state—but Prime Minister Sato and the Japanese public were understandably dismayed and embarrassed that their government was given no advance notice of the impending public announcement. In his memoirs, Kissinger has admitted to a "serious error in manners" in not finding a way to moderate the shock his secret mission to Beijing caused in Tokyo. He has not admitted to any error in strategy, however, because he believed then and later that Japan had no option but to adjust to the new American line on China.

Some at the time took a very different view. U. Alexis Johnson, the U.S. ambassador to Japan just before Nixon came into office and one of the most influential Japan hands in the State Department, drew a much more severe conclusion in his memoirs, noting that Kissinger's "passion for secrecy, combined with his contempt for the [State] Department and disdain for the Japanese, threw a devastating wrench into our relations with Japan on the question of China."[1]

Considering developments in U.S.-China-Japan relations over the nearly thirty years since Kissinger's first Beijing trip, it is clearly not the case that the Nixon administration's secret diplomacy with the Chinese had a "devastating" impact on U.S.-Japan relations with respect to China. No doubt it sowed seeds of suspicion in Tokyo about U.S. policy and established a pattern—one all too enthusiastically embraced by Carter's national security adviser, Zbigniew Brzezinski—of downplaying the importance of consultations with the Japanese on China policy. Nonetheless, embarrassed and angry as they were, Japanese government leaders, who had already suspected for months that U.S. China policy was going to change, quickly adjusted to the new situation. They moved with remarkable speed not simply to catch up with the United States but to get out in front of it, establishing formal diplomatic relations with the PRC in 1972, seven years before the United States did so.

In terms of the longer term consequences for U.S. policy in East Asia, what Kissinger said about Japan during his visit to Beijing and what both he and Nixon reiterated in subsequent meetings with Mao and Zhou Enlai, are far more important. Neither Nixon nor Kissinger sought to convince PRC leaders that postwar democratic Japan was determined to pursue a peaceful foreign policy and to avoid a resurgence of military power. Instead, the thrust of their remarks was that the best way to prevent Japan from once again becoming an important military factor in the region was to keep it allied with, and subordinated to, the United States.

In Nixon and Kissinger's geopolitical perspective, it was imperative that the United States remain a military power in East Asia and continue to be able to forward deploy its forces on bases in Japan. They wanted to convince Chinese leaders that it was in their interest for the United States to keep the security treaty in force and U.S. military forces in Japan, and they did so by playing on Chinese fears of revived Japanese militarism.

As Kissinger himself notes in his memoirs, he stressed to Mao that "China's fear of Japan could best be assuaged by a continuing U.S.-Japanese alliance."[2] Both Kissinger and Nixon emphasized the role of the U.S.-Japan alliance in keeping a lid on Japanese military power, or, as Kissinger put it, serving as a "rein on Japanese unilateralism."[3] Here, for example, is Nixon, talking to Zhou Enlai: "[T]he United States can get out of Japanese waters, but others will still fish there. If we were to leave Japan naked and defenseless, they would have to turn to others for help [a warning that the Japanese would look to the Soviets?] or build the capability to defend themselves. If we had no defense arrangement with Japan, we would have no influence where they were concerned." Since a Japanese-Soviet military alliance was too far-fetched for Zhou or anyone else to take seriously, this was in fact a thinly veiled warning that the only alternative to a U.S.-Japan alliance was an independent, militarily powerful Japan. Nixon went on to drive the point home: "If the United States is gone from Asia, gone from Japan, our protests, no matter how loud, would be like firing an empty cannon. We would have no effect, because thousands of miles away is just too far to be heard."[4]

Nixon and Kissinger claimed, in other words, that the way to avoid a triangular U.S.-Japan-China relationship in East Asia was to keep Japan in the snug embrace of the United States, which would at least delay, if not avoid altogether, Japan's military revival. They no doubt took this posture in part for opportunistic reasons, seeing it as a persuasive argument for gaining Chinese acquiescence to continuing the security treaty and the presence of U.S. forces in the region. But it was an easy task, because their view of Japan was remarkably compatible with Mao's and Zhou's views.

Nixon and Kissinger prided themselves on being "realists" in international affairs, and realist theory predicted that as Japan became more economically powerful, it would seek to become more politically and militarily powerful in its region and in the world. Kissinger made this argument when he held public office, and he has continued to adhere to the view that Japan will soon decide to develop a military posture commensurate with its economic capabilities. (That might happen one day, and when it does, realists will claim that their theory has been confirmed, but of what use is a theory that has been consistently wrong about Japan for at least the past thirty years?)

Like other realist theorists, Nixon and Kissinger both believed that pressures at the international level would overwhelm pacifist opinion in Japan and drive it in the direction of major rearmament. They may not have shared the Chinese fear of the Japanese as inherently militaristic, but their penchant for realist thinking gave them a perspective on Japan far more compatible with views they heard in China than in Tokyo.

In February 1970, shortly after the Okinawa reversion agreement was completed, Nixon predicted that Japan would no longer be reluctant to become involved in world affairs and that he "wouldn't be surprised if in five years we didn't have to restrain them."[5] This is a rather astonishing statement for someone with a reputation as a brilliant analyst of international affairs. Nixon later boasted that he was tough with the Chinese: "We told them that if you try to keep us from protecting the Japanese, we would let them go nuclear," as if the only thing holding the Japanese back from becoming a nuclear power and a menace to the region was the United States and its security treaty arrangement.[6]

The popularity of the idea that the security treaty is the "cap in the bottle" of Japanese militarism is a legacy of the Nixon-Kissinger era, even if the phrase itself (which was coined in March 1990 by Major General Henry Stackpole III, the commander of marine corps bases in Japan) is not. The Chinese accepted this interpretation and gave passive, if not open, support to the security treaty until the mid-1990s. Their view changed, however, when President Clinton and Prime Minister Hashimoto Ichiro issued a joint declaration on security cooperation in April 1996, and a subsequent revision of the guidelines for U.S.-Japan defense cooperation that gave Japan an expanded role in supporting U.S. forces engaged in hostilities in the "areas surrounding Japan." Chinese leaders appear to view these developments as an attempt to pull the "cap" at least partway out of the Japanese military "bottle."

Nixon and Kissinger were all too ready to reinforce Chinese fears of revived Japanese militarism, whatever the cost to U.S. relations with Japan. Armin Meyer, the U.S. ambassador to Japan at the time, warned Nixon and Kissinger against trying to "persuade the Chinese that the United States—

Japan security relationship had a restraining effect on Japanese 'militarism.' This would inevitably get back to Japan, undermining Japanese confidence in the U.S. and weakening the U.S.-Japan relationship just as Beijing desired."[7]

Nixon and Kissinger were more realistic about the short-term consequences of their position. They understood that the Japanese had little choice but to acquiesce to American policy toward China. Their worldview convinced them that sooner or later, Japan would become a more normal country and an independent force in international affairs. And they were not inclined to pay much attention to Japanese sensibilities, especially when there was little Japan could do to upset U.S. China policy and when the United States was engaged in a historic effort to mobilize China in an attempt to create a new balance of power with the Soviet Union.

From Kissinger to Brzezinski

The election of Jimmy Carter as president in 1976 and his appointment of Zbigniew Brzezinski as his national security adviser, even though it meant a shift from a Republican to a Democratic administration, did not alter the basic lines of U.S. policy toward Japan already established by Nixon and Kissinger. Brzezinski was intent on pushing the U.S.-Chinese strategic relationship further than Kissinger had been able to take it. On China matters, Japanese leaders were for the most part ignored by the new U.S. administration, as they had been during the administrations of Ford and Nixon. Kissinger's success in taking control of China policy and keeping the State Department out of the loop set a precedent that Brzezinski was all too eager to continue. It was not long before he and Secretary of State Cyrus Vance were engaged in a struggle for influence with the president on a range of foreign policy issues, including China.

Brzezinski's inattention to the Japan relationship is somewhat surprising. He was a key figure in establishing and providing intellectual leadership to the Trilateral Commission, which was created in the belief that Americans and Europeans needed broader dialogue and closer consultation with the Japanese. Perhaps all this indicates is that unlike university professors, policymakers become preoccupied with immediate issues needing resolution. The Carter administration had decided to push forward an effort to establish formal diplomatic relations with China and saw little reason to involve Japan, which had established its own diplomatic relations with China several years earlier.

The changes in U.S.-Japan relations with respect to China during the Carter-Brzezinski years grew out of the Carter administration's skepticism about détente. Kissinger had tried to play a China card to draw the Soviets into accepting the premises of détente, but Brzezinski was a severe critic of détente. He saw his China card as a way to maximize the power of forces opposed to Soviet expansionism. Concerned about containing Soviet power, the Carter administration wanted Japan to strengthen its own military capabilities and take on more of the burden of its own defense. Reacting to these pressures, the Japanese eventually proposed that the two countries establish clear guidelines for U.S.-Japan defense cooperation. The United States responded positively to this initiative, viewing the 1978 Guidelines on U.S.-Japan Defense Cooperation as a way to more closely integrate Japanese defense forces with U.S. forces. Japan saw them as a way to specify the limits to its own security role. The guidelines did not change Japan's "defensive defense" strategy, but they did consolidate a shift in roles between the U.S. and the Japanese military. In the event of an attack on Japan, Japanese forces would not merely supplement U.S. power. Japan would take primary responsibility for its own defense, and American military action would focus on regional security threats. These guidelines remained in effect for twenty years, until they were revised by the next Democratic president, Bill Clinton.

President Carter's demand for stringent controls over the operation of nuclear fuel reprocessing plants turned out to be more controversial. Since the Japanese were in the process of building a reprocessing plant at Tokaimura (the site of a nuclear accident in October 1999), they became a major target of Carter's nonproliferation campaign. In Japan the issue sparked a great deal of hostility toward the Carter administration. To the Japanese, U.S. policy demonstrated a lack of trust in their commitment not to develop nuclear weapons and was seen as an effort to restrict the development of peaceful nuclear energy resources in a country lacking other significant domestic energy sources. The matter was eventually resolved, but during Carter's one term in office, little was accomplished to ameliorate tensions over security issues and China.

The Ron-Yasu Relationship

Ronald Reagan's election produced important changes in the Japan policy laid down by Nixon and Kissinger and continued by Carter and Brzezinski. Reagan was not enthralled with China, as Nixon and Carter and their national security advisers had been, and he did not have to deal with the problems of opening a dialogue or establishing formal diplomatic relations with China. Unlike Nixon, the conservative practitioner of realpolitik, Reagan was a right-wing ideologue whose anticommunism ran deep and whose sympathy for Taiwan made him less than enthusiastic about embracing the Chinese to fight the "evil empire" of the Soviet Union.

Reagan, who was more inclined to embrace Japan, found himself dealing with a kindred spirit in the person of Prime Minister Nakasone Yasuhiro. Nakasone was a well-known nationalist who took pride in his knowledge of international affairs and in his ability, rare among Japanese political leaders, to think in global and strategic terms. The two leaders established what seems to have been a genuinely warm "Ron-Yasu" relationship, based on a common view of the Soviet threat and rooted in an understanding of the importance of close relations between their two countries.

When Reagan and Nakasone first came to power, few observers would have guessed that they would get along so well. Reagan and his defense secretary, Caspar Weinberger, believed in confronting the Soviet Union with overwhelming military power and, at least during Reagan's first years, in strengthening ties with Taiwan. It would have been reasonable to expect that Reagan would pressure the Japanese to increase their defense budget and take on a larger security role and to move closer to his administration's position on Taiwan. Nakasone, for his part, was a well-known nationalist when he assumed office. He had worn a black tie to every Diet session during the postwar American Occupation because he believed the nation was in mourning until the occupying army left. Many thought he wanted to see a loosening of Japan's bonds with the United States in favor of a more "autonomous" defense.

Their behavior confounded these expectations. After an initial period in which, following the example of his predecessors, Weinberger demanded that Japan spend more on defense, the Reagan administration fundamentally shifted its strategy toward Japan on defense matters, focusing its attention and its negotiations on "missions" and "roles." The earlier emphasis on budgetary expenditures, a carryover from the Occupation, involved American officials in Japan's domestic decision-making process. The idea now was that if the United States could reach an agreement with Japan defining new roles and missions for Japan's Self-Defense Forces, the Japanese would decide what it would cost to fulfill the terms of the agreement. The "roles and missions" approach quickly produced positive results, the first being the decision by the short-lived Suzuki government, which preceded Nakasone's administration, to expand Japan's defense perimeter to sea lanes extending a thousand miles southeast and southwest of Japanese shores.

The image of Nakasone as a proponent of an autonomous defense who wanted to distance Japan from the United States on security matters was quickly shown to be misleading. Nakasone sought every opportunity to demonstrate to the Japanese public that Japan's security was ineluctably linked to U.S. power and that U.S. and Japanese policies must be formulated in the context of a global, and not simply a regional, balance of power. Nakasone succeeded in convincing Reagan that any arms control agreement with the Soviet Union concerning its removal of SS-20 missiles aimed at Western Europe should also prohibit their redeployment to East Asia. Nakasone also publicly declared that Japan was an "immovable aircraft carrier" in the cause of free world security and criticized the pacifism-in-one-country mentality so dominant in Japan. The sharp differences over China policy and the tensions in defense relations that characterized U.S.-Japan relations in the 1970s were muted during the years Ron and Yasu were in charge.

Another reason for the positive turn in U.S.-Japan relations during the Reagan years was the role played by George Shultz, who succeeded Alexander Haig as Reagan's secretary of state in 1982 and remained in that post until the end of the Reagan era. He was a professional economist whose worldview seemed to have been shaped more by considerations of relative economic power than by the kind of geopolitical thinking favored by Kissinger and Brzezinski. Shultz was skeptical about China's importance to the United States, arguing that fascination with China "has tended to make U.S. foreign policy in Asia Sinocentric. . . . For me, the centerpiece has always been Japan. By far the largest economy in Asia, Japan is a key strategic partner and a dramatic example of successful democratic governance in an area where that is scarce."[8] Shultz insisted that his first trip to Asia as secretary of state should be to Japan rather than to China, and he made a point of stopping off in Tokyo after visiting China, as his predecessors had not done and as his successors would not do, to report to Japanese government leaders on his discussions there.[9]

Shultz was against Japan's development into a major military power, and he probably played a role in countering the influence of Defense Secretary Weinberger on the issue of a Japanese military buildup. Again, his economist's view of the world drove his views on Japan: "America must ensure that Japan is not tempted, because of Western neglect, shortsightedness, or hostility, to build an economic and military zone of its own in Asia. A strong Japan severed from America would be unnerving to Asia and the rest of the world. The other side of the coin is that Japan, through its intense competitive challenge, can help keep the massive potential and achievements of the American economy from declining through our own complacency."[10] Together, Reagan and Shultz, in a close working relationship with Nakasone and his foreign minister, Abe Shintaro, repaired some of the damage that had been done to U.S. relations with Japan during previous administrations. But they were unable to stem the tide of anti-Japanese sentiment in the United States arising from the gross imbalance in trade relations, and they were no longer in office when the Tiananmen incident posed new challenges to the U.S.-Japan relationship.

The Impact of Tiananmen

The Tiananmen incident played out in U.S.-Japan relations in a curious way. George Bush, who succeeded Reagan as president in 1989, had been head of the Liaison Office in China and unlike Reagan, was enthusiastic about developing closer ties with the PRC. But the Chinese government's brutal suppression of the demonstrations in Tiananmen Square and the intense criticism provoked by the incident in Congress and among the American public upset his plans. Along with the United States and European countries, Japan imposed sanctions on China, but it did so reluctantly and looked for the first opportunity to remove them.

Japan's seeming lack of outrage over the actions of the "butchers of Beijing" and its alleged indifference to human rights produced a chorus of criticism in Congress and the American media, but the Bush administration did not join in. Kaifu Toshiki, the Japanese prime minister at the time, found himself in a politically advantageous position: he was able to pursue a China policy that served Japanese economic interests and made him look like a leader who would stand up to the United States on behalf of Japanese interests, and he enjoyed the quiet blessing of President Bush. At the Group of Seven (G7) summit in Houston in July 1990, when Kaifu proclaimed Japan's intention to resume loans to the PRC, he was announcing the kind of policy President Bush would have liked to pursue if domestic political pressures had not prevented him. Kaifu had discussed China during a phone conversation with Bush before he left for Houston, and I remember his telling me at the time that he had secured Bush's blessing for his policy, the assumption being that Japan would ease the way for the United States to resume normal relations with Beijing. Bush's public comment on Kaifu's announcement that Japan would move forward with a $5.6 billion package for China was more supportive than many Americans wanted him to be. Japan, Bush remarked, "is a sovereign nation that can make up its own mind on a lot of questions."[11] Kaifu almost certainly would not have been the first leader from a G7 country to visit China after Tiananmen if he had not had the implicit support of the U.S. government. Actions that appeared to break ranks with the West[12] were the result of close, if not exactly public, consultations with the United States.

The Underlying Trends

It was unavoidable that during the two decades under consideration, U.S. leaders would give far more attention to China than to Japan. The president, national security adviser, and secretary of state, with the singular exception of George Shultz, all viewed foreign policy in almost exclusively political and military terms; economics was a second-order issue. Japan was a given in the larger context of the cold war struggle with the Soviet Union. It was China that offered an opportunity for innovative diplomacy: strategists could design a China policy aimed at strengthening the position of the United States in relation to the Soviet Union. Major changes in U.S. relations with Japan, however, could only cause problems, domestically in Japan and regionally in U.S. relations with China and with South Korea and Southeast Asia. Thus, a great deal of thought and energy went into designing a new China policy, but there were no comparable incentives for innovative thinking about relations with Japan.

Moreover, in the 1970s in particular, American leaders were not concerned that Japan might take action in ways that would complicate U.S. relations with China. Given Japan's weakened position, Nixon and Kissinger, and later Carter and Brzezinski, could safely assume that although Japan had wanted to normalize relations with Beijing back in 1950, it would follow in the tracks the Americans laid down, grumbling about not being consulted but accommodating itself to the new U.S. position.

Another factor, the importance of which it is impossible to measure, was that strategists like Kissinger and Brzezinski obviously enjoyed discussing global issues with the Chinese but were bored to tears by discussions with the Japanese. Kissinger had enormous difficulty engaging with the Japanese and chalked it up to the fact that Japan was "a society whose structures, habits, and forms of decision making are so unique as to insulate Japan from all other cultures."[13] Since there was little worry in the administration that Japan would do anything to upset its evolving China policy and little to be learned from listening to the views of Japanese leaders, busy U.S. officials had little incentive to discuss China policy with Japanese leaders, even if those leaders represented the most important U.S. ally in East Asia.

The Trade Conundrum

It hardly seems necessary to note that beginning with the Nixon administration, the most difficult and contentious but important issue in U.S.-Japan relations was not China but bilateral trade relations. Throughout the 1970s and 1980s, while the United States confronted mounting budget and trade deficits, Japanese trade surpluses rose inexorably. Whatever its ideological inclinations, no administration could ignore the intense domestic pressure to "do something" about trade with Japan and about what some regarded as Japan's unfair trade practices.

Yet despite its importance, the Japan trade issue did not engage the focused attention of either the president or his top foreign policy advisers. Trade was a second-order issue not to be compared with matters of military security. Congress and the agencies within the administration, such as the Department of Commerce and the Office of the Special Trade Representative, that continued to press for action did so because it was part of their assigned mission. There is no evidence that any of the presidents' chief foreign policy advisers—Kissinger, Brzezinski, Richard Allen, Robert McFarlane, Colin Powell, or Brent Scowcroft, among others—thought of trade, or international economic relations more generally, as a necessary part of a comprehensive foreign policy strategy. Trade relations were treated more as a matter between the administration and Congress than as a matter between the U.S. government and Japan. The Japanese understood this situation quite accurately and did what they could to support the administration in fighting off congressional demands for action, while keeping Japanese concessions to a minimum. Until the "textile wrangle" broke into public view in the early 1970s, the Japanese had known little about the critical role of the U.S. Congress. They immediately began building up resources in Washington to represent their interests in Congress. Their success caused intense frustration among many U.S. trade negotiators.[14] Clyde Prestowitz, who was involved in trade negotiations with Japan in the 1980s, emerged from the trenches complaining that "The negotiation thus changed direction: originally a matter of US government requests, it became one of mutually calibrating just how much action would be necessary to keep Congress leashed. Instead of a negotiator, the US trade team became an adviser to the government of Japan on how to handle the US Congress."[15] The result was increased hostility toward Japan and growing frustration in Congress and U.S. public opinion.

Neither Nixon nor Kissinger was interested in trade, except, in Nixon's case, insofar as it affected his domestic political power base. International economic relations did not figure into the calculus of top "strategic" thinkers. In his memoirs, Kissinger makes light of his ignorance of trade issues, but in terms of U.S.-Japan relations, the fact that the president's senior adviser on international affairs had little interest in or knowledge of international economics was particularly unfortunate. Issues such as how to manage trade relations or how to deal with important structural changes in the world economy received little attention.

The "textile wrangle" was the most politically charged trade dispute in postwar U.S.-Japanese history up to that point, but it was not the first time the United States and Japan had dealt with a serious bilateral trade problem, nor was it the first time the United States sought a solution by asking Japan for voluntary export restraints. What made the textile case significantly different from previous trade disputes was its timing: the position of the United States in the world economy was undergoing a fundamental change. In 1971 the United States experienced its first overall merchandise trade deficit—$2.27 billion—in nearly a century. The trade deficit with Japan swelled to $3.2 billion on two-way trade of almost $11.5 billion. Ten years later, the U.S. bilateral trade deficit with Japan was $16 billion, and by 1987 it had reached a staggering $59 billion.

The appearance of red ink on the current account of the U.S. balance of payments led to the second "Nixon shock," the New Economic Policy announced on August 15, 1971. Among other things it imposed a 10 percent surcharge on all imports and suspended the convertibility of the dollar into gold. The failure of the Smithsonian agreement signed in December to stabilize exchange rates (it had pegged the dollar at ¥308 instead of ¥360) produced a new regime of floating exchange rates. It also inaugurated a new era in U.S.-Japan economic relations in which the American administration grasped at macroeconomic measures, multilateral trade negotiations, sectoral-specific trade agreements, results-oriented managed trade agreements, and other strategies in an effort to contain the growing, and increasingly politically explosive, Japan trade problem.

Throughout the 1970s—that is, during the Nixon, Ford, and Carter presidencies—congressional hostility toward Japan over trade issues grew exponentially. All three administrations tried to deal with the problem in essentially the same manner: they strong-armed Japan to adopt voluntary export restraints, they threatened to unleash Congress and impose harsh protectionist measures against Japan if it did not comply with American demands, and they kept a high firewall between trade and the security dimensions of the U.S.-Japan alliance.

This was still an age when trade was best left to government trade specialists and those in the White House responsible for managing relations with Congress. The State Department had not emphasized economic expertise in training its foreign service offices and, whether under Rogers, Kissinger, or Vance, did not aggressively seek to influence trade policy. According to the White House National Security Council, economic relations did not fall under the rubric of national security. Given the exigencies of the cold war and the critical role of the Japan alliance in U.S. Asia strategy, the president's foreign policy advisers had no enthusiasm for a policy that would put the U.S.-Japan alliance at risk in order to achieve a better import-export balance.

Yet Nixon, Ford, and Carter made no attempt to try to decrease trade tensions. In their rhetoric, they echoed congressional criticism of Japanese trade practices, but they did not develop coherent practical strategies to engage Japan over trade conflicts, nor did they openly contest the popular view that Japanese trade policies were at fault. The result was a pattern of piecemeal protectionist measures adopted in order to avoid the imposition of harsher measures by Congress.

When Ronald Reagan came into office, presidential rhetoric changed. Reagan was a committed free trader, as were the key people in his administration, including George Shultz. Shultz's equanimity in the face of growing trade deficits reflected his training in modern economic theory, but his views were far from those gaining strength in the Congress, the business community, and the mass media: "As an economist and a believer in the benefits of free trade, I worried less about such developments [Japan's trade surplus and overseas investment] than did most people in Washington. If the Japanese, as a producer-dominated and protected society, want to pay astronomical prices for goods that are cheaper elsewhere, that is more their problem than ours. . . . If we are worried about foreign financing of investment in the United States, let us increase our own savings to finance our own investment. In other words, I felt, if we wanted to see our real problems, we should look in the mirror."[16]

But precisely because Reagan and Shultz did not consider the bilateral trade imbalance with Japan a burning issue, as did so many others, they came into office without a strategy for coping with it. They found themselves in much the same position as their predecessors: having no strategy, they had to improvise one to deal with a Congress that was threatening protectionist measures to contain Japanese imports. A failure to head off Congress would not only produce congressional action that Reagan considered unwise, it would demonstrate that the Democrats controlled Congress's power over the Republican administration, and thus weaken the president politically.

The Reagan administration's benign neglect approach to the bilateral trade problem with Japan allowed Congress to dictate policy, and it demanded further voluntary export restraints. Within months of taking office, Reagan was forced to seek voluntary export restraints on Japanese automobiles. Later in his first term, he did the same for Japanese steel. In the meantime, the political mood became ever more bitter.

The MOSS (Market-Oriented Sector Specific) Talks

Even if Reagan agreed with Shultz that trade account imbalances are a symptom rather than the cause of economic problems, politically he had to try to get out in front of the trade problem with Japan. In 1985 the Reagan administration announced that it was initiating the MOSS—market-oriented sector specific—talks, a new round of trade negotiations with Japan. High-ranking officials committed an enormous amount of time to trying to open Japanese markets in electronics, telecommunications equipment and services, medical equipment and pharmaceuticals, and forest products to foreign access.

The MOSS talks produced some progress but did little to relieve tensions in bilateral trade relations. According to Shultz, they "produced positive results in a painful, tooth-pulling effort that left everyone a little ragged and frustrated."[17] Given the structure of the U.S. government, any strategy requiring intense involvement by senior officials over an extended period of time for modest results was ultimately unsustainable. The Japanese government, by contrast, could give the issue high priority, and it trained many senior officials whose entire raison d'être was to deal with trade issues.

If the MOSS talks achieved only limited success, they did shift the focus of congressional criticism. During the Nixon, Ford, and Carter administrations, the major objective of trade negotiations with Japan had been to restrain Japanese exports to the U.S. market. The MOSS talks shifted the focus of U.S. concern to market access. The United States then emphasized changing the rules and procedures that shut out foreign firms seeking to export to or invest in the Japanese market. MOSS represented an important turning point in U.S. trade policy toward Japan and served as a leading indicator of a more basic change in U.S. trade policy. Reagan and Bush (and Clinton, for that matter) argued that in U.S.-Japan trade relations, the core challenge was not how to protect U.S. companies from Japanese competition in the U.S. market but how to give U.S. and other foreign companies a fair chance to compete in the Japanese market. Market access became the key objective, and threats to restrict Japanese access to U.S. markets were used as leverage.

By emphasizing expanding trade through increased market access rather than restricting trade through voluntary or coercive restraints on Japanese exports, the policies of the U.S. Trade Representative (USTR) and Commerce became better synchronized with the macroeconomic policies being pursued by Treasury and supported by the White House Council of Economic Advisers. The coordinated intervention achieved by the Plaza Accord in 1985 to force a depreciation of the dollar in relation to the yen and other major currencies removed the handicap that an overvalued dollar had imposed on American manufacturers in the world market. It sought to drive policy where "market access" advocates in the USTR wanted to take it: toward an expansion of U.S. exports rather than a contraction of U.S. imports.

However, neither the MOSS talks nor the Plaza Accord was sufficient to calm the roiled waters of anti-Japanese opinion in the U.S. Congress and the business community. Demands for more and tougher measures against Japan continued to mount at roughly the same pace as the increase in the U.S. trade deficit with Japan. In March 1985, by a vote of 92–0, the Senate passed a resolution condemning Japan for unfair trade practices and urging retaliation if U.S. exports to Japan did not significantly increase. In 1988, Reagan's last year in office, the Senate passed the Omnibus Trade and Competitiveness Act. It included the so-called Super 301 provision compelling the administration to compile a list of countries that maintain a consistent pattern of unfair trade practices and requiring it to negotiate the removal of barriers within a set period of time.

Guaranteeing Market Share

Amid growing pressure, in 1986 the Reagan administration forged an agreement with Japan that violated its own strictures about free trade and provided a model for the kind of "results-oriented" trade agreements that formed the heart of the Clinton administration's Japanese trade strategy. The 1986 Semiconductor Agreement sought, through the Japanese government's efforts to promote relationships between Japanese firms and foreign semiconductor manufacturers, to prevent Japanese firms from dumping semiconductors abroad and to increase sales by foreign semiconductor firms within Japan. The agreement's most important provision was included in a confidential side letter, quickly leaked, that committed Japan to seeking a 10 to 20 percent increase in the share of foreign semiconductor sales in Japan by 1991.

Although the Japanese government denied that the agreement amounted to a government guarantee of market share, the United States insisted that Japan had made a firm commitment to see that the goal was attained. In 1987, the U.S. government imposed economic sanctions against Japan, having determined that dumping had not ceased and that access to the Japanese market continued to be restricted. The dumping portion of the sanctions was soon lifted, but the market access portion, amounting to $165 million, was suspended only in 1991, when the Bush administration revised and extended the agreement.

Supporters of the semiconductor agreement argued that trying to get Japan to change its rules and procedures would be time consuming and would produce little of benefit for American exporters. A new "revisionist" theory now became prominent in the debate over trade relations with Japan. Advocates of this theory argued that Japan should be free to organize its economy in any way it preferred. What mattered to the United States were the results, not how Japan achieved them. Simply sticking to the mantra of free trade would get the United States nowhere in terms of access to the Japanese market. The only sensible strategy for dealing with a mercantilist country like Japan, which stacked the deck against foreign competitors in its domestic market through formal and informal means, was to set targets industry by industry, identify measurable indicators of progress, and demand results. Given its ideological commitment to free trade, the Reagan administration did not accept this revisionist theory. But in its efforts to manage the domestic political problems generated by trade tensions with Japan, it ended up forging a semiconductor agreement that became the darling of the revisionist community and produced a new model invoked by those who advocated managed trade deals with Japan. The Clinton administration implemented this new strategy, replacing a process-oriented strategy with one that focused on quantitative indicators and results.

From MOSS to the Structural Impediments Initiative (SII)

The trade policy of the Bush administration toward Japan also reflected the tensions between the White House and the Congress, between the trade-specialized agencies and the macroeconomic-oriented Treasury Department and Council of Economic Advisers, and between the State Department, concerned to keep political relations on an even keel, and the administration's trade hawks. The public debate over trade relations with Japan during the Bush administration soon became polarized. On one side were those who adopted the "revisionist" position that the organization of the Japanese political economy was so fundamentally different that special results-oriented measures were imperative. On the other were those, often referred to as members of a "Chrysanthemum Club," who argued variously that bilateral trade imbalances were unimportant or that the relevant issue was not Japanese barriers to imports but a lack of competitiveness or effort by U.S. companies, or that trade relations should not be permitted to threaten the all-important U.S.-Japan political and security relationship.

Japanese trade relations posed a difficult domestic political issue for the Bush administration, and it responded by trying to accommodate the conflicting pressures. It came to repeat the familiar pattern: tough rhetoric toward Japan, combined with a concerted attempt to derail strongly protectionist measures in Congress by emphasizing multilateral trade negotiations to reduce barriers to global trade, and with the pursuit of bilateral sector-specific agreements.

The Uruguay Round—multilateral negotiations intended to reduce barriers to market access—was at the top of the Bush administration's trade priorities, its goal being to conclude an agreement by December 1990. The Japanese government joined European countries in opposing U.S. proposals for agricultural liberalization, since farmers formed the core constituency for the ruling Liberal Democratic Party (LDP). Where Japan "chose to be vocal on specific issues," as Merit Janow, the deputy assistant U.S. trade representative during the Bush years, put it, "it took positions that were either opposed to outcomes sought by the United States or less ambitious than those hoped for by the United States."[18] The negotiating parties eventually compromised, and the Uruguay Round concluded successfully in 1994, when Bush and the LDP were no longer in power.

The Japanese government's performance in the Uruguay Round reinforced its image as determinedly protectionist. Japan was not primarily responsible for the slow progress of the talks, and once the Americans and the Europeans had cut a deal, Japan quickly got on board with the concessions needed to conclude an agreement, but its actions did little to weaken the anti-Japanese sentiment on Capitol Hill.

In its bilateral dealings with Japan on trade, the Bush administration introduced a new approach, the structural impediments initiative (SII), which signaled how far U.S. trade policy had evolved since the Nixon administration's textile wrangle with Japan. The administration sought to get Japan to implement reforms across a wide range of areas believed by the United States to pose structural barriers to expanded foreign penetration of the Japanese market. These areas included macroeconomic policies, the organization of the distribution system, bidding practices for public works projects, relations among firms in keiretsu groups, and other issues.

SII was based on an optimistic assumption, quite contrary to the views of the "revisionist" school, that changes in Japanese practices and institutions could "level the playing field" of trade relations. It was also rooted in the belief that simply negotiating sector-specific agreements, as Reagan's MOSS talks sought to do, would only wear the American negotiators out and could never get to the nub of the problem. To truly deal with the problem meant attacking the entire array of Japanese economic practices, which combined to produce trade policies the world economy could not sustain and the American political system would not tolerate. The U.S. Trade Representative set out on this path with a limited staff but with unlimited energy and enthusiasm. At one point in the SII process, the Japanese media counted a total of 240 separate American demands for change in Japan.[19]

Although SII's success in achieving its stated goals was mixed,[20] it did have a positive, longer-term impact that was generally underestimated at the time. As Lynn Williams, the chief U.S. negotiator in the SII talks, put it, "The only way we were going to succeed was if we could appeal to the public interest."[21] A key assumption of SII strategy was that the United States had to bypass the Japanese government and appeal directly to the Japanese people if it hoped to create a domestic constituency that would press for this kind of change. The coverage SII received in the Japanese media educated the Japanese public about the outrageous pricing practices that made some Japanese goods cheaper in New York than in Tokyo, provided graphic examples of how much more expensive it was to live in Tokyo than in other major metropolitan cities and how inferior its living conditions were in terms of public infrastructure and housing, and revealed patterns of oligopolistic practices and government-business collusion that not only were disadvantageous to foreigners but also penalized the Japanese people themselves. SII had a greater impact in triggering a vigorous debate in the 1990s about the need for structural reform in the Japanese economy than is usually recognized.

If one of its purposes was to significantly reduce congressional and domestic political demands for tougher action against Japan, however, SII was a failure. Facing domestic pressure while pursuing SII, President Bush also pressed hard for agreements with Japan that would show the business community and Congress he could get "results." (This was the impetus for his ill-fated January 1992 trip to Tokyo with a score of American businessmen, where he became ill in Prime Minister Miyazawa Kiichi's lap.) The Bush administration enjoyed considerable success in opening the Japanese market to more U.S. exports: According to some estimates, exports in the sectors covered by the thirteen bilateral sectoral agreements signed by the United States and Japan increased about twice as fast as exports to Japan overall.[22] But despite its rhetorical emphasis on "results," the Bush administration remained committed to a process-oriented approach. Its achievements did not stem revisionist demands for a results-oriented, managed-market approach to Japan.

Even former secretaries of state Henry Kissinger and Cyrus Vance, neither of whom had exercised any leadership over, or showed any interest in, international economic relations when they were in government, hopped onto the revisionist bandwagon. In a 1988 *Foreign Affairs* article, they declared that the United States and Japan should seek to "establish an overall trade balance the United States would find tolerable; within that balance, Japan would have the choice of either reducing its exports or increasing its imports, thus removing the need for sector-by-sector industrial negotiations." They did not spell out what the United States should do if Japan did not agree with this scheme, nor did they explain why, in terms of its impact on the U.S. economy, they considered a reduction in Japanese exports to the United States equivalent to an increase in U.S. exports to Japan.

In February 1989, the Advisory Committee on Trade Policy and Negotiations (ACTPN), the U.S. trade representative's most senior private sector advisory committee, issued a report calling on the government to adopt a "results-oriented trade strategy." The advisory committee recommended that the United States identify those sectors where "an increase in US exports could be expected if Japan were to act like other industrial countries with similar economic attributes," and "insist on appropriate sectoral import levels that properly reflect the international competitiveness of US" and other foreign suppliers. This report was issued near the end of the Bush presidency, and Bush did not act on it, but his successor, Bill Clinton, did, leading to the most contentious, least productive period in postwar U.S.-Japan trade relations.

The Semiconductor Agreement, originally hammered out in 1986, embodied what was to become the guiding spirit of the Clinton approach. In 1991 the Bush administration had negotiated an extension of that agreement in which the Japanese government explicitly recognized the U.S. industry's "expectation" that foreign semiconductors would secure more than 20 percent of the Japanese market by the end of 1992. The Japanese added that it "considers that this can be realized," which was all but a government promise.

According to the 1991 accord, the 20 percent figure was not a floor or a ceiling or a guaranteed market share, and other "quantitative and qualitative factors" would be taken into account in measuring progress under the agreement. Given the decided lack of enthusiasm for this extension later expressed by Carla Hills, the U.S. trade representative responsible for negotiating it,[23] it seems clear that it was not the Bush administration's idea of a desirable trade policy but an assessment of what was politically unavoidable or expedient. It was left to Bill Clinton and to his trade representative, Mickey Kantor, to draw inspiration from this semiconductor agreement and design a managed trade strategy toward Japan.

The Pluses and Minuses of Trade Frictions

In looking back on this period, it is important to recognize that trade problems with Japan had significant salutary effects for the United States. Japanese economic success truly frightened American business leaders and forced them to focus more directly on issues of productivity and competitiveness. American managers became avid students of "just-in-time" inventory systems and other Japanese management techniques. Corporate boards of directors also became more concerned about what management was doing to improve quality standards to better compete with high-quality Japanese goods. Competition from Japanese automobile companies eventually forced the Big Three of U.S. auto makers to take decisive steps toward improving the quality of the cars they produced. Little did anyone at the time anticipate the ironic outcome: that Japanese competition would in fact strengthen American industry and that continued restrictions on foreign competition in Japan's own markets would weaken some of Japan's manufacturing sectors and inhibit its financial institutions in adapting to the globalization of financial markets.

Japan's success, and the opportunities SII gave the Japanese to tell the United States what was wrong with its economy, also had a positive impact. Each government was able to articulate its concerns about structural issues in the other country. The Japanese harped on the importance of reducing the U.S. budget deficit if the United States hoped to enjoy economic growth and decrease its trade deficit. These lectures on how the United States should run its economy—often delivered with the same kind of hubris Americans now display when they give the Japanese advice on how to rebuild their economy—were not responsible for, but surely contributed to, the determined American effort to bring the U.S. budget deficit under control.

The complicated domestic politics engendered by the Japan trade problem produced another positive effect. Each administration wanted to avoid protectionism, and yet each felt the heat of congressional pressure to do something about Japan. By the mid-1980s the dominant response was to emphasize market access in Japan, channeling protectionist pressures so that they became a wedge, or a crowbar, in Trade Representative Hills's apt phrase, in breaking down barriers to access.

Through MOSS and SII, the United States could plausibly claim to be pressing for the expansion of a rules-based liberal trading regime while insisting to those sectors in the U.S. economy most intensely concerned about Japanese competition that it had their interests at heart. Through SII, moreover, the United States was able to strengthen domestic constituencies in Japan in support of market liberalization measures. In the end, despite popular assumptions about Japan's inability to reject *gaiatsu* (that is, foreign—namely, U.S.—pressure) if exercised intensely and long enough, SII demonstrated quite persuasively that the way to elicit meaningful change in Japanese commercial and economic policies was to ally with domestic constituencies powerful enough to demand it.[24]

The negative side of two decades of trade wars hardly needs elaboration. U.S.-Japan trade disputes exacted a heavy price in terms of American attitudes toward Japan, especially among the policy elite. By the time the Clinton administration took office, the revisionist view of Japan as an unfair trader and a threat to the United States had become the dominant view in Washington, and it was to have a substantial impact on the thinking of top officials in the new government. Persistent trade tensions with Japan, and the resort to bilateral ad hoc agreements and to unilateral actions, also weakened support in the United States for a multilateral, rules-based trade regime. In terms of its impact on the overall tenor of the U.S.-Japan relationship, the trade conflict produced no winners. Although there is little to be gained by constructing counterfactual arguments about "what might have been" if trade disputes had been handled differently, many opportunities for cooperative action on a range of issues of common interest were undoubtedly lost because of the animosity generated by the failure of the two governments to manage trade relations more effectively.

Concluding Thoughts

Implicit in the preceding analysis is a troubling question: If one U.S. administration after another ignored Japan in formulating its China policy and battled with Japan over trade, why is the U.S.-Japan relationship as positive as it is? Indeed, political and security relations have grown closer, even with the loss of the "glue" of cold war confrontation with the Soviet Union. Economic interdependence has increased dramatically. Yet for years Japanese and American Japan specialists have been bemoaning the sorry state of U.S.-Japan relations and complaining that the United States does not give enough attention to Japan. Is it simply this, or has the pattern of U.S. diplomacy recounted here imposed real costs?

The reason the China issue does not appear to have done much damage to anything besides Japan's amour propre is not difficult to assess. Nixon's "China shock" was embarrassing to the Japanese government, which was left scampering to catch the China bus; Japan was also annoyed that Nixon and Kissinger played up the Japanese militarist threat with the Chinese. But precisely because there was not a hint in U.S. strategy of a U.S.-China-Japan triangle, whether under Nixon or the other presidents considered here (Clinton is another matter), the China initiative did not generate fear in Japan of U.S. abandonment. Whatever rationale they presented to the Chinese, Nixon and Kissinger, and then Carter and Brzezinski, emphasized the importance of the U.S.-Japan security treaty, thus assuring Japan that this key prop in its postwar security policy would remain in place, thus providing Prime Minister Tanaka a firm basis for moving forward with Japan's normalization of relations with China.

The nervousness Clinton's China policy inspired in Tokyo throws this point into sharp relief. Without the power dynamics of the cold war to hold the U.S.-Japanese alliance together, the possibility not so much that the United States would abandon Japan but that it would drift away seems far more real. In addition, given China's growing economic importance and the U.S. penchant for exaggerating that importance, the possibility that the United States might bypass Japan to forge a close relationship with China is taken far more seriously than in the pre-Clinton years. Thus, actions that in earlier years might have been merely irritating, such as not stopping off in Japan on the way into or out of China, now raise questions about U.S. intentions. And if the president of the United States stresses the importance of his country's "strategic partnership" with China when the only meaningful strategic U.S. partnership in East Asia is with Japan, or uses a joint press conference with the president of China to reflect on their common "problem"—Japan's inadequate economic performance—it is hardly surprising that Japan would speculate about a shift in the U.S. strategy in East Asia.

The manner in which administrations from Nixon to Bush pursued their China policy—by rejecting close consultation with Japan—has exacted a cost, setting a pattern of diplomatic behavior the Clinton administration all too readily adopted. If the United States had developed a habit of consultation instead of unilateralism, the two countries might have been better prepared to avoid friction as they pursued their post–cold war policies toward China. The failure of one U.S. administration after another has made the task of coordination much harder now, when the need is all the greater.

What about the cost of trade friction? Trade and economic disputes did not lead to unrestrained protectionism in the United States or spill over into the security dimension of the U.S.-Japan relationship, and they probably did prod Japan to move farther along in the direction of market liberalization. American and Japanese political leaders were in basic agreement that trade conflicts should not be allowed to cause a serious rupture in the relationship. To achieve this end, they engaged in a kind of "game" whose goal was to contain congressional pressure for protectionist measures. In the course of developing the game's rules, and as part of the more general phenomenon of economic globalization, their focus shifted from restricting Japanese access to the U.S. market in the 1970s to expanding U.S. access to the Japanese market in the 1980s, a shift that still characterizes U.S. trade policy toward Japan today.

But trade disputes exacted a heavy price in eroded trust and goodwill on both sides of the Pacific. It is not difficult to imagine that a significant downturn in the U.S. economy would prompt American invective against Japan all too similar to that of the 1980s. There is no guarantee that a heating up of trade tensions would not have an adverse affect on political and security relations now that the cold war is over. Furthermore, in spite of its economic problems, Japan is stronger economically and more willing to undertake its own diplomatic initiatives, especially with respect to East Asia, than in the past.

Every president and his chief policy advisers, from Nixon to Clinton, seem to have been convinced that the most effective way of dealing with Japan was to use "pressure." Those who argued for a different approach, especially the Japan hands in the State Department, were mostly sidelined from key policy-making positions. Except for Reagan's adviser Gaston Sigur, for the past thirty years Japan specialists have also been kept out of key positions in the president's National Security Council and the upper reaches of the State Department, and there is no sign that this pattern is about to change.

It is impossible to measure the cost of opportunities lost as a result of the failure of Japan and the United States to develop a more robust pattern of consultation on regional issues, nor is it possible to anticipate how a decline in mutual trust might affect the relationship in the future. What is clear, however, is that the uncertainties of international relations in East Asia place a higher premium on close U.S.-Japanese consultation than ever before. Unfortunately, the diplomatic practices of the administrations in power and the policies and practices of the Japanese government did not foster such consultation. The question now is whether the next U.S. president will be able to overcome this legacy and develop new strategies for sustaining the alliance and infusing it with new purpose.

CHAPTER SEVEN

Japanese Relations with the United States

Nakanishi Hiroshi

Postwar Japanese relations with the United States underwent a clear break between 1969 and 1972. Prior to 1969, the U.S.-Japan relationship was based on a simple framework, that of the former victor and the formerly vanquished, the protector and the protected. The international framework for the bilateral relationship was also clear-cut: in the politico-strategic sphere of high politics, it was the East-West rivalry, and in the politico-economic sphere of low politics, it was the Bretton Woods free trade regime dominated by American economic hegemony.

During the 1969–72 transition, the Okinawa reversion and the two "Nixon shocks" took place, and the bilateral relationship between Japan and the United States changed significantly. Japan had become a major actor in the global economy, which the United States could no longer manage singlehandedly. International pressure on Japan—primarily but not solely from the United States—for a more active contribution to the costs of waging the cold war grew stronger, especially during the period of increased tension following the Soviet invasion of Afghanistan in 1979. At the same time, the gap between the size of the Japanese economy and that of the U.S. economy rapidly narrowed, and in the late 1980s Japan became the world's largest creditor, with a technological edge in manufacturing. Japan and the United States remained allies, but they had become economic rivals.

This essay describes Japanese relations with the United States during the two decades from 1972 to 1992. During these years, their common interest in the global system enabled them to maintain a relatively cooperative bilateral relationship. They shared the Western camp's interest in resisting Soviet expansionism, and both were intent on maintaining a liberal global capitalist free trade regime and inducing developing countries to join. At the time, the trilateral relationship between Japan, the United States, and China had little impact on the U.S.-Japan bilateral relationship.

From the late 1980s, however, the international system showed signs of change, and these changes became more apparent in the 1990s, creating a new context for the bilateral relationship. The drastic transformation in the relationship between state and society spearheaded by the Reagan-Thatcher reforms had international implications for rulemaking in the increasingly global economy. Greater American pressure to open the Japanese market exemplified this new stage of "globalization," in which the traditional boundary between international and domestic affairs was weakened.

The gradual ending of the cold war in the late 1980s required that the U.S.-Japan relationship adapt to a different strategic setting. In the new world order symbolized by George Bush's leadership in assembling the major powers of the world in the fight against the "rogue" state of Iraq, Japan was supposed to play a completely new role. When the intractability of regional and local conflicts became more apparent and the "new world order" proved to be a mirage, regional frameworks gained renewed importance, and the U.S.-Japan-China relationship began to develop as a pillar in the Asia-Pacific region. The Tiananmen incident of 1989 may have been a harbinger of this new trilateral relationship. The 1989–92 period seemed to be a transition to a new era.

Healing the "Shocks"

The twin surprises delivered by the Nixon administration in July and August 1971, first suddenly announcing Nixon's planned trip to Beijing in February 1972 and then unilaterally taking economic measures that included raising import levies and halting the exchange of gold for dollars, were severe blows to Japan's political leaders, especially Prime Minister Sato Eisaku and his supporters. These actions, dubbed the *Nikuson Shokku* ("Nixon shocks"), left the Japanese angry about being treated so casually. But for several reasons these moves did not result in a fundamental reorientation of Japanese policy toward the United States. Although Sato was discredited, the Liberal Democratic Party (LDP), a coalition party consisting of several factions, was flexible enough to provide alternative leadership. Tanaka Kakuei, a self-made politician of nonelite origins, became prime minister in a virtual revolt against Sato and his protégé, Fukuda Takeo, and grasped the opportune momentum for refashioning Japanese diplomacy. The formal dialogue between the United States and China had long been viewed as being in Japan's interest. It not only allowed Japan to have closer economic relations with China but formalized their political relationship, thereby avoiding such headaches as the Nagasaki flag incident of 1958, when China responded to the desecration of the Chinese flag in Nagasaki by almost eliminating trade with Japan and insisting that it would not allow the continuation of economic relations without improved political relations. Japan viewed Nixon's drastic economic policy initiative in a more negative light, but a readjustment in its economic relationship with the United States had been thought necessary even before August 1971. After all, Japan had become one of the biggest beneficiaries of the free trade system, and its bilateral trade balance with the United States was growing in Japan's favor, so the advantage of continuing cooperation was all too obvious.

Tanaka won the race against Fukuda to become the next LDP leader in July 1972 by usurping the Sato faction and gaining support from the Ohira, Nakasone, and Miki factions. A primary reason these three faction heads supported Tanaka was his readiness to normalize relations with China at an early stage. Fukuda, successor of the faction of Kishi Shinsuke (ex–prime minister and elder brother of Sato), had strong ties with Taiwan and was therefore handicapped in meeting the Chinese demand that political and diplomatic ties with the island be cut off. Just after becoming prime minister, Tanaka quickly met with Nixon in Honolulu and joined in a joint communiqué stating that the U.S.-Japan security relationship would be maintained and that Japan would normalize its diplomatic relationship with China. (The meeting later played a notable role in the alleged Lockheed scandal, in which Tanaka was said to have accepted bribes, promising to wield his influence on Japanese airline companies to purchase planes from Lockheed.) Tanaka visited Beijing the following month and succeeded in normalizing relations with China, although not without some difficulty.

The change in the relationship between China and the United States, and between China and Japan, therefore, did not have a negative impact on the U.S.-Japan relationship. However, there was very little coordination between Japan and the United States about the implications of their changed relations with China. For Richard Nixon and Henry Kissinger, détente with China constituted one part of a global strategic readjustment among three powers: the United States, the Soviet Union, and China. Secondarily, the logic of a regional power balance between Japan and China was used to persuade China of the merits of the U.S.-Japan security relationship as a hedge against a remilitarized Japan. For its part, Japan viewed U.S. diplomatic normalization with China as a necessary step in working out its own relations with China, which had been left unresolved since 1945. In addition, Japan regarded China as both a major market and a source of raw materials. The China question also had a domestic dimension. Earlier, those opposed to the Japanese security tie with the United States had attacked the government, claiming that the United States had discriminated against Japan by opposing its diplomatic opening to China while allowing European countries such as Great Britain and France to have normal diplomatic relations with China. In the eyes of the Japanese public, therefore, the normalization of U.S. relations with China, along with the ending of the Vietnam War, significantly improved the U.S. image.

However, in the 1970s, the need for economic coordination had far more significance than the China question in improving the U.S.-Japan relationship. At the end of 1971, the Smithsonian agreement on a new exchange rate was reached among the major powers, but by early 1973 it had run into difficulties. The United States recognized the prime importance of achieving an agreement with Japan in persuading European powers to allow an exchange rate readjustment. The United States had decided to devalue the dollar by 10 percent against gold, but unless the yen could also be revalued by 10 percent or more, reaching an agreement with the European countries on revaluation seemed unlikely. In February 1973, U.S. Treasury officials, led by Paul Volcker, flew to Japan to argue their case. The Japanese side, headed by Minister of Finance Aichi Kiichi, understood the need for an exchange rate readjustment but was not inclined to make a clear commitment to another revaluation, not least because February, when the budget was debated in the Diet, was a sensitive time in Japanese politics. A formal agreement to readjust the dollar-yen rate would require a revision in the budgetary plan, which was the last thing Ministry of Finance officials would be willing to entertain.

When American and Japanese officials met, therefore, they reached a somewhat ambiguous agreement. Japan did not commit to any specific exchange rate but agreed to float the yen, while the United States understood that the yen would be revalued. The Americans then flew to Europe to negotiate with officials there. Japanese officials also flew to Europe, aiming for a united front against the United States. On their arrival, however, Japanese officials found that Japan was totally isolated. Helmut Schmidt, the German minister of finance, coolly told them that if Japan would not agree to reevaluation, Japan and the United States would enter into economic warfare.[1]

In the event, the exchange agreement came to naught because of the severe inflationary pressure caused by the oil shock of late 1973. But the important legacy of this Nixon shock and its aftermath was the new awareness, among the advanced economies, of the need to coordinate their economic policies. The United States realized that to bring about cooperation among the Western economies it was important to reach an agreement with Japan, the second-largest economy in the West and, with West Germany, the major exporting country. Japan realized that the mere appearance of shared frustration with the United States did not constitute diplomatic cooperation with the Europeans and that in order to avoid isolation, its first priority must continue to be cooperation with the United States.

Japan's experience in coping with the oil crisis in 1973 reaffirmed this realization. When the Arab countries initiated their "oil strategy" later that year, Japanese society was hit by severe panic, not so much because of objective statistics—more than 70 percent of Japan's energy was provided by oil; Japan was the world's largest importer of crude oil and was dependent for almost all its oil on imports, mostly from the Middle East—as because of the psychological shock of realizing that the Arabs were not treating Japan as a "friendly country." In response, Japan sought desperately to improve relations with the oil-producing countries. The Tanaka cabinet sent Miki Takeo on a special mission to the Middle East to discover how Japan could contribute to the economic development of the Arab nations. The United States, in contrast, took the stance that the oil-consuming countries should not succumb to the threats of the Arab oil producers. Kissinger visited Japan in mid-November, at the height of the crisis, and demanded that Japan follow the American lead and resist Arab pressure. There was some tension within the Tanaka cabinet between concern for the U.S. relationship and interest in sustaining oil imports. In the end, Kissinger left Japan without obtaining any concrete commitment.

Because of Japan's vigorous efforts to increase its ties with Arab oil-producing countries and to make pro-Arab statements, the Arab countries placed Japan in their "friendly countries" category. After its initial panic over oil supplies had subsided, Japan tried to cooperate with the Western countries on oil issues without sacrificing its relationship with oil-producing countries. At the same time, the United States launched its mediating diplomacy in the Middle East. In cooperation with Japan, it established the International Energy Agency in late 1974, under the Organization for Economic Cooperation and Development (OECD) framework, as a forum for dialogue between oil producers and consumers. In addition, Japan also supported U.S. Middle Eastern diplomacy by agreeing to provide economic assistance to Egypt in 1975.

Partners in Global Economic Management

The political and economic turmoil of the early 1970s caused some turbulence in the U.S.-Japan relationship, but by the mid-1970s each country had clearly realized the critical importance of the other in its foreign relations. The reasons for this perception were multilayered, and the relative importance attached to each of these layers has varied over time. From the Japanese perspective, global economic cooperation to uphold the free trade regime under American hegemony was of the most fundamental importance, while global politico-strategic cooperation against the Soviet threat did not loom large until the Nakasone cabinet (1983–87). From the U.S. perspective, Japan had emerged as a major global economic power that had to be included in dealing with global economic issues and as a major ally on regional security issues. Regional issues such as policies toward China or the Association of Southeast Asian Nations (ASEAN) did not hinder the bilateral relationship, nor did they become topics of critical importance that required close bilateral coordination.

U.S. recognition of the importance of Japan in the global economy was reflected in the launching of the economic summits that began at Rambouillet, France, in 1975. The 1975 summit was the first regular meeting in which top Japanese political leaders joined with top Western leaders in a multilateral setting. Even though Kissinger sarcastically described Prime Minister Miki Takeo as being asleep at Rambouillet, the Japanese came to refer to this annual meeting as *Samitto* ("the Summit"). It symbolized the complementarities of the close bilateral relationship as well as the multilateral framework.[2]

The respective roles prime ministers Fukuda Takeo and Ohira Masayoshi played at the summit meetings in which they participated illustrates the importance Japanese leaders attached to these diplomatic occasions. Fukuda first participated in the London summit in May 1977, impressing other members with his knowledge of economic issues and his comments on his personal memory of the Great Depression era and the dangers of international protectionism. Fukuda actively supported the "three-locomotive theory" (the argument that, like locomotives, the U.S., Japan, and West Germany should lead global economic growth) and pledged to undertake expansionary fiscal measures to achieve high growth. At the Bonn summit in 1978, Fukuda again pledged 7 percent GNP growth and followed through with expansionary policies.

Ohira succeeded Fukuda in December 1978, after a fierce intraparty battle. In addition to being a personal and factional rival of Fukuda, Ohira differed in his view of the soundness of the fiscal expansionist policy Fukuda had pursued. Because of his concern about continuing budget deficits, he quickly scrapped Fukuda's pledge to achieve 7 percent economic growth, which prompted an angry response from the Carter administration. In late April 1978, Ohira hurriedly flew to Washington, and the personal relationship between the two leaders was repaired, not least because of the fact that Ohira was a pious Christian of great personal character. Another factor was the shift of focus in international economic management issues. The "second oil shock," the sudden oil price hike caused by the Iranian revolution in early 1979, meant that the supply of oil replaced growth as the basic economic issue at the next summit.

Ohira became the first Japanese prime minister to host a summit, which was held in Tokyo in mid-1979. The main theme of the Tokyo summit was how to counter Organization of Petroleum Exporting Countries (OPEC) moves. It was proposed that each member country would accept oil import quotas in order to limit total global oil demand. But Ohira, the summit chair, was excluded when concrete import quotas were first discussed informally among representatives from the United States, France, West Germany, and Great Britain. Later, when they presented their agreed on plan to the formal session, Ohira discovered that the oil import quota assigned to Japan was far lower than the amount Japanese officials estimated to be the minimum level needed to sustain the Japanese economy. Ohira faced a serious dilemma: whether to oppose the arrangement and destroy the summit agreement or agree to an import quota that would be severely criticized at home. In the end, the United States came to Ohira's aid by allowing a modest increase in the Japanese import quota.

These early summit experiences demonstrate the growing cooperative relationship between Japan and the United States in global economic management. To be sure, there were still occasions of conflict between the two. A case in point was the U.S. Iranian embassy hostage crisis. During the standoff, the United States retaliated against Iran by imposing an oil import boycott. Iran, however, was one of Japan's major sources of oil, and Japan had just begun to make connections with the Iranian Revolutionary Government to proceed on a large-scale oil refinery project. Frustrated by the hostage crisis, Secretary of State Cyrus Vance criticized Japan's continued purchasing of Iranian oil as "insensitive." The Ohira cabinet was again in a serious dilemma, but this time Iran came to the rescue. By asking for a price increase, it provided Japan with an excuse for discontinuing the purchasing agreement without destroying the Japan-Iranian relationship. But Japan's approach to Iran differed from that of the United States; it preferred a "softer" stance to avoid rupturing its relations with a major oil producer.

In general, Japan took what American international relations specialists call a "liberalist" perspective, believing in the ability of nations to harmonize their international relations policies on the basis of mutual interests, especially economic interests. In contrast, the United States took a relatively more "realist" view, holding that sanctions should have a larger role, including threatening retaliation against noncooperation. Needless to say, the Japanese stance reflected Japan's economic self-interest, following the country's basic postwar foreign policy of keeping a low profile on contentious issues and maintaining good political relationships where its economic goals, which remained its highest priority, were concerned. Anchored by its liberalist worldview and its economic self-interest, Japan's foreign policy tended to aim at widening economic relations in Asia and the Middle East or even the Soviet Union, but within the constraint that its actions not harm its relationship with the United States.

Détente and the Reformulation of Japanese Defense Policy

The chief concern surrounding the reversion of Okinawa to Japanese control, which went into effect in 1972, was the political significance of stabilizing the U.S.-Japan security relationship beyond 1970. At that time, the security treaty concluded in 1960 entered the period during which it could be terminated with one year's advance notice by either side. Prime Minister Sato had made Okinawan reversion the key issue of his premiership, and the United States believed that the importance of Japanese political support for the security relationship outweighed the military convenience of preserving direct political control over Okinawa. The Okinawa reversion also reflected another dimension: the U.S. desire that Japan play a larger security role. In this sense, the reversion was part of the general reassessment of American strategy articulated in the Nixon Doctrine of 1969, which demanded that Asian allies bear primary defense responsibility against local insurgencies and conventional threats, while the United States would continue to provide a "nuclear umbrella" against the nuclear threat.

The Nixon Doctrine following the Vietnam War aimed to limit U.S. involvement in land wars in Asia. The implications for Japan were twofold: (1) directly, the United States called for Japan to take primary responsibility for its own defense by more clearly defining the role its defense capability would play, and (2) indirectly, the United States desired that Japan, which had emerged as a major global economic power, take a more active stance in contributing to regional security, including sharing the defense burdens of the United States. In both cases, implementing measures providing for a greater Japanese contribution was no easy matter.

Sato's choice of Nakasone Yasuhiro in 1970 as chief of the Defense Agency was intended to signal Japan's willingness to tackle defense issues more seriously. Nakasone, long viewed as a nationalist, and formerly a critic of the Allied occupation, probably went beyond what Sato wanted him to do: he demanded a large-scale defense budget increase for the Fourth Defense Program (*Yojibo*); he advocated a change in the Basic Policy of National Defense stipulated in 1957; and he pursued the reversion or joint use of American bases, sought to increase endogenous military production, and omitted the three nonnuclear principles (no production, creation, or possession of nuclear weapons on Japanese soil) from his White Paper on Defense.

In Prime Minister Sato's view, Nakasone's activism was excessive. Sato tried to control him and replaced him at the next cabinet reshuffle.

The Fourth Defense Program, which contained large budget increases, was adopted in 1972; because of the high rate of inflation, however, it was discarded before it was implemented. Nevertheless, efforts to define the role of Japan's self-defense capability were continued under the Miki cabinet by the defense chief Sakata Michita. In 1976, the Defense Program Outline was agreed to, which spelled out Japan's role in defending against aggression more clearly than ever before. The basic doctrine was that the Japanese Self-Defense Forces (SDF) would meet "limited and small-scale aggression" with their own power, while in case of aggression on a larger scale the SDF would resist aggression until American assistance arrived. As political compensation to those who opposed an enlarged military role, the cabinet agreed to a budget ceiling limiting the Japanese defense budget to within 1 percent of the country's GNP.

In the meantime, what role Japan should take in the regional and global politico-strategic sphere remained a nebulous question. Nakasone's show of activism as chief of the Defense Agency caused concern among the countries in the Asia-Pacific region, and even some in the United States voiced uneasiness. Moreover, the change in the relationships between Japan and China and between the United States and China in 1971–72 greatly changed the politico-strategic landscape. In effect, Japan and China reached a kind of détente in the Asia-Pacific region. However, the Nixon Doctrine, as well as the withdrawal of American forces from the Vietnam War, also prompted some anxiety about U.S. withdrawal from the area. The concern in the region over an increased security role for Japan, combined with the fear that the United States might withdraw, resulted in Japan's continued low-profile stance on politico-strategic matters but a clear affirmation of its desire to see the American presence maintained. While Japan sought to strengthen détente in East Asia by improving its relations with both China and the Soviet Union, it began to formalize a clearer, though still limited, role in its U.S. military alliance through the new Guidelines on U.S.-Japan Defense Cooperation agreed to late in 1978.

As to the Japanese-Chinese relationship, after the normalization of bilateral relations was achieved in 1972, negotiations over the Treaty of Peace and Friendship became the major focus. Japan was generally willing to sign the treaty: it was favored by the public as well as by the business sector, which viewed Chinese energy resources and markets with great enthusiasm. The major obstacle was the so-called "antihegemony" clause, whose inclusion China regarded as crucial. The clause was clearly intended as an anti-Soviet statement, and the U.S.S.R warned Japan not to sign a treaty that included such wording. In Japan the clause was viewed as not only detrimental to improving relations with the Soviet Union but dishonorable, since it would allow China to constrain Japanese foreign policy options.

The Japanese attempt to improve relations with the Soviet Union produced limited results. Tanaka began to move toward "détente" with the Soviet Union with his visit to Moscow in 1973. In the context of the first oil shock, he aimed to strengthen mutual interest in investment in resource exploitation projects and to lay the basis for possible resource development and importation. He also hoped potential Japanese funding for Soviet resource development might lead to concessions from the U.S.S.R. on the Northern Territories issue. The Soviet Union responded somewhat ambiguously, which heightened Japanese hopes for progress on these issues. But the relationship advanced no further. In 1976 a Soviet MIG-25 fighter airplane, whose pilot was seeking asylum, flew to Hokkaido. The Soviet government put firm pressure on Japan to return the plane, but the Japanese government allowed the Americans to inspect the fighter to gather information about Soviet technology. From around this time, the Soviet attitude toward Japan became increasingly inflexible. The U.S.S.R. unilaterally declared, for example, that its fishery zone extended in the Sea of Okhotsk, and it increased its military presence in the Kurile Islands.

Thus, in the late 1970s, in response to these factors, the Japanese government proceeded toward negotiating a treaty with China and freezing its "détente" with the Soviet Union. First, Fukuda, who did not enjoy high opinion poll ratings when he took office as prime minister, was particularly eager to conclude the treaty with China. Second, Soviet intransigence appeared to render meaningless any attempt to engage in reasonable dialogue. Third, the United States, which increasingly leaned away from the Soviet Union and toward China, indicated to Japanese leaders that it favored an early conclusion of the Japan-China treaty. When Fukuda visited the United States in May 1978, Carter conveyed this message to him directly. Later that month, Carter's national security adviser, Zbigniew Brzezinski, visited Beijing and discussed normalization of U.S.-China relations. It was evident that Brzezinski wanted to work with China in taking a tougher stance against the Soviet Union. Chinese leaders confessed their frustration over the Japanese reluctance to sign the China-Japan treaty, so Brzezinski decided to talk with Fukuda when he briefed him on the Beijing visit on his way home to the United States. If there was anything like trilateral cooperation in the U.S.-Sino-Japanese relationship during 1972–92, this was perhaps its peak.

These factors all combined to encourage Japan to agree to the treaty with China, including the antihegemony clause. Japan only agreed, however, on the condition that an additional clause be inserted stating that no clause in the treaty would unfavorably affect either party's relationship with a third country. The treaty was signed in August 1978.

At the same time, Japan tried to step up its strategic dialogue with the United States by way of the Defense Guidelines formalizing the U.S. commitment to Japan's defense, and to secure a stable, long-term U.S. presence in the region. The guidelines, agreed on by the two governments in November 1978, were the first attempt by the United States and Japan to specify the military aspects of their security treaty. They officially confirmed that the United States would provide a nuclear umbrella over Japan against a nuclear threat. They also provided the framework for combined defense planning under the U.S.-Japan security treaty, which was designed to apply in two cases: in the defense of Japan (Article 5) and in the use of Japanese bases for U.S. military operations (Article 6). But as was agreed in the course of their preparation, the guidelines would not override the interpretation of the Japanese constitution stating that Japan would prepare itself for defensive activities only and thus would not contribute directly to military operations beyond its own borders, as specified in Article 6. Later, planning for the defense of Japan progressed relatively smoothly, and Japanese and American military services were able to work closely together. Planning for activities beyond Japan, however, did not achieve much progress because aiding U.S. forces in combat activities other than in Japan's defense was interpreted as unconstitutional.

There may have been additional reasons for Japan's reluctance to aid U.S. forces except in its own defense. The Carter administration's announcement of its plan to withdraw American land troops from Korea shocked the Japanese government and Japanese security analysts. Although Fukuda avoided expressing outright opposition, he conveyed his concern at his first meeting with Carter in March 1977. The joint communiqué issued afterward declared that the United States would withdraw its land forces in South Korea only after consulting South Korea and Japan. In May 1978, Fukuda frankly asked Carter not to withdraw a battalion until the United States had given clear and sufficient military support to South Korea. If U.S. troops left Korea, any show of Japanese willingness to take part in regional military affairs might arouse Asian concerns about Japanese remilitarization, while adding a further excuse to Carter's desire to withdraw American forces. Later, under strong pressure from South Korea and from domestic critics, Carter postponed his withdrawal plan, and Ronald Reagan discarded this attempt completely.

So the "new look" Japanese defense policy was in fact highly constrained. The guidelines advanced strategic thinking within the Japanese defense policy community and opened the way for wider U.S.-Japanese security cooperation. But they also clarified the domestic and international limitations on Japanese defense policies. To the United States and other Western powers who wanted additional countries to bear a fair share of the security burden, Japanese security efforts seemed insufficient. Since the United States was spending more than 5 percent of its GNP on defense and the Western European countries 3–5 percent, Japanese spending, at less than 1 percent, appeared conspicuously inadequate.

Concern about pressure to assume a greater share of the defense burden led to what the Japanese called the "sympathy budget," whereby the Japanese government assumed more of the costs of U.S. troops stationed in Japan. According to the earlier status of forces agreement, the United States was expected to pay the personnel costs of Japanese workers on these U.S. bases as well as miscellaneous charges for services such as electricity and water. But because of the rapid appreciation of the yen in the 1970s, paying these fees became a strain for the U.S. forces in Japan. So, starting in 1978, Kanemaru Shin, the chief of the Defense Agency under the Fukuda cabinet, agreed to pay for these items out of the Japanese budget, calling it a "sympathy budget." This arrangement continues to this day, although after Japan's financial problems in the 1990s, the Japanese government expressed its hope for a reduction in these expenses.

The "sympathy budget" was ¥6.2 billion in 1978 but soon reached several hundreds of billion yen a year. The U.S. government voiced appreciation for this arrangement, and the Japanese considered this their contribution to the security burden of the West, but many Americans viewed the "sympathy budget" as less than a proper fulfillment of the shared defense burden. In order to avoid being criticized as a "free rider," Japan still needed to find other ways to contribute.

"The Most Important Bilateral Relationship in the World"

From the late 1970s into the 1980s, when East-West tensions increased rapidly, Japan chose to make its main contribution to world order through active aid for political and economic ends, not through a military buildup. This focus, representing the Japanese share of the burden of maintaining world order, reflected both the postwar liberalist foreign policy ideology and the realistic calculation that an indirect approach—strengthening economies and free markets—would contribute more to world peace than a direct military buildup. Moreover, after Japan's role in World War II, the countries of Asia did not necessarily welcome Japanese rather than U.S. protection. As secretary of state during the Reagan administration, George Shultz wrote in his memoir, "The United States, with Secretary Weinberger pushing particularly hard, had sought to persuade Japan to increase its defense spending and to take on more of the burden of its self-defense, making more tangible the responsibility announced earlier for a 1,000–mile perimeter of defense out into the Pacific. When I visited in the Philippines, the Filipinos were anxious to know where that 1,000 miles began. If it started on the Japanese-owned island of Okinawa, then the arc would include the Philippines, but if it started in Tokyo, then it wouldn't include the Philippines. One thing was clear: the Filipinos didn't want to be included."[3]

Still, beginning in the late 1970s, as its economic power and trade balances surged ahead, Japan was increasingly castigated by the United States and Europe for not doing enough to contribute to global military efforts to counter the Soviet threat. Partly as a response to this criticism, Japan increased its aid contributions. In 1977 Japan pledged to double its official development assistance (ODA) in five years. During his visit to the United States in May 1978, Fukuda announced Japan's decision to shorten this period to three years because of the rapid appreciation of the yen. The doubling was achieved in 1980, the total amount reaching $3.3 billion. During the 1980s, the Japanese contribution to ODA rose even more rapidly, and Japan began to use ODA as a political tool to complement, if not substitute for, Western efforts against Soviet expansionism, especially in developing countries. This policy line was named a "comprehensive security strategy" by the Ohira cabinet, implying a wider definition of security going beyond military affairs. The Ohira cabinet decided to provide what it designated as "strategic aid" to Thailand, Pakistan, and Turkey. The active aid policy was viewed as a key contribution to comprehensive security strategy.

The major focus of this comprehensive security strategy was China. An economic approach to China formed one of the pillars of the Pacific rim strategy advocated by the Ohira cabinet in 1979–80. Ohira also instituted the official aid policy to China, offering ¥50 billion in yen loans and stating three principles for this aid, which took the interests of other countries into account: (1) there would be no military cooperation, (2) the loans would have no negative effect on Japanese aid to ASEAN, and (3) there was no intention to hinder American and European interests that sought to enter the Chinese economy. In the course of the 1980s, the amount of yen loans to China skyrocketed: in 1984 Nakasone offered ¥470 billion, and in 1988 Takeshita Noboru offered ¥810 billion over six years. The United States tended to view China in terms of the global geopolitical confrontation against the U.S.S.R., while Japan tended to view China in regional and economic terms. Japan therefore focused more on stimulating Chinese growth, encouraging Chinese policies of reform and opening, and helping to extend China's Asia-Pacific economic network.

Prime Minister Nakasone, who came to power in November 1982, built on the complementary relationship between Japan and the United States by adding a more strategic dimension. His active support for America's security strategy and his willingness to take political risks made him a valuable political partner of President Reagan. The two formed the so-called Ron-Yasu relationship. When Prime Minister Suzuki Zenko, Nakasone's predecessor, used the word "alliance" in the joint communiqué that followed his meeting with Reagan in May 1981, it caused a sensation in the Japanese media and resulted in the resignation of Foreign Minister Itoh Masayoshi. But Nakasone bravely embraced the term. He also made an exemption to Japan's virtual ban on exporting military-related technology, responding positively to the U.S. request that Japan pass its new military technology on to the United States. Nakasone admitted F-16 squadrons at the Misawa base and approved Japan's participation in the technological research for the Strategic Defense Initiative (SDI). Active not only in strengthening defense and alliance, he also supported Reagan's "zero option" for complete elimination of intermediate-range nuclear forces at the Williamsburg summit in May 1983. Nakasone's performance at Williamsburg has been viewed as the most effective of any Japanese prime minister at a summit meeting. He also repealed the 1 percent ceiling on the defense budget that had been set by the Miki cabinet; in fact, the actual percentage stayed at around 1 percent of the GDP because the Japanese GDP grew speedily in the 1980s.

Nakasone also searched for an expanded political role in the region for Japan. He chose South Korea for his first foreign visit. In conjunction with the visit, he solved the entangled aid issue, releasing funds for South Korea. Nakasone's first decision as prime minister in 1983 was to provide $4 billion in yen loans to South Korea through the Japan Export-Import Bank. Given the domestic criticism against the Korean military regime, this took political courage. South Korea appreciated his action and welcomed him during his visit. But Nakasone's security stance related primarily to global confrontation, and thus regional security issues were less conspicuous. The question of what role, if any, Japan should play in the regional security context remained unanswered. Overall, the policies of the United States and Japan during this period were complementary. Mike Mansfield, the American ambassador to Japan, expressed this relationship in the famous phrase, "The U.S.-Japan relationship is the most important bilateral relationship in the world, bar none."

From Trade Frictions to Structural Frictions

Even though Japan and the United States recognized each other's importance during the 1970s, the bilateral relationship suffered from friction in economic relations. Japan's growing trade surplus with other advanced economies strengthened U.S. determination to use political pressure to limit Japanese imports. Trade talks between the two countries on such goods as color television sets, steel, automobiles, semiconductors, and videotape recorders became continuous, and the negotiation process was almost always frustrating to both sides. The U.S. side tended to view Japanese market openings as "too little, too late," while the Japanese side felt that it was constantly forced to give in to American political pressure, which included the threat of protectionist measures in Congress.

The commitment of the Reagan administration to free trade and deregulation eased U.S. pressure on Japan to restrict its exports to the U.S. market. After Japan accepted voluntary export restrictions on automobiles in 1981, curbing Japanese exports was no longer the number one priority of the

American government. But new pressures demanding conformity to rules often defined by the United States and a further opening of the Japanese market then became the focus. As the Reagan administration spearheaded deregulation, it increasingly came to view the governmental regulations of other countries as trade barriers. The hegemony of the dollar as a foreign reserve currency, coupled with the large-scale current-account deficit of the United States, made the situation even more complicated. On the one hand, in Japan American pressure for deregulation was viewed as a heavy-handed attempt to make other economies accept the U.S. definition of what in the 1990s came to be called the "global standard." On the other hand, the importance of the U.S. economy, despite the occasionally confrontational style that upset Asians, led other countries to recognize the wisdom of assisting the United States. After all, as long as deregulation and globalization reflected technological developments in communications and information technology, some kind of adjustment was necessary. The U.S.-Japan yen-dollar commission that began in February 1984 held the first of a series of talks, through which Japan began to open up its financial markets.

As cold war tensions waned, as U.S. deregulation and globalization of its economy proceeded, and as the Japanese trade surplus and the American trade and fiscal deficit became less politically tolerable, U.S. pressure for structural changes in the Japanese economy increased. The market-oriented sector specific (MOSS) talks that began in 1985 were later replaced, under the Bush administration, by the structural impediment initiative (SII). The Japanese government accepted the framework of the MOSS talks because it understood that protectionist pressure in the U.S. Congress was mounting. The ratio of Japan's current-account trade surplus to its GNP steadily increased, from 0.8 percent in 1982 to 4.5 percent in 1986. The bilateral trade surplus with the United States also increased, from $16.8 billion in 1982 to $55 billion in 1986. Although it was pointed out that this huge bilateral trade imbalance was due to the artificially strong American dollar as well as massive fiscal expansion under Reaganomics, Japan was seriously concerned about the political implications of these numbers and sought to take action. The MOSS talks were supposed to be a better approach than setting up negotiations for each item.

Although after the peak years of 1986 and 1987 the Japanese current-account surplus and bilateral trade surplus gradually declined, American frustration showed no sign of decline. The focus of friction now shifted to such items as semiconductors in the high-technology sphere, which led to the infamous "numerical targets," the import targets demanded by the United States. At the same time, it was disclosed that a branch company of Toshiba had exported machine tools to the Soviet Union, knowingly violating Coordinating Committee for Multilateral Export Controls (COCOM) regulations. This angered the U.S. Congress, and news footage of American senators crushing a Toshiba cassette radio was widely replayed in Japan.

In the late 1980s, as the Japanese economic presence in the world economy reached its peak, U.S. concerns focused on Japan's foreign investment in the United States and on America's "decline." The United States saw Japan as a major rival, and these events reinforced the so-called revisionist contention that Japanese society was operating under norms and values that differed from those of Western societies. Writings by authors such as Theodore White and Karel van Wolfren in particular caused a great sensation in Japan. The massive Japanese investment boom in the United States and other parts of the world, which made sense in economic terms as a way to recycle current-account surpluses, also had the effect of worsening its image as a country that was aggressively buying out other economies. Japanese companies invested in the United States and elsewhere seeking business profits, but there was also some element of hubris. Carrying over rivalries in domestic Japanese markets, Japanese companies competed to buy conspicuous foreign assets such as the Rockefeller Center in New York or Columbia Pictures and MGM. Even though these real estate and corporate assets then appeared cheap because of the appreciated yen, these companies were surprisingly insensitive to the American public's antagonistic reaction.

But at the end of the decade, Japan's frustration with the apparently endless criticism of its closed markets also heightened. Japanese officials leaned toward the view that low American savings rates, which led to the so-called twin fiscal and current-account deficits, were the root cause of America's troubles. When Japan accepted the SII framework, it was thus explained in Japan that the discussion was to be two-way, the Japanese side pointing to American deficit issues, the American side to the closed nature of the Japanese markets. The United States soon made it clear, however, that it wanted concrete results in the SII talks, and that the negotiations were not two-way.

On the other hand, macroeconomic management through the Group of Five (G5) and the later Group of Seven (G7) framework began to take a more active role in financial coordination after the Plaza Accord of September 1985. At that meeting, Minister of Finance Takeshita Noboru had voluntarily expressed Japan's willingness to accept more than a 10 percent appreciation of the yen. Japan also initiated a comprehensive review of its economic structure, which resulted in the so-called Maekawa report of April 1986. There is no doubt that the Nakasone cabinet was seriously concerned about high Japanese trade surpluses, especially with the United States. Nakasone made a special television appearance to appeal to the public to buy more imported goods. He also walked into a department store and bought himself a few nice ties (although they were made in France, not the United States).[4]

Although the exchange rate moved from about ¥230/dollar to ¥200/dollar in January 1986, for the moment the Japanese trade surplus was not substantially reduced. The Nakasone cabinet was heavily criticized by small- and medium-sized Japanese companies for the difficulties caused by the appreciation of the yen. In early 1986, to boost the domestic economy and stabilize the exchange rate, the Bank of Japan (BOJ) repeatedly lowered the interest rate. But the yen continued to appreciate against the dollar, reaching the level of ¥150/dollar by July of that year. Around this same time, Nakasone wrote to Reagan asking for cooperation in stopping the yen's appreciation, but Reagan responded negatively, citing the strong protectionist pressure in Congress. In fact, James Baker, the secretary of the treasury, had expressed his willingness to accept further yen appreciation, apparently as a tactic to press Japan in trade negotiations.

After the general election of July 1986, Miyazawa Kiichi replaced Takeshita as minister of finance. He and Baker met in San Francisco and reached an agreement that Japan would pursue an expansionary fiscal and monetary policy, while the United States would cooperate in stabilizing the yen-dollar exchange rate. The BOJ lowered the interest rate further, and the Japanese government introduced a supplementary budget of more than ¥3 trillion. The Louvre agreement, finally reached in February 1987 at the G7 finance ministers' meeting, stated that the G7 countries would cooperate in their respective domestic economic policies and maintain the current exchange rate. This meant that the United States would reduce its fiscal budget, while Japan would further expand its domestic demand. Japan implemented this agreement by further reducing the interest rate to a historical low of 2.5 percent and announcing a ¥6 trillion fiscal package. The worldwide "Black Monday" stockmarket crash in October 1987 prevented Japan from reviewing its low interest rate policy. The Japanese interest rate was not raised until May 1989.

The U.S. trade deficit with Japan gradually declined, from $56 billion in 1987 to $41 billion in 1990. Japan also continued to finance the American shortage of savings in the form of private investment and the purchase of U.S. Treasury bonds by Japanese financial companies. It is not yet clear whether Japan's actions were based purely on business judgments or whether political judgments were involved. On the one hand, investment in American assets made economic sense. The rapid appreciation of the yen put strong deflationary pressure on the Japanese economy, which reduced domestic business investment opportunities. The only good investment opportunities were, ironically, the already competitive export-oriented industries. This sector retained its competitiveness even under the strong yen. Other domestic investment led to land and other asset speculation, which caused the inflationary bubble. Investing in foreign assets was therefore viewed as a sound choice.

At the same time, the policymakers of the period recognized that Japan should bear its fair share in supporting activities for the "international public good." Both U.S. leadership in the West in the cold war setting and the free trade regime collectively managed by the G7 countries were viewed as the key international framework from which Japan benefited greatly, hence the argument for a greater "international contribution" by Japanese political and bureaucratic leaders. While talks on trade and structure remained tense, macroeconomic management, in terms of the interest rate and the promotion in financial recycling of the Japanese current-account surplus, was successful. Still, this success was not widely recognized by the public or even by many political leaders in either country, especially in the United States.

Toward the Post–Cold War Era

When George Bush replaced Ronald Reagan as president in 1989, the cold war was clearly heading toward its final stage. The period 1989–92 was one of transition to a post–cold war era and a new context for the U.S.-Japan relationship. Three examples illustrate this transition: the FSX controversy, the response to the Tiananmen incident, and the experience during and after the Gulf crisis.

Japan's FSX was a new Fighter Support airplane expected to replace the F-1 type, which the Defense Agency intended to build domestically. But the

United States demanded that Japan either purchase an American plane or jointly develop a new plane. In 1987 the Defense Agency decided to pursue joint development, adopting the U.S. F-16 airplane as a prototype. The next year a memorandum of understanding (MOU) on the cost and the technology to be shared was signed by the two countries. But in 1989, just after the Bush administration took office, some members of Congress began to denounce the joint development framework as unilaterally releasing American technology to Japanese industry. Bush failed to oppose this pressure effectively, and as a result, the MOU had to be renegotiated. Its revised form met some U.S. demands, but the obvious failure of the American side to keep its pledge prompted a sense of uneasiness among the Japanese media as well as the Japanese officials concerned. The episode suggests the strength of the forces in the United States that saw Japan as the chief competitor in the post–cold war world.

The Tiananmen incident on June 4, 1989, revealed another post–cold war dimension of the U.S.-Japan bilateral relationship. Seeing China use military force against its own citizens, the United States and European countries strongly denounced the Chinese government. Japan joined in the denunciation, but soon downgraded its sanctions. At the 1990 Houston summit, Prime Minister Kaifu Toshiki told President Bush about the Japanese belief that isolating China was not in the best interests of international society. This belief reflected Japan's long-standing view that human rights was an important, but not the sole, objective in its relations with China—and that improving human rights conditions would take a long time and would first require improved economic and social conditions. After the Tiananmen incident, regional international relations began to assert their importance. The Asian-Pacific area was a complicated and potentially conflict-prone region with widely divergent value systems. How to manage the U.S.-Japan bilateral relationship within this regional context became a new assignment for the two countries in the 1990s.

The experience of the Gulf War taught Japan that the foreign policy stance it had developed and maintained during the cold war was ill-suited to the post–cold war era. Japan's liberalist foreign policy had combined a number of factors reasonably well: Japanese economic self-interest, the Japanese political consensus on the pacifistic interpretation of the Japanese constitution, lingering fears about Japanese political and military assertiveness, and the country's need to contribute to the international system, chiefly by providing economic aid and by accepting the need for policy coordination. But Japan was totally unprepared for an era in which United Nations activities could have military implications or large-scale warfare could take place. The Japanese financing of the Gulf War through a $13 billion tax increase was not only unappreciated, it was also dubbed "checkbook diplomacy." Later, Japan sent a squadron of minesweepers to the Gulf, but this was also seen as another example of doing "too little, too late" in contributing to international order. The Gulf War experience posed a dilemma: should Japan adhere to its postwar principle of not using military force beyond its border or should it contribute more to international security? Although President Bush's "new world order" did not materialize, in the post–cold war era the major powers occasionally resorted to the use of force. For Japan, the Gulf War was a shock at least comparable to the "Nixon shocks" or the first oil shock. This time, however, the shock proved the impetus for an overall reassessment of Japan's postwar political, economic, social, and ideological arrangements, which produced a series of reforms.

Above all, the events since 1989 illustrate the fact that the U.S.-Japan relationship needed to adjust to different circumstances: the continuing and far-reaching influences of globalization, the newly recognized importance of regional activities, and the new global management of international affairs.

Concluding Observations

The U.S.-Japan relationship was managed reasonably well during the 1970s and 1980s, despite the initial "shocks" of the early 1970s. Perhaps the chief reason for its general success was the need for mutual cooperation in global economic management and in uniting the market economies against the communist world. The two countries' understanding of each other, however, was not very deep. This was especially true of top American leaders such as Henry Kissinger, Zbigniew Brzezinski, and James Baker, who were more interested in advancing American interests in global geopolitics than in cultivating a relationship with Japan per se. Japanese leaders were inevitably more concerned about Japan's relationship with the United States than U.S. leaders were about the United States' relationship with Japan. And Japan's slow political adjustment to its increasing economic power, especially in comparison to its slower progress during the early postwar era, led to mutual frustration. Nevertheless, through a series of compromises, day-to-day affairs were managed relatively well.

One may thus conclude that the relationship was well managed not because of deep mutual understanding and political statesmanship but because of the international structure and the correspondence of interests within it. The global cold war framework not only buttressed the U.S.-Japan security relationship, it also provided an opportunity for Japan to articulate Western interests, as Nakasone did most clearly. The United States remained frustrated with Japan's limited contribution to the Western security effort, while Japan often considered America's stance and rhetoric too bellicose. But Japan's basic perception that the United States was the leader of the West and the U.S. perception that Japan was its key ally in Asia fundamentally oriented the two countries in a collaborative direction.

Moreover, the experience of the successive economic shocks in the early 1970s made it clear that the global economy would have to be jointly managed by the major advanced economies. By then it was also clear that Japan was an indispensable member of that group. The institutionalization of various meetings, which now included Japan, was central to the management of global economic issues. In this context, the importance of the G7 summit cannot be overemphasized.

The global international setting made the two countries' approach to the Asia-Pacific region complementary, although there was little conscious coordination between them. The United States embraced China in the early 1970s chiefly because it found entente with the Chinese to be a strategic asset in its rivalry with the Soviet Union. Japan then took the initiative to promote greater economic interdependence in East Asia, including China. The different motives for improving relations with China did not produce problems between the United States and Japan and allowed the U.S.-China-Japan trilateral relationship to remain generally stable. Japan promoted economic cooperation with those ASEAN members not necessarily on good terms with the United States, but the Cambodian conflict and the close relationship between Vietnam and the U.S.S.R. again made the West's interest in the region complementary with that of the other Southeast Asian countries.

The changing global context, especially after the late 1980s, strained the U.S.-Japan relationship in new ways. The waning of the global confrontation between the superpowers weakened the shared sense of a common strategic interest among the Western countries. It also blurred the standard measures of national strength, which complicated the management of international affairs. What counted: nuclear force, economic competitiveness, democratic values, or technological prowess? What did other nations seek, and which one would be the next rival? These questions were increasingly difficult to answer.

At the same time, the forces of globalization, promoted by the Reagan administration but more fundamentally a response to progress in information technology, undermined the collective management of the global economy by government representatives. Globalization created strong pressure for worldwide conformity. The institutions, rules, and cultural codes previously thought to be under domestic jurisdiction were now under international scrutiny, which all too often evoked a strong public response.

During the late 1980s and early 1990s the U.S.-Japan relationship faced new challenges. The global flow of goods and money reached far beyond the level that government officials could effectively manipulate by coordinating economic policies. In addition, for most countries international policy coordination, although important, was not the first priority. Economic difficulties naturally led to a search for scapegoats. This happened in the United States in the late 1980s with the so-called revisionist stereotyping of Japanese society, and it was also reflected in the FSX fiasco. Compared to the United States, Japan seems to have placed a high priority on policy coordination during the period, but this approach backfired when the government missed important cues in the domestic economy. Japan's version of a conspiracy theory gained support among Japanese observers in the 1990s, who traced their country's problems to U.S. attempts to regain economic supremacy: in yielding to policy coordination efforts, Japan's interest rates went down, thereby driving Japanese financial resources out of Japan in the form of foreign direct and portfolio investment. This line of argument misses the main point: in the late 1980s, Japanese leaders still considered cooperation with the United States vital to Japan's self-interest.

The Tiananmen incident exemplified the new international setting of the Asia-Pacific region. The restrictions on technology exports and other sanctions imposed by Western nations on China after the Tiananmen incident indicated the waning importance of China as a strategic asset for the West because of the end of the cold war. The growth in regional activities was reflected in the 1989 decision to launch the Asia Pacific Economic Cooperation forum (APEC), the first association to cover the entire Asia-Pacific region. Whether to pursue further economic interdependence or put a higher priority on human rights and thus expose differences in views within the region became a highly salient issue.

The Gulf crisis and the Gulf War demonstrated that Japan's combination of economic diplomacy and political silence had degenerated to "checkbook diplomacy" and that its postwar foreign policy stance was increasingly inadequate. Japan failed to articulate the values it would uphold in the post–cold war environment. Paradoxically, globalization has brought peoples with different values closer, so that the violent conflicts often associated with those differences occur more frequently. Regionalism has also emerged, which may modify, mitigate, or counter the effect of global uniformity. How the United States and Japan respond to these issues will decide the character of the bilateral relationship in the future.

IV

Sino-Japanese Relations

CHAPTER EIGHT

China's Relations with Japan

Zhang Tuosheng

Sino-Japanese relations underwent profound changes and made great progress in the two decades after 1972, when the Joint Statement for the normalization of relations between China and Japan was issued. In general, these advances benefited not only the two countries and the two peoples but also regional and global peace and development. Since the end of the cold war, major changes occurred internationally, which in turn have brought major ups and downs in Sino-Japanese relations. At this juncture it is important to review the history of the relationship during these decades to deepen understanding, introduce new interpretations, and draw lessons from both the failures and the successes. This essay seeks thereby to shed light on current issues in the bilateral relationship in the hope of furthering the development of Sino-Japanese relations in the new century.

An Overall Review of Sino-Japanese Relations, 1972–1992

In 1992, when the twentieth anniversary of the normalization of relations between China and Japan was celebrated, both nations evaluated the course of their interaction over the intervening two decades. The Chinese side pointed out that with the Joint Statement, China and Japan opened a new chapter in their relationship and that bilateral ties had made great progress. The Chinese announced that the fruits achieved resulted from long-term joint efforts by the two countries and the two peoples, and that these accomplishments should be treasured.[1] In addition, as some Chinese scholars and experts have stressed, there is an enormous difference between the relationship at the time of normalization and the relationship twenty years later. Tremendous changes have occurred as two major powers with different social systems have learned to coexist peacefully and cooperate in international affairs.[2]

While fully recognizing these accomplishments, the Chinese side has also acknowledged that during these two decades there was some friction between the two countries, some quarrels, and some twists and turns. It pointed to, for instance, the disagreement over the antihegemony clause in the 1970s, the differences in perspective on the historical period from 1895 through World War II, when Japan waged aggressive wars against China and other countries, the differing perspectives on the Taiwan issue, the disputes over the Diaoyu Islands (called Senkaku by the Japanese), the frequent economic friction concerning economic and trade relations, and Japan's imposition of sanctions on China at the end of the 1980s. None of these differences, however, prevented the two countries from maintaining a positive relationship. All these problems were side currents, while the primary relations between the two nations were friendly.[3] It is my understanding that in Japan many scholars had the same view at that time. To be sure, there were also differing views. For example, some Japanese put more emphasis on the political, economic, and social differences between the two countries and argued that the two had been friendly only superficially and that problems had often occurred behind the scenes.[4] Other Japanese viewed this period negatively. But generally speaking, theirs were minority opinions that did not persuade the Japanese mainstream.

More recently, sharp differences between China and Japan on a number of issues, such as the interpretation of history, Japan-Taiwan relations, and the U.S.-Japan military alliance, have intensified. It must be acknowledged that beginning in the mid-1990s, bilateral relations suffered major frustrations, even setbacks. By the end of the decade, however, these problems had basically been resolved, or at least brought under control. Bilateral relations had begun to improve, but the friendly atmosphere between the two peoples was still not what it had been before 1992. Therefore it is appropriate to ask whether the progress achieved during the years 1972–92 has been overestimated while the seriousness of existing differences that were then under control has been underestimated. The answer is clear: we have not overestimated the progress in these two decades. On the contrary, the problems and the complications that have occurred since the mid-1990s reflect the significant progress and the valuable experience achieved earlier. Before spelling out that experience, it is worth summarizing the major achievements in Sino-Japanese relations during this twenty-year period. I would stress the following four points:

First, politically, the Sino-Japanese Joint Statement and the Sino-Japanese Treaty of Peace and Friendship built a legal framework of major principles for developing friendly cooperation between the two countries. On this basis, both sides conducted high-level multilayered and multichannel consultation and dialogue and their top leaders exchanged many visits, thus greatly enhancing mutual understanding and confidence.[5] In 1992 General Secretary Jiang Zemin visited Japan and Emperor Akihito visited China. This high-level exchange reflected a new level of bilateral political relations. During these two decades, both sides seized opportunities to improve and develop the two countries' relationship.

Second, economically, imports and exports increased rapidly, from a very low level to a comprehensive, large-scale level of trade. Economic relations have expanded in all areas—investment, technical cooperation, and governmental financial cooperation (including programs such as the Japanese ODA to China,[6] loans for energy development, and recycling plan loans). The total volume of the export-import trade rose from $1.038 billion in 1972 to $25.38 billion in 1992, a twentyfold increase in twenty years. Trade content also underwent restructuring as the percentage of Chinese exports of finished industrial products continued to increase. In addition, from 1979 to 1992, the various loans to China made by the Japanese government, together with outright grants to China, totaled some ¥1,394.22 billion. Bilateral economic and trade cooperation, with strong complementarity, helped strengthen Sino-Japanese relations.[7]

Third, in security and international affairs, the two countries put an end to long-term hostility. The U.S.-Japan security alliance stopped targeting China,[8] and China and Japan achieved a measure of indirect strategic cooperation. Both countries opposed hegemonism, neither tried to seek hegemony, and both made positive contributions to world peace, security, and development, particularly in the Asia-Pacific region. After political turmoil broke out in China during the late spring and early summer of 1989, Japan joined seven Western countries in imposing sanctions on China. Still, Japan clearly opposed isolating China and took the lead in lifting the sanctions, which in turn aided China in persuading the West to reduce and remove its sanctions. During this period, Sino-Japanese cooperation in international affairs was achieved because of improved bilateral relations. Although their cooperation was mostly indirect, it provided an important basis for further international collaboration in the future.

Fourth, in terms of friendly activities such as cultural exchanges and the exchange of visits, substantial progress was made through both official and unofficial efforts. The exchanges covered all fields, including culture, education, fine arts, and science and technology. The large number and extensive variety of participants in nongovernmental exchanges far exceeded the numbers in formal exchanges during the same period. By 1991 there were 127 pairs of sister cities in Japan and China, and the large-scale visit of 3,000 Japanese youth to China in 1984 was unprecedented. These activities played an indispensable role in deepening mutual understanding and promoting the development of friendly relations.

In short, the two decades from 1972 to 1992 formed the most successful period in Sino-Japanese relations in the twentieth century.[9] The progress in these four areas represented the primary direction of the bilateral relationship in the first twenty years after normalization. These developments allowed the two countries to manage their differences and provided an important base for furthering bilateral relations in the complex environment of the post–cold war era. In the new post–cold war period, China and Japan confronted new international issues, but China is now much stronger economically, more open, and much more active in international affairs than it was in 1972.

The Root Causes of Differences and Friction

Although friction in Sino-Japanese relations during the 1970s and 1980s did not deter the two countries from maintaining good overall relations, it is important to understand these differences, for while some have been thoroughly resolved and some are basically under control, others crop up time and again, and still others have intensified under the new circumstances. Analyzing and summarizing these problems is one way to reduce their impact on smooth relations between the two countries in the future. The six major problems included:

1. *Disagreement on the Antihegemony Clause.* Disagreement on the antihegemony clause was the principal obstacle to the conclusion of the Treaty of Peace and Friendship between China and Japan in the 1970s after the normalization of relations. Between 1975[10] and 1978, through long-term effort and compromise, the two sides gradually resolved the disagreement and were finally able to conclude the treaty. How do we analyze the problem? I believe there are four factors.

First, the two countries had real policy differences toward the Soviet Union. China intended to establish a united front against Soviet hegemony and therefore insisted that the antihegemony clause of the Joint Statement be incorporated into the treaty. Although Japan viewed the U.S.S.R. as the major threat to its security, it believed that its interests lay in maintaining a diplomacy of equal distance between China and the Soviet Union. After signing the Joint Statement with China, Japan began to retreat from the position expressed in that document in the face of repeated diplomatic pressure and intimidation from the U.S.S.R.[11] The Japanese first opposed the incorporation of the antihegemony clause in the treaty, and then agreed to do so but gave various explanations of the clause in an attempt to weaken it. This is the main reason for bilateral differences on this issue.

Second, this disagreement reflected the determined efforts of pro-Taiwan right wingers in Japan to hinder the development of friendly relations between the two countries, which may in fact be the deeper cause of the problems over the hegemony clause. When the Tanaka administration resigned because of the Lockheed scandal, Miki Takeo succeeded Tanaka Kakuei as prime minister. Miki's faction within the Liberal Democratic Party was small, and his coming to power was accomplished only with the cooperation of various factions that had opposed the Tanaka administration. Anti-China hard-liners, who had opposed the Tanaka and Ohira factions and who dominated the LDP coalition that controlled the government, played a role in constraining Miki's policies toward China. In 1974, in a meeting with visiting Japanese delegations, then Vice Premier Deng Xiaoping had explained why negotiations on the business agreements and the Treaty of Peace and Friendship had been prolonged. Evaluating the efforts of Prime Minister Tanaka and Foreign Minister Ohira positively, he held that the difficulties had been the work of a handful of people, namely the hawks and the members of the pro-Taiwan right wing in Japan, including Kishi

Nobusuke, Sato Eisaku, Shiina Etsusaburo, and the Seirankai group, which steadfastly supported Taiwan because of Japanese financial interests there.[12] After Miki came to power, their influence remained strong, and they constituted the backbone of those opposed to the antihegemony clause. In the spring of 1978, Deng Xiaoping unambiguously pointed out that the antihegemony clause had become a card in the hands of the right wingers.[13] It is easy to understand why China insisted that it would not back down from its position on the antihegemony clause in the Joint Statement; it was determined to continue to struggle against pro-Taiwan forces in Japan.

Third, the Chinese position on the antihegemony clause was not aimed exclusively, as some Japanese have speculated, at inducing Japan to join China in opposing the Soviet Union. Of course at the time, China was deeply concerned about the U.S.S.R. But through this clause, China also intended that both China and Japan would obligate themselves not to seek hegemony in the Asia-Pacific region. Deng explained to Japanese visitors that China was prepared to use this clause to restrain itself, and that its inclusion in the treaty was beneficial to Japan and necessary in reassuring China, given the legacy of Japanese behavior in World War II. The clause was meant to oppose any country or bloc of countries that might seek hegemony in the region, although it mainly targeted the Soviet Union.[14]

Fourth, new elements arose in 1978. In Japan, the number of people demanding that the treaty be concluded apparently grew, not only in the various parties and pro-China organizations but also in the business community. At the same time, both the increasing tension with the U.S.S.R. and the supportive attitude of the United States toward an early conclusion of the treaty drove Japan to soften its position. But the key factor was that China, which desired to advance Sino-Japanese bilateral relations quickly, demonstrated flexibility on the relevant policies. As a result, the Chinese negotiators consented to the incorporation of a clause stating that the treaty did not affect the relations of any third party with a signatory to the treaty. In view of China's flexibility, the Japanese could argue that the antihegemony clause did not change its relations with the Soviet Union. In this way, China and Japan were able to compromise, finally ending their bilateral disagreement.

The inclusion of the antihegemony clause in the treaty, a pioneering undertaking, was a significant historic step in the struggle against hegemony in general, and the hegemonic strategy of the U.S.S.R. in particular. More important, once the disagreement was resolved, the two peoples finally signed the treaty, the realization of their long-held wish, which furthered bilateral relations. In particular, it aided the development of economic and cultural relations and generated a new wave of friendly relations between the two countries.

Since the signing, profound changes have occurred, internationally in the former Soviet Union and elsewhere, and domestically within China and Japan. Yet the antihegemonic principle is not obsolete. The fact that neither China nor Japan seeks hegemony undoubtedly has practical significance, since both have themselves become influential major powers.

2. *Differences in Perspective on the History Issue.* The 1982 history textbook issue, the official and respectful 1985 visit of the Japanese prime minister to the Yasukuni Shrine, and continuing "slips of the tongue" by Diet members, taken together, have generated serious problems for the development of friendly bilateral relations. The history issue forms the core of the friction between the two countries. In order to ensure the healthy development of Sino-Japanese relations in the future, this issue must be clearly and objectively understood and correctly addressed.

As I interpret the issue, the Japanese side—particularly the right wing—must bear primary responsibility for the emergence and intensification of the problem. Their mistaken words and actions, which glorify the invasion and honor the Japanese invaders, have repeatedly sent great tremors throughout China. Under these circumstances, it is only natural for the Chinese government to express serious objections. As someone just over thirty years old in 1982, I found it hard to understand how Japanese textbooks could openly alter historical facts. China and Japan had normalized relations, China had given up its demand for war reparations, and the two countries had signed the Treaty of Peace and Friendship. But the textbooks approved by the Japanese Ministry of Education still referred to the invasion of China as "entering and leaving China." For those who had suffered the horrors of the war, it was like rubbing salt in old wounds.[15] The Chinese people became increasingly outraged because such statements were repeated, and in late 1985, university students in China staged anti-Japanese demonstrations.

Is it true, as some say, that China always overreacts or picks on Japan over the history issue? Absolutely not. Beginning in the 1950s, when meeting with Japanese friends, the Chinese national leaders constantly repeated certain remarks. One was that a handful of militarists, but not the Japanese people as a whole, should be held accountable for the wars, since the Japanese people were also victims. The second was an acknowledgment that an apology had been expressed and that the two sides should let bygones be bygones; both China and Japan should focus on the future. Precisely because of these beliefs, as relations were being normalized in 1972, the Chinese side did not make larger demands, even though it was not fully satisfied with the Japanese response on the history issue.

The Japanese side first proposed the wording "had caused great trouble to the Chinese people" and "we offer an expression of deep self-examination." They later changed the wording to, "We feel deeply that the Japanese bear responsibility for causing major damage to the Chinese people by the wars, and we express deep self-examination." They still avoided using the word "invasion." Later, when receiving Japanese friends, Premier Zhou Enlai explained that past problems had been resolved in the Joint Statement, and that efforts should now be made to maintain sound and enduring relations between China and Japan.[16] In accord with these guidelines, the Treaty of Peace and Friendship signed in 1978 was a forward-looking treaty.

In the 1980s, however, as the Japanese negated or "beautified" their aggression in case after case, their actions triggered strong reaction in China. Again, in 1985, when Prime Minister Nakasone Yasuhiro, in his official capacity, paid homage at the Yasukuni Shrine, where the name of Tojo Hideki, a first-class war criminal, was on display, his visit heightened the friction between the two countries.

Students in Beijing, Xi'an, and elsewhere took to the streets in September 1985 to protest against Japan with such slogans as "Down with the Japanese militarists!" and "Boycott Japanese Goods!" An authorized article, "Treasure the Hard-Won China-Japan Friendly Relations," carried in the *People's Daily* at the end of October, was well received by the Chinese people. The article provided systematic guidance to help the Chinese people distinguish the handful of Japanese who were bent on a militarist stance from the broader Japanese public. The article correctly recognized the existing problems but emphasized that further improvement of Sino-Japanese friendship was inevitable. It expressed the clear-cut objective of maintaining and promoting friendship between the two countries. This article was written at the suggestion of Hu Qiaomu, then in charge of publicity and ideology work for the CCP Central Committee. He revised the article himself before publication and personally added the concluding paragraph.[17]

During this same period, at a meeting with the representatives of the China-Japan 21st Century Friendship Committee, CCP General Secretary Hu Yaobang put forward "Four Points for Developing China-Japan Relations." Hu Yaobang emphasized that any idea or act that belittled and underestimated Sino-Japanese friendship showed a lack of vision and incorrect judgment in the long run. As these statements make clear, Chinese leaders have given much care and thought to maintaining the Sino-Japanese relationship. They do not "pick on Japan."

It must also be acknowledged that when Japan's effort to whitewash atrocities was criticized, the Japanese government took measures to handle each case of denial or whitewashing individually. The Japanese government also reiterated its adherence to the principles on the history issue that had been expounded in the Joint Statement and the Treaty of Peace and Friendship. Sometimes the Japanese government did acknowledge wartime behavior more directly. For example, in 1983, in the first such statement by any prime minister, Prime Minister Nakasone admitted in the Diet that the Japanese war on China was an aggressive one,[18] and he reiterated the point in 1986.[19] In general, after 1982 the history issue gradually became the main irritant between the two countries, but it did not constitute a major obstacle to advancing bilateral relations.

Fourth, the Japanese Diet has refused, even in 1995 on the centenary of the occupation of Taiwan, to pass a self-examination, apology, and no-war bill. The bill the Diet finally adopted was ambiguous, and the wording empty and short of self-examination. Japan repeatedly lost opportunities to put aside historical burdens. Why has Japan consistently attempted to cover up its aggressive history and why does its level of self-examination concerning its history lag far behind that of Germany? It is now clear that Japan's democratic reforms were inadequate and that militarism was not totally liquidated. As far as public attitudes toward Japan's aggressive history are concerned, there are large differences among the Japanese people. These differences can be grouped into four categories. The first is that the wars launched by Japan since 1894 were aggressive, imperialist wars in search of hegemony, a view accepted by a small number of people; the second, that there was some aggression; the third, that the Japanese nation committed some aggressions but that the wars were not launched intentionally by the Japanese government; and the fourth, an across-the-board denial of aggression by a small number of people like Ishihara Shintaro.[20] Given such views among the Japanese public, the differences in historical perspective can hardly be settled in a short time. In retrospect, China somewhat underestimated the difficulties involved in resolving these problems. In the long run, however, the history issue will not prevent progress in bilateral relations. Both China and Japan have paid a grievous price for this dispute. As far as China is concerned, history is, after all, past, and current and future policies in Japan are more important. Yet the Japanese concept of history is only one of the elements that can influence Japan's policies. If leading Japanese policies adhere to the postwar model of peaceful development, differences between China and Japan over history will gradually become less important with the passage of time and the furtherance of mutual understanding.

3. *Differences over the Taiwan Issue.* In 1987 the Chiang Kai-shek Legacy Association was set up in Japan. In the same year, the Osaka High Court's incorrect ruling in the Kokaryo dormitory case, that the Kyoto building belonged to the Taiwan government rather than to the Chinese government, generated major political and legal disputes between China and Japan.[21] For several years, these incidents adversely affected the bilateral relationship. In addition, since the late 1970s, the Japanese have not strictly observed the oral promise about restricting Japan-Taiwan exchanges that was made by Japanese leaders at the time of the normalization of relations.[22] But in general, from 1971 to 1992 friction over this issue was not serious, especially in comparison to other periods after World War II. For several decades before normalization, however, the Taiwan issue was a major obstacle, and in recent years it has again come to the forefront and caused increasing trouble between the two countries.[23]

As a result of Japan's long rule over Taiwan, there are many varieties of pro-Taiwan forces in Japan that have very close economic ties and emotional connections with Taiwan. Some of them have been deeply involved in the activities of "Taiwan independence." Those in Japan with great ambitions for Taiwan tried to resist the normalization of Sino-Japanese relations, but during the 1972–92 period they had little success. The reasons for this lack of success are worth studying. One important factor is that the Japanese government, out of consideration for overall Sino-Japanese relations, could remain behind the "one China principle" (even though many Japanese +believed that Taiwan's status was undecided) embedded in the Joint Statement. This made it possible for Japan to handle the friction in a low-key manner as problems arose, and prevented deterioration of Sino-Japanese relations. Besides, at the time, the issue of Taiwan independence was not as powerful as it is at present.

On the issue of Taiwan, the Kokaryo case was the most important event during the years 1972–92. Japan's behavior clearly violated its international obligations with respect to recognizing the Chinese government. The Chinese government had hoped that the Japanese government would proceed in terms of the overall interests of the bilateral relationship and take necessary measures to resolve the issue appropriately. However, under the pretext of the government's "checks and balances" mechanism—the separation of the government from the courts—the Japanese government shirked its responsibilities and was silent on the wrongdoings of judicial authorities, triggering strong opposition from China. Deng Xiaoping warned of the revival of militarism by an extremely small number of people in Japan.[24] He also pointed out that there were some in Japan who constantly kept Taiwan in mind, and that the Kokaryo case was related to the principal matter of the "one China" or "two Chinas" issue. Further, he said that the Japanese government owed China something because the outcome of the Kokaryo case departed from the Treaty of Peace and Friendship. In the meantime, the *People's Daily* carried articles that sharply criticized the behavior of the Japanese government in paying homage at the Yasukuni Shrine, putting out textbooks that whitewashed Japanese aggression, compiling a defense budget that violated the limit of 1 percent of its GNP, and declaring that the Kokaryo building belonged to Taiwan rather than to the government of China.[25]

The concerns of the Chinese side over these issues reflect three points, which should be highlighted. First, Chinese leaders and the Chinese people consider Taiwan to be of utmost importance. Second, the Taiwan issue is a practical problem between China and Japan, but it is also connected with the history issue, and is thus an especially sensitive matter. Third, the tensions over the history issue, the Taiwan issue, and the issue of Japanese military growth are interwoven, and they will have a strong psychological effect on the Chinese. If Japan pulls away from its promises on all three, China will lose trust in Japan.

4. *The Diaoyu Islands (Diaoyutai) Dispute.* Settlement of the territorial dispute between China and Japan over the Diaoyu Islands has been pending for some time. In the 1970s, in order to normalize Sino-Japanese relations and sign the Sino-Japanese Treaty of Peace and Friendship, the leaders of both

countries wisely shelved the issue. Since then, occasional quarrels over the Diaoyu Islands have erupted. For example, on several occasions Japanese right wingers tried to build a lighthouse on the island. The Chinese criticized the Japanese over these actions, but the situation did not get out of control. Three factors have been influential in stabilizing the disagreement. First, although the stances of both sides are inherently confrontational and any incident evokes an emotional response, this dispute carries very little weight in terms of the overall interests of Sino-Japanese relations. Second, Chinese leaders are following broad-minded, long-range, visionary policies concerning the Diaoyu Islands. Zhou Enlai's concept of temporary avoidance[26] and Deng Xiaoping's concept of "leaving it to future generations" and "shelving the dispute and seeking common development"[27] have provided a practical way for the two countries to handle the problem and also opened broad vistas for its final solution. The Chinese side has also called for vigilance to prevent the problem from being used to poison the general atmosphere of Sino-Japanese relations. Third, given the Northern Territories dispute between Japan and Russia, Japan needs to take a more cautious attitude toward the Diaoyu Islands.

China and Japan differ in significant ways over how to understand and settle this issue. Japan insists that theoretically, "there is no territorial dispute." In reality, however, it now and then gives implicit support to right-wing activities on the islands even as it tries to confine these activities within certain limits. This approach became clearer after the incident in 1996, when Japanese right wingers built a temporary lighthouse on one of the Diaoyu Islands.

5. *Economic Friction.* After the normalization of relations between China and Japan, bilateral economic and trade relations expanded rapidly. However, this still didn't stop many problems from arising, such as China's request, as it corrected its overheated economy of 1977–78, to cancel some contracts with Japanese enterprises, the trade imbalance, disputes over technology transfers, and the fluctuation in Japanese investment in China. In addition, in the name of safeguarding the Coordinating Committee for Multilateral Export Controls (COCOM), Japan adopted measures to control exports to China after the "Toshiba machinery incident," in which the United States criticized Japan for exporting technology with security implications. It also implemented limited sanctions against China after the June 4 Incident of 1989, which also had a negative impact on trade between the two

countries. But in general, these problems were small bumps on the path forward and did not affect the overall expansion of bilateral economic relations that had begun in the early 1980s.

The frictions in trade and economic relations proved to be very different from political frictions between the two countries. The former originated in both China and Japan, while the latter was brought about by Japan. Fluctuations in economic relations have three possible causes. The first is the effect of China's efforts to readjust its overheated economy. The second is related to problems in political relations. The third is the incompatibility of economic and trade structures between two countries at different levels of development.[28] Among them, the economic factors rather than the political ones played a major role. In fact, economic frictions are endemic between countries engaged in trade, even between developed capitalist countries with identical economic systems. Therefore, from 1972 to 1992, as Sino-Japanese trade increased, it was only natural for friction to increase. Yet the complementary benefits of trade between the two countries are enormous, and increased experience, understanding, and standardization of bilateral exchanges have made it possible to find ways to handle conflict and strike a new balance. In the mid- and early 1980s, however, trade friction, combined with disagreement over the history issue, caused strong mutual psychological friction that complicated Sino-Japanese economic relations. The situation changed considerably as the Chinese economy grew stronger and the role of the market expanded.

6. *Chinese Concern About Japanese Militarism and Its Military Buildup.* In the early 1970s, China judged that Japanese militarism had revived, but the majority of its visiting Japanese friends disagreed. Before long, in accordance with the response on the issue he had received from relevant departments, Premier Zhou Enlai decided to change the wording "has revived" to "is reviving" and instructed his staff to mobilize experts to do further research on this matter. After normalization of relations in 1972, the issue of Japanese militarism was no longer brought up. Now it is clear that the dangers of the revival of Japanese militarism had been overestimated. Fortunately, a correction was quickly achieved.[29]

In the 1980s Chinese leaders once more raised the issue of vigilance in relation to the revival of Japanese militarism. In his political report to the Twelfth National Congress of the CCP in 1982, Hu Yaobang mentioned this danger, and Deng Xiaoping mentioned it again to visiting Japanese friends in 1987. Chinese apprehension was linked to a series of developments in Japan: for example, the history textbook cases, the Kokaryo dormitory case, the excessive defense budget, and Japan's search for great power status. The arguments at the time, however, were different from previous ones, and during this period, Chinese spokesmen always pointed out that only a handful of people had attempted to revive militarism and that the majority of the Japanese people opposed them.

Around 1987, Chinese academics began to raise more questions about whether Japan might become a military power. After the Persian Gulf War, in the wake of increasing U.S. pressure to assume more military responsibility, Japan quickened the pace of its military development. Discussion about amending the Japanese Pacific Constitution to allow armed forces to go outside the country increased. Whether Japan will indeed embark on the road to becoming a military power is a focus of concern in Chinese diplomatic and academic circles. I would argue that rather than revive militarism, Japan will become a military power. Logically, a militarist state must take the path of a military power, but military power does not necessarily require a militarist state. In Japan at present, support for a stronger military is much stronger than support for militarism, and China should remain vigilant.

In recent years, following the strengthening of the U.S.-Japan military alliance, this issue, which increased China's concerns that Japan is becoming a military power, has become a major source of friction between China and Japan. To resolve the issue, China should try to make an accurate and objective evaluation of Japanese military development, and Japan should keep its promise not to seek to become a great military power and to follow the path of peaceful development, thus encouraging the confidence of its neighbors.

Guidelines for the Future

Between 1972 and 1992 China and Japan developed a good working relationship. Both sides now have a rich store of experience and knowledge that can help their relations continue to prosper into the twenty-first century. In view of current realities, I offer three conclusions to guide future actions.

1. The establishment and development of Sino-Japanese friendship and cooperation are determined by the fundamental interests of the two peoples. Maintaining good relations is conducive to the prosperity and development of the two countries, but it also contributes to peace, stability, and development in the Asia-Pacific region and in the world as a whole. In the new cen-

tury, both China and Japan should commit themselves to continuing friendship and cooperation.

Some have concluded that during these twenty years, their common opposition to Soviet hegemony pushed China and Japan to normalize and rapidly develop bilateral relations. There is some truth to this, but it is not the fundamental reason their relations achieved such noticeable progress. History shows that by the early 1980s, China had already changed its international strategy of presenting a united front against the Soviet Union by working with the United States, Japan, and Europe. Even when China and Japan were united against the U.S.S.R., their policies toward the superpower reflected differences as well as similarities. It is, rather, the deep and fundamental cultural linkage resulting from over two thousand years of friendly exchanges between the two countries that has played a long-term role in pushing bilateral relations toward rapid development. In answer to Dr. Kissinger's question, "Why are you so anxious to visit China?" Prime Minister Tanaka replied simply but clearly, "Japan-China relations are much longer than U.S.-China relations."[30] Deng Xiaoping once remarked to some Japanese friends, "I feel that Sino-Japanese friendship is very special."[31]

China and Japan have drawn profound lessons from their shared tragic disasters. Both sides recognize the truth of the adage "Harmony brings common prosperity and fighting brings common damage." Even before normalization, strong people-to-people interactions through nongovernmental organizations, unique to China's relations with Japan, were important in shaping Japanese government policy. The relationship began developing even in the 1950s, despite strong resistance. After normalization, relations flourished because of the huge potential in the economic complementarity between the two nations and the unprecedented opportunity for trade and economic cooperation offered by China's reform and opening.

In fact, by the early 1950s, Chinese leaders had already formulated a new approach to Japan based on clear-cut general principles: they sought to normalize relations between the two countries, restore friendship, and realize common prosperity for future generations. Premier Zhou Enlai frequently expressed this view of Japan in his routine daily work. In March 1955, the Political Bureau of the CCP Central Committee adopted a resolution, "The Principles and Policies Toward Japan," which spelled out these principles. Over time, of course, there were adjustments. In the 1950s and 1960s, China stressed unity with the Japanese people in waging a common struggle against

U.S. policies of control and interference, in an effort to isolate the United States and pressure the Japanese government to alter its China policy. From the 1970s to the early 1980s, in confronting the Soviet threat, China emphasized unity with Japan to oppose Soviet hegemonism. In 1982 China and Japan formulated four basic goals to guide their relations: "peace and friendship, equality and mutual benefit, mutual trust, and long-term stability." They hoped to promote Sino-Japanese relations in an all-encompassing way to make their bilateral relationship a model for peaceful relations and common prosperity between major powers.

Since the mid-1990s, in the wake of the changing global situation, deepening bilateral exchanges, and in particular, the emergence of a new era when both countries are strong (the traditional structures have been strong China and weak Japan or strong Japan and weak China),[32] tension and suspicion have increased. There is a growing tendency in both China and Japan to belittle and underestimate their long-term friendship, and those who constantly oppose this friendship have become more active. Vigilance must be maintained. The people and especially the leaders of both countries must keep history's lessons in mind, recognize the objective foundation for friendly cooperation and the fundamental interests of the two peoples, and strengthen their unwavering determination to carry Sino-Japanese friendship forward for generations to come. Only by remaining firm in their joint commitment can China and Japan achieve a new pattern of bilateral relations and strengthen their partnership.

2. The Joint Statement and the Treaty of Peace and Friendship signed by the two governments correctly sum up the history of bilateral relations and lay the foundation for future relations. A firm adherence to the spirit embodied in the Joint Statement and the Peace Treaty and better implementation of their basic principles are the fundamental guarantees of productive bilateral relations in the future. These four basic principles are as follows:

Admit and correctly understand the stretch of unfortunate history between China and Japan.

Accept the principle that there is only one China and Taiwan is part of China.

Develop amicable long-term relations on the basis of the Five Principles of Peaceful Coexistence and settle all bilateral disputes by peaceful means rather than by force.

Do not seek hegemony and oppose any other country's efforts to establish such hegemony.

The most important idea embodied in these principles is that of "seeking common ground while reserving differences." This spirit and these principles lay down a solid political foundation for both China and Japan to transcend cold war realities and the differences in their ideologies and political systems, and to establish and develop normal state relations.

What remains worrisome as we enter a new century is that the history issue, which should have been resolved long ago, still generates irritation and frustration. In recent years, the issue of Taiwan has intensified feelings on both sides, and may worsen enough to cause further trouble in the years to come. Furthermore, the emergence of the era when both countries are strong may actually increase mutual suspicion. A strong China may be seen as a threat by Japan, and a strong Japan as a military power by China. On the basis of the spirit of the principles enshrined in the Joint Statement and the Peace Treaty, as well as the Joint Declaration issued by the two countries in 1998, both China and Japan should engage in dialogue and adjust their relations to include precautionary measures.

3. The development of a triangular relationship between China, Japan, and the United States that includes frequent interaction and an effort to maintain a relative balance can play an important role in promoting and guaranteeing good Sino-Japanese relations. Nowadays China-U.S.-Japan triangular relations are assuming a bigger role, although some imbalances remain. To help to guarantee the healthy development of bilateral relations, an effort should be made to keep these triangular relations in relative balance.

From the end of World War II to the early 1970s, the China-U.S.-Japan triangle had always had a negative effect on Sino-Japanese relations. Bound by U.S. foreign policy, Japan was constrained to follow the American lead, which encouraged Japanese hostility toward China. In the 1970s and 1980s, however, the China-U.S.-Japan triangle supported better Sino-Japanese relations. President Nixon's February 1972 visit to China improved China-U.S. relations, which in turn made possible the normalization of Sino-Japanese relations and the conclusion of the Treaty of Peace and Friendship. Similarly, the ongoing development of Sino-Japanese relations following normalization in 1972 exerted a positive impact on the establishment of Sino-American diplomatic relations in 1979.[33]

The emergence of this healthy triangle—China, the United States, and Japan—occurred within a context of common resistance to the U.S.S.R., but the real motivating force, an inner impetus among them, was deeper and more complicated. In the early 1980s, China made a strategic readjustment, keeping its distance from the United States and no longer implementing the policy of uniting with it to resist the Soviet Union.[34] At the same time, China gave more attention to Sino-Japanese relations.

Through its continued economic growth, Japan had consolidated its position as the world's number two economic power by the middle of the 1980s. Japan then made clear its objective: to become a political power and gain further independence from the United States. While economic friction between the United States and Japan intensified, China's economic relations with both countries rapidly improved and its economic ties with each strengthened. These elements all helped the triangular relationship achieve a relative balance and advance step by step.

After the political turmoil in China in 1989, Japan demonstrated a strong capacity for making its own decisions and assuming its own posture in international affairs. It pursued an independent position on China and chose not to go along with the policy of overall sanctions imposed by the United States. It took the lead in sending members of the Japanese cabinet to visit China and in lifting its limited economic sanctions on China. In 1992 Prime Minister Kiichi Miyazawa suggested that Japanese diplomacy had two wheels—relations between Japan and China and relations between Japan and the United States—and that both were needed if diplomacy was to function properly.[35] As a result, Sino-Japanese relations avoided a serious setback and soon moved ahead. At this stage, the progress of Sino-Japanese relations again played a positive role in promoting the restoration and improvement of Sino-American relations.

Since the end of the cold war, and especially since the mid-1990s, the role of China-U.S.-Japan triangular relations is becoming prominent, but the actual performance reflects certain difficulties and certain large imbalances. During this same period, Sino-Japanese relations have also suffered rather serious ups and downs, corresponding to the ongoing transition in international patterns after the cold war. There has been extensive debate inside Japan about the post–cold war structure of China-U.S.-Japan relations: Should Japan "focus on Asia" or "on America" or "on relatively balanced relations"?[36] The debate continues, but Japanese foreign policy currently emphasizes "balanced relations," although in its actual policies Japan tends to be closer to the United States.

Within China there are also many opinions on this matter, but a dominant view has already taken shape. China, the United States, and Japan need to establish among themselves the balanced, long-term, stable relations that will serve the fundamental interests of all three countries. Further improvement and development of Sino-Japanese relations in the near future is, I believe, the key to a new breakthrough. Former U.S. defense secretary Robert MacNamara once said that if China and Japan could reach a true and thorough reconciliation like the one between Germany and France, it would be the most important guarantee of peace and prosperity in Asia. This is a penetrating judgment reflecting a profound sense of history. From a long-term perspective, China and Japan, separated by only a strip of water, must establish good, neighborly relations in order to safeguard their interests. There is no other alternative.

Through a serious analysis of history, I hope a consensus on the nature of China-U.S.-Japan relations can gradually be reached, not only among scholars in China and Japan but also among scholars in China, Japan, and the United States. Through these concerted efforts, we can help the governments of the three countries make the best policy choices. I very much admire a Chinese scholar's judgment: "We must build a balanced, stable triangular relationship. If we can pursue such a policy, it would bring tidings of joy to the three countries and to the Asia-Pacific region."[37]

CHAPTER NINE

Japan's Relations with China

Soeya Yoshihide

This essay examines Sino-Japanese relations in the 1970s and the 1980s after the normalization of diplomatic relations in 1972. This was a distinct period in the postwar history of Sino-Japanese relations, since the relationship ostensibly did not concern itself with the "strategic" imperatives of the U.S.-China-Soviet triangle, although it was of course affected by the strategic triangle.[1] Japan's policy toward China therefore did not interfere with its fundamental security alliance with the United States, and Japanese policymakers could concentrate on developing a special relationship with China, independent of "strategic" considerations. The new relationship China had established with the United States in 1972 eventually allowed China to gain confidence about its strategic relations not only with the United States but also with the Soviet Union, and thus to have room to opt for an independent foreign policy. China and Japan were able to develop ties whose peculiar logic was deeply embedded in the bilateral relationship and separated from security considerations, setting off the previous two decades as a distinct period.

Between 1989 and 1992, Japan began to shift the premises of its approach to China, from a nonstrategic focus on the bilateral relationship itself to a strategic focus on China and its role in a new and changing post–cold war international environment.[2] The three-year period from the Tiananmen incident in 1989 to the emperor's visit to China in 1992 marked the transition to the new relationship. The Japanese government's decision to promote the emperor's visit demonstrated its determination to base its China policy on its long-standing postwar emphasis, the importance of the two countries' special bilateral relationship. This policy dictated the decision not to isolate China at the time of the Tiananmen incident, although thereafter, the Japanese perception of China began to deteriorate. China's growing regional role, which followed from its economic growth, also aroused Japanese concern about its intentions and future course.[3] There was tension between Japan's traditional postwar approach on the one hand, and a newly emerging post–cold war strategy for coping with the rise of China on the other. In retrospect, the 1989–92 period can be seen as a prelude to Japan's new approach to China.

Although Japan had become an economic power before 1989, it was not a player in the global political structure comprised of the relationships between the United States, China, and the Soviet Union. It did not have an independent strategy for taking part in this structure, nor was it prepared or equipped, either domestically or internationally, to carry out such a strategy. Japan's foreign policy, especially its security policy, had been the result of its inability, even its unwillingness, to develop an independent strategy, rather than the result of any centralized intention or "conspiracy." Since World War II, after all, Japan had not been a strategic power in the style of the United States or China.

In order to highlight the nature of Japan's role in the context of the triangular relationship, this essay contrasts the development of U.S.-China-Soviet relations, influenced by the strategic dynamics among the three powers, with the development of Japan-China relations, which had its own bilateral momentum. By examining the patterns and the characteristics of the interaction between these two different levels of development, the essay provides a Japanese perspective on the triangular relationship.[4]

Diplomatic Normalization

THE STRATEGIC ENVIRONMENT

The United States' diplomatic overture toward China in the early 1970s represented a truly strategic move to overhaul U.S. diplomacy and gave rise to a new U.S.-China relationship that had a significant impact on U.S.-Japan relations. The Nixon administration, which took office in January 1969, simultaneously pursued three major diplomatic goals: withdrawal from Vietnam, détente with the Soviet Union, and rapprochement with China. In short, Nixon and his team, led by National Security Advisor Henry Kissinger, aspired to create a new international environment by remaking what had been a black-and-white cold war strategy into a traditional balance of power. This in turn was expected to allow the United States to reduce its excessive overseas commitment in the Vietnam War. Nixon and Kissinger thought they would be able to withdraw from Vietnam in a credible fashion only if they succeeded in establishing a "structure for peace" sustained by sound relations with both communist giants.

Rapprochement with China was to provide a breakthrough in this ambitious plan. For U.S. diplomacy, the greatest asset was the intensifying Sino-Soviet rift, which served as a significant impetus for both China and the Soviet Union to give priority to improving relations with the United States over Vietnam. China needed the United States to cope with the Soviet threat, and the Soviet Union needed a stable relationship with the United States to reconstruct its trouble-ridden society and revise its diplomacy, which was further aggravated by the intensifying conflict with China.[5] In the context of this grand strategic picture, the American plan was to isolate Hanoi by approaching both Beijing and Moscow and then draw its belligerent leadership into a negotiated settlement of the Vietnam War.

After a series of Romanian and Pakistani backchannel contacts, Kissinger secretly visited Beijing on July 9–11, 1971, paving the way for Nixon. On July 15, Nixon disclosed Kissinger's secret trip and announced that he would visit China before May 1972. North Vietnamese premier Pham Van Dong visited China in November 1971 and requested the cancellation of Nixon's visit, but Mao Zedong flatly rejected the plea, advising him instead to accept a negotiated settlement of the Vietnam War that would keep the South Vietnamese government intact.[6] Nixon visited China in February 1972 and signed the Shanghai Communiqué declaring a historic U.S.-China rapprochement.

JAPAN-CHINA DIPLOMATIC NORMALIZATION

Although the Japanese embassy in Washington had suspected that the United States might be making overtures to China, Nixon's move still came as a shock to Japanese policymakers. Ushiba Nobuhiko, Japan's ambassador to Washington, was informed of Nixon's announcement on July 15, less than an hour before it was made public.[7] Prime Minister Sato Eisaku is said to have learned the news only minutes before it was announced (on July 16,

Japan time), and it also came as a great shock to him, since both governments had previously agreed to remain in close consultation on the China question.

Even after the Nixon shock, Sato was prepared to cosponsor, with the United States, the dual representation formula for China and Taiwan in the United Nations in the fall of 1971, but he soon decided that Japan should normalize its relations with China at the earliest possible moment. Indeed, among Japanese policymakers, there was a strong feeling of having been betrayed by the United States. A Foreign Ministry official who played a key role in normalization stated, "There was resentment over the fact that the United States had gone ahead of Japan in opening up contact with China. Unless Japan got ahead of the United States in the actual normalization, the Japanese people would not accept such a verdict."[8]

Unlike the U.S. decision, Sato's response to the Nixon shock was based not on a strategic analysis of international relations but on the "weight" of China in the long history of the special relationship between the two countries, which had dictated Japan's China policy during the U.S.-China confrontation of the 1950s and 1960s. Japan's dealings with communist China during those years were little affected by security considerations, despite the premium Japan placed on its security relations with the United States.[9] Japan's rapid and overall tilt toward Beijing in the 1970s was thus a manifestation of its pro-China inclinations and its long-held desire for continuing economic relations with China despite the cold war security structure and its own alliance with the United States. In the judgment of Japanese leaders, the move did not involve fundamental changes in the security relationship with the United States, nor did it have implications for the regional security structure.

Despite this strong inclination on the part of the Japanese government to maintain its security relationship with the United States while normalizing its diplomatic relations with China, Nixon was concerned that Japan's decision might have implications for the regional security structure. In particular, Nixon feared that Japan's hasty move would lead to unnecessary concessions to China over the question of Taiwan. Here, a gap apparently existed between the U.S. preoccupation with the highly strategic dimensions of the development and the Japanese preoccupation with the imperatives, which was conditioned by their inclination to maintain nonstrategic relations with their neighbors.

After the Nixon shock, Sato's early attempts to contact China by various means were met with a firm Chinese denial. In Japan, too, the dominant feeling was that Sato had been around too long and should step down with the reversion of Okinawa on May 15, 1972, for which he had worked so hard. On June 17, soon after the return of Okinawa, Sato announced his resignation. An important aspect of the public mood was the sense that Sato would be unable to improve relations with China.

In the Liberal Democratic Party presidential election in July, Tanaka Kakuei defeated Fukuda Takeo, who had received Sato's full support. On July 7, after the first cabinet meeting, Tanaka declared that he would hasten diplomatic normalization with China, a statement to which Zhou Enlai responded positively two days later. Thus, with the establishment of the Tanaka administration, diplomatic normalization was already a foregone conclusion. Tanaka was determined to seize on the momentum of U.S.-China rapprochement and achieve normalization as quickly as possible.

The Chinese side presented its draft version of a joint communiqué to establish diplomatic normalization to Takeiri Yoshikatsu, chair of the Clean Government Party, who visited China on July 25. Within the Japanese Foreign Ministry, these Chinese proposals were closely examined. At the end of July, a small working group of officials was established in the ministry, and by early September it had completed a Japanese draft of a joint communiqué.[10]

In the meantime, Tanaka met with Nixon on August 31 and September 1, 1972, in Honolulu. Kissinger's memorandum for Nixon reiterated the importance of the U.S.-Japan alliance and the security of Taiwan, saying that the objectives at the Honolulu meeting should be:

> To reaffirm the U.S.-Japan alliance, not only as a general proposition—which Tanaka accepts—but also as a relationship which requires concrete contributions by both sides to keep it going. E.g., while we furnish nuclear protection, the Japanese must make it possible for us to use Japanese bases.
>
> To assure that Japan's move to normalize relations with Peking will not inhibit our use of our Japanese bases in fulfillment of our defense commitments to Taiwan and South Korea.[11]

In Honolulu, Tanaka in fact reaffirmed Japan's strong continuing commitment to the U.S.-Japan security relationship after diplomatic normalization with China. In particular, he made it clear that the disruption of diplomatic relations with Taiwan would not mean a change in the status of

Taiwan in the U.S.-Japan security arrangements.[12] This position was a natural extension of the Japanese government's fundamental security policy, which was premised on its security relationship with the United States.

Actual negotiations between Japan and China were brief, and the joint communiqué to establish diplomatic normalization was signed on September 29, 1972, less than three months after the inauguration of the Tanaka cabinet. The Japanese negotiators concentrated their main efforts on the legal issues, particularly the question of compatibility between the communiqué and the Japan-Taiwan peace treaty signed in 1952.[13] These issues were settled primarily through concessions on the part of the Chinese government, a clear indication that Chinese leaders were eager to establish normalization. Domestically, they were concerned that political opposition might gain strength, while externally, strategic considerations prevailed over legal details. This was demonstrated by article 7 of the joint communiqué, which stated that "The normalization of relations between Japan and China is not directed against any third country. Neither of the two countries should seek hegemony in the Asia-Pacific region and each is opposed to efforts by any other country or group of countries to establish such hegemony." The anti-Soviet implications of this clause were obvious to Chinese leaders.

The Japanese accepted this "antihegemony" clause as a quid pro quo for Chinese concessions, since it did not concern strategic issues.[14] This is not to say, however, that the Japanese side was unaware of the anti-Soviet nature of the clause, which was reflected in its own insistence on the third country clause. Nonetheless, what stood out in the Japanese response was a determination not to be involved in the strategic dynamics of the Sino-Soviet rift, U.S.-China rapprochement, and U.S.-Soviet détente.

Prime Minister Tanaka later summarized his views on the Japan-China normalization of relations. First, for Japan the China issue was "a domestic issue rather than a diplomatic issue," and "the settlement of the China issue removes two-thirds of the domestic problems." Second, the combined population of the two nations "comprises one-fourth of the world's population. Without the settlement of such relations, Japan would have no stability." Third, "Japan should establish friendly relations with China alongside [maintaining] the Japan-U.S. security treaty. With the formation of the triangular relationship among Japan, the United States, and China, peace in the Far East is secured."[15] For Tanaka, as these remarks reveal, Japan-China diplomatic normalization, a domestic problem, came first; then his version of the special relationship with China; and finally, regional security considerations.

This last point, however, did not reflect the same strategic imperatives motivating the United States or China or even, for that matter, the Soviet Union. It simply reveals that Tanaka was excited about the fact that the Japan-U.S. security relationship and Japan-China diplomatic normalization were finally compatible because the United States no longer objected to closer relations between Japan and China. For many others in charge of policymaking, this change was the most significant in postwar Japanese diplomacy. Domestically, "two incompatible objectives that had divided Japanese domestic politics for more than two decades" were now reconciled.[16] Those Japanese who wanted to improve relations with China were no longer in opposition to those who wanted to continue good relations with the United States. On the external front, Japan-China diplomatic normalization was considered to be the beginning of a new era: Japanese diplomacy could now develop diversified relations with Asian countries that were also compatible with its most important alliance, that with the United States.

Peace and Friendship Treaty

THE STRATEGIC ENVIRONMENT

In the new international environment of U.S.-China rapprochement and U.S.-Soviet détente, the U.S. government attempted to avoid appearing to be aligning with either China or the Soviet Union against the other and encouraged both to seek a stronger relationship with the United States to gain leverage in their own strategic calculations with the other.

Under the Nixon and Ford administrations U.S. officials endeavored to maintain this "swing" position, despite emerging domestic pressure to use a "China card" against the Soviet Union's intervention in Angola in 1975–76.[17] Naturally, China was not happy about the expansion of U.S. relations with the Soviet Union brought about by SALT II negotiations, grain sales, technology transfers, and the Helsinki Accords signed in the summer of 1975. To continue diplomatic balancing, the Ford administration agreed in December 1975 to the British sale to China of Rolls-Royce Spey jet engines and to the construction of a Spey engine factory in China.[18] Similarly, in October 1976, the United States approved the sales of the Cyper-172 computer systems to both China and the Soviet Union.[19]

With the advent of the Carter administration in January 1977 and the return of Deng Xiaoping to power in July, however, U.S.-China relations shifted into a distinct post–Nixon/Kissinger phase. Toward the end of the 1970s, America's desire to keep its "swing" position was gradually eroded due to Soviet adventurism in the Third World and increasing frustration and doubt among the cold war warriors in the United States about the effectiveness of the détente scheme. As the United States set out to normalize diplomatic relations with China under the Carter administration, U.S. priorities gradually shifted to alignment with China at the expense of the Soviet Union.

By mid-1977 the new Carter administration decided that it would pursue diplomatic normalization with China by accepting the Chinese demand to put an end to U.S. diplomatic relations with Taiwan.[20] For the time being, however, the Carter administration continued to seek improved relations with the Soviet Union, and thus in August 1977, sent Secretary of State Cyrus Vance, a strong proponent of détente with the Soviet Union, to China.[21] In the meantime, Soviet-Cuban intervention in the Ethiopia-Somalia conflict in the Horn of Africa in early 1978 began to affect the Carter administration's approach toward China and the Soviet Union. The turning point was President Carter's decision to send his national security adviser, Zbigniew Brzezinski, to China in May 1978.

At this juncture, Carter himself still hoped for an early conclusion to a SALT II agreement and decided in mid-March to send Vance to Moscow to balance Brzezinski's trip to Beijing.[22] But China and the Soviet Union— and Brzezinski himself—perceived the China trip differently. China was happy about Brzezinski's emphasis on common strategic interests vis-à-vis the Soviet Union,[23] and the Soviet Union saw the visit as the turning point in Carter administration policy "from a relatively considered and even-handed 'triangular diplomacy' to a single-minded pro-Peking and anti-Soviet orientation."[24] The U.S.-China joint communiqué signed in mid-December announced the establishment of diplomatic relations as of January 1979.

In the course of these developments, East Asian international relations again became fluid, especially in Indochina. Amid the uncertain shifts in U.S.-China-Soviet strategic relations, Vietnam, in its desperate effort to recover from the devastation of war, had sought improved relations with the international community, particularly with the Association of Southeast Asian Nations (ASEAN) members and Japan, and diplomatic normalization with the United States.

In the beginning, the Carter administration had also explored the possibility of diplomatic normalization with Vietnam. As a first step in this direction, it had lifted restrictions on travel by Americans to Vietnam on March 9, 1977, and in May began talks with Vietnam on improving relations. After Brzezinski's China visit in May 1978, however, the administration realized that normalizing relations with Vietnam would antagonize China. In October 1978, in order to complete the China transaction, Carter formally decided to suspend negotiations on diplomatic normalization with Vietnam.[25]

The new strategic development in U.S.-China-Soviet relations after May 1978 thus crushed Vietnamese hopes for improved relations with the United States and clouded the political situation in Indochina toward the end of that year. Vietnam still clearly remembered, and strongly resented, its betrayal by China at the end of the Vietnam War. Since 1975, China had stood firmly behind the anti-Vietnam Khmer Rouge government of Cambodia that had severed diplomatic relations with Hanoi in December 1977. In the spring of 1978, Sino-Vietnamese relations worsened further because of Vietnamese treatment of Chinese residents, and in July China decided to suspend all aid to Vietnam. On June 29, shortly before the aid suspension, Vietnam joined the Council for Mutual Economic Assistance (COMECON) and, on November 3, signed a treaty of friendship and cooperation with the Soviet Union. In December, Vietnam invaded Cambodia, with Soviet backing. China meanwhile played the America card: when Deng Xiaoping visited the United States in January 1979, he stated that the Chinese "consider it necessary to put a restraint on the wild ambitions of the Vietnamese and to give them an appropriate limited lesson," and asked the United States to provide "moral support."[26] In February, China invaded Vietnam.

The U.S.-China strategic entente to check Soviet adventurism thus became the central element in the strategic environment toward the latter half of the 1970s. China was linked with the mainstream of the international community. The Khmer Rouge, as a close friend of China, represented Cambodia in its coalition government in the United Nations, while Vietnam, a Soviet ally, was isolated through an economic embargo and sanctions imposed by the international community.

JAPAN-CHINA TREATY OF PEACE AND FRIENDSHIP

In the 1970s, in essence, Japan's basic diplomatic stance toward China was to retain its "autonomy," free from the strategic rivalries between the United States, China, and the Soviet Union. This diplomatic propensity was a peculiar creation of postwar international politics and of Japan's domestic politics. In this context, the pursuit of "autonomous diplomacy" was not equivalent to a quest for an independent strategic role; rather, it reflected hope of remaining independent of military-strategic considerations.

An important example of Japan's pattern of diplomacy in the rapidly changing security environment that followed U.S.-China normalization was the signing of the Japan-China Treaty of Peace and Friendship in August 1978. The treaty was controversial because of the antihegemony clause, which was widely understood to be anti-Soviet. Initially, the Japanese government, fully aware of the clause's implications, resisted its inclusion. Facing China's determination, however, it agreed to the clause but only in tandem with the so-called third country clause, which read: "The present Treaty shall not affect the position of either contracting party regarding its relations with third countries."

This treaty is often interpreted as a sign of Japan's strategic tilt toward China, along the lines of Brzezinski's later strategy, which tilted toward China and away from the Soviet Union. Brzezinski understood the Japanese move in this strategic context as the Japanese government's concurrence with his presentations on his way back from China in May 1978.[27] Both China and the Soviet Union interpreted the major implications of the treaty in the same vein.

Japanese motives, however, lay elsewhere, and the Japanese government argued that the third country clause negated the treaty's anti-Soviet nature and brought it into conformity with Prime Minister Fukuda Takeo's "omnidirectional diplomacy." The Fukuda administration's central motives were in fact much like those of his predecessors, Tanaka Kakuei and Miki Takeo: to solidify friendly, stable relations with China purely at the bilateral level. His considerations remained "nonstrategic." The policy debate in Tokyo gave no indication that the American attitude was of much concern, and by March 1978, well before Brzezinski's trip to China and Japan, Fukuda had decided on the terms of negotiations over the antihegemony clause and the third country clause.[28]

The Japanese government, under Prime Minister Miki Takeo, had already agreed to the inclusion of the antihegemony clause in November 1975 and subsequently proposed its own draft treaty, which included the antihegemony clause. In approaching China, the Miki government attempted to neutralize the treaty's anti-Soviet strategic implications by insisting on four conditions, which were conveyed to Foreign Minister Qiao Guanhua by Foreign Minister Miyazawa Kiichi: (1) hegemony will be opposed not only in the Asia-Pacific region but also anywhere else; (2) antihegemony is not directed against a specific third party; (3) antihegemony does not mean any common action by Japan and China; and (4) a principle that is contradictory to the spirit of the United Nations Charter cannot be accepted.[29]

In 1978, therefore, the issue was not whether Japan would comply with the antihegemony clause but whether China would agree to a third country clause desperately supported by the Japanese side. When the Japanese government proposed its draft treaty in November 1975, the Chinese side was not yet ready to negotiate over a third country clause. The year 1976 was filled with political turmoil in both Japan and China: the Miki cabinet was preoccupied with the handling of the Lockheed scandal and had to resign after a fatal defeat in the lower house elections in December, and China was bogged down in the leadership struggle that followed the deaths of Zhou Enlai and Mao Zedong. The return of Deng Xiaoping to the Chinese leadership group in July 1977 became an important turning point for Sino-Japanese negotiations, just as it was for the process of U.S.-China diplomatic normalization.

The final negotiations in Beijing, from July 21 to August 8, 1978, centered on the third country clause. The wording finally agreed to in Article 4 of the treaty was the result of a compromise between the Japanese proposal ("The present Treaty is not directed against any specific third country") and the Chinese version ("The present Treaty is not directed against any third country that does not seek hegemony").[30]

The Japanese government subsequently insisted that this clause concerning a third country effectively freed Japan from entanglement in the Sino-Soviet rift. Sonoda Sunao, then foreign minister and the Japanese signatory to the treaty, summarized the significance of the peace and friendship treaty with China as follows: First, it opened the way for an expanded development of Japan-China relations. Second, it contributed to the stability of the Asia-Pacific region. Third, it expanded the basis of Japanese diplomacy.[31]

Complexities in the 1980s

STRATEGIC ENVIRONMENT

China in effect used the U.S. card in the process of diplomatic normalization with the United States. Throughout the 1980s, the United States generally regarded China with a bit of romanticism, expecting it to become "like us" through its experiments in reform and its open door policy, which were unprecedented for a socialist country. In China, economic growth and diplomatic advances created a mood of "confident nationalism."[32]

This Chinese confidence was an important part of the background for Deng Xiaoping's open door policy, beginning in the late 1970s, and led to a more complex political and strategic environment in the Asia-Pacific region in the 1980s. With this growing confidence, it was natural for China to incline toward an independent foreign policy. Its relations with the United States in the 1970s constrained China somewhat because the United States held the swing position in the Sino-Soviet rift. Following diplomatic normalization with the United States, the Chinese strategic position improved markedly, and the United States and China now formed a united front against the Soviet Union.

Reflecting upon this improved strategic situation, China in the ensuing years reassessed the international strategic environment and its own place within it and declared its new "independent foreign policy" at the Twelfth Party Congress in 1982. It looked as if China had now assumed a swing position in the heightened cold war between the United States and the Soviet Union, one that allowed China to distance itself from the United States in relative strategic terms.

China's new drive was a source of complications in U.S.-China relations, as seen in the issue of escalated arms sales to Taiwan with the advent of President Ronald Reagan in January 1981.[33] China's perception of its new strategic position also played an important role in its relations with the Soviet Union, for China now felt confident enough to move toward gradual normalization of relations.[34] Despite problems associated with the new strategic imperatives emanating from China, however, U.S.-China relations basically developed apace, and included arms sales and technology transfers from the United States to China, until the Tiananmen incident.

In sum, the strategic environment in the 1980s was composed of a complex mix of key imperatives: the U.S.-China strategic partnership against the

Soviet Union under the dominant new cold war atmosphere, the momentum of improved relations between China and the Soviet Union in the second half of the 1980s, and the Chinese move toward an independent foreign policy in the strategic triangle formed by the three powers.

SPECIAL BILATERAL RELATIONSHIP

This complex strategic environment made it easier for Japan to maintain its "nonstrategic" approach toward China. In the context of heightened tensions between the United States and the Soviet Union, the congruence of interests between the United States and China freed Japan from the difficult problem of defending the U.S.-Japan alliance from Chinese criticism, allowing it to continue to concentrate on "nonstrategic" domains in its relations with China. The importance of the momentum for gradual Sino-Soviet normalization also became obvious in the advent of Mikhail Gorbachev as the Soviet leader in the mid-1980s. The increasing independence in China's foreign policy stance allowed it to continue its special bilateral relationship with Japan, free of strategic considerations vis-à-vis the United States and the Soviet Union. This in turn allowed Japan to continue the "nonstrategic" posture of its China policy throughout much of the 1980s.

Chinese independence, however, became a formidable issue for Japan. The largest and most effective tools available to the Japanese in consolidating a special bilateral relationship with China were economic assistance and business dealings. The Japanese in general, including the government and the business community, were highly motivated by a sense of mission to help China modernize and to strengthen bilateral relations. However, the natural economic logic that gave Japan an important role in the Chinese economy aroused Chinese concern, even suspicion in some cases, about China's economic dependence on Japan and the resulting imbalance in the relationship.

The first such instance was the Chinese cancellation of plant exports, a symbol of new economic relations between Japan and China after the conclusion of the Treaty of Peace and Friendship and the Long-Term Trade Agreement in 1978. In February 1979, China requested a suspension of business contracts, including the contracts for the Baoshan Steel Complex near Shanghai, and in January 1981, it abruptly canceled them.[35]

Although these unilateral decisions shocked Japan, the Japanese government responded with a decision to start massive "official development assistance" (ODA) programs, including yen loans to China, to save the canceled contracts at the initial stage. According to mainstream Japanese thinking at the time, the political rationale underlying this new phase of Japan-China relations was that helping the modernization programs of the current regime in Beijing and securing the stable development of China would best serve Japanese national interests.[36]

The net result of this new development, however, was an imbalance in trade and financial flows, which increased Chinese wariness of excessive dependence on Japan. In addition, as China embarked on an independent foreign policy, it appeared to have reassessed Japan's role and to have begun to believe that Japan, with its economic might, was now interested in growing into a "political power."[37] Here, the "history card" proved an effective way to attempt to redress an overall imbalance.

The first occasion, indeed the very first one in the postwar period, occurred in July 1982, when China made a diplomatic issue out of Japan's textbook inspection results.[38] According to several sources, the Chinese decision came from the very top, from Deng Xiaoping himself, and was designed to close the issue diplomatically by September, when Japanese prime minister Suzuki Zenko was to visit China to celebrate the tenth anniversary of diplomatic normalization. (China in fact accepted Japan's explanation on September 8.) Suzuki visited China on September 26 and reaffirmed the three basic principles of the bilateral relationship (peace and friendship, equality and reciprocity, long-term stability) first articulated by Chinese premier Zhao Ziyang during an official visit to Japan in May-June 1982 and reiterated by General Secretary Hu Yaobang at the Twelfth Party Congress in early September.

Bilateral relations over the ensuing two years were widely believed to be "the best in the two-thousand-year history" of the relationship. Hu Yaobang came to Japan in November 1983 and cemented the relationship with Prime Minister Nakasone Yasuhiro by adding "mutual trust" to the three original principles. Nakasone in turn visited China in March 1984 and committed himself to the second round of Japanese ODA to China totaling ¥470 billion for the 1984–88 period, a huge increase over the total of ¥300 billion provided for the first round in the 1979–83 period.

Nakasone, who became prime minister in November 1982, had stated in the National Diet on February 18, 1983, that the war conducted by Japan in the past was one of aggression; in Beijing he said to an audience at Beijing University that "as the top leader of Japan, I declare without any hesitation that my country would never allow the revival of militarism." Zhao Ziyang was reported to have said to Nakasone that he had no concern about the defense policy of the Nakasone cabinet.[39]

Without changing its fundamental policy of friendship with Japan, China engaged in a delicate balancing act over the history issue as the fortieth anniversary of Japan's defeat in World War II approached. The anniversary occasioned a flood of articles, meetings, special events, and political campaigns in China to educate the Chinese people.[40] Across the Sea of Japan, in Tokyo, Prime Minister Nakasone paid an official visit on August 15 to the Yasukuni Shrine, a memorial to all those who died for their country, including the 2.5 million war dead during World War II. On September 18, the anniversary of Japan's 1931 invasion of Manchuria, a thousand Chinese students marched through Tiananmen Square shouting, "Down with Nakasone," "Down with Japanese militarism," and "Down with Japanese economic invasion." There were hints that the students' frustration was also directed against the Chinese government, which therefore had to balance cooling down the students' spontaneous demonstrations with requests to the Japanese government to stop damaging the feelings of the Chinese people. In the meantime, the Chinese government continued to reaffirm the fundamentally stable bilateral relationship with Japan, and when Zhao Ziyang met Nakasone at the United Nations on October 23, he did not mention the Yasukuni issue.[41]

This balancing act was closely connected to the overall strategic environment. China was highly motivated by its confident nationalism and independent foreign policy. To the extent China felt comfortable in this strategic environment, it felt equally comfortable establishing a stable bilateral relationship with Japan as an independent entity. The Chinese assessment of Japan as a "political power" may have been based on this overall situation.

Naturally, however, a preoccupation with the bilateral context would also highlight negative aspects of the relationship in the eyes of the policymakers, causing cyclical patterns of ups and downs in its overall development. The Japanese decision in December 1986 to exceed the 1 percent of GNP ceiling for its national defense budget and the Kokaryo case in February 1987, in which the Osaka High Court recognized Taiwan's ownership of a Kyoto dormitory for Chinese students,[42] contributed to such a cycle over the remainder of the 1980s.

The climax was Deng Xiaoping's remarks on June 4, 1987, to the effect that the Japanese government should be able to do something about the Kokaryo case, since its system of checks and balances was different from that of the United States. He added that exceeding the 1 percent ceiling of the defense budget would fuel Japanese militarism and continued in these terms: from a historical point of view, Japan should contribute more to assist Chinese development; to be frank, Japan is the country in the world most indebted to China; we did not demand war reparations at the time of diplomatic normalization.[43] Deng's remarks were the first official statement linking the reparation issue and Japan's commitment to Chinese modernization and development.

Two years later, during Gorbachev's visit to China to complete the normalization of Sino-Soviet relations, the Tiananmen incident occurred, ushering in a new period of Japan-China relations in response to the major transformation of the international system.

Conclusions

This essay has portrayed the nature of Japan's approach to China as basically "nonstrategic" and has indicated that the key to understanding the structure of the U.S.-China-Japan triangle is to regard it as fundamentally asymmetrical. Throughout the postwar years, the United States and China have both been prepared to play highly strategic games by recognizing each other as a strategic counterpart. In contrast, neither has been ready or willing to recognize Japan as such, albeit often for different policy reasons.

Many policymakers (as well as many analysts) in Washington and Beijing, however, have not really appreciated the fact that Japan's junior status in the asymmetrical triangular relationship has been more or less recognized and accepted by the central decision-makers in the Japanese government. This lack of appreciation for Japan's willingness to accept a lesser political role has been an important source of confusion in conceptualizing the place and role of Japan in the triangular relationship and, by extension, in the management of the triangle.

One specific indication of such failure is the confusion over Japan's move toward "autonomous diplomacy," which had begun to emerge in the late 1960s and gained momentum in the 1970s; during that decade, the phrase became a catchword to characterize Japanese diplomacy after the Nixon shock and U.S.-China rapprochement. Diplomatic normalization and nego-tiations over the peace and friendship treaty between Japan and China were conducted in this political atmosphere.

U.S.-China relations were influenced by the strategic considerations of both countries, which shaped the overall political and strategic environment of the time. Japanese diplomacy, however, did not necessarily present itself as a deviation from or a challenge to this dominant strategic environment; rather, it attempted to distance Japan from the strategic imperatives moving the United States, China, and the Soviet Union without contradicting them.

Thus, from a Japanese point of view, Japan's aspiration for "autonomous diplomacy" did not necessarily run counter to the fundamental importance of the U.S.-Japan security relationship, nor did it reflect any alternative stra-tegic imperative. What stood out in Japan's approach was its unwillingness to be involved in strategic rivalries among the United States, China, and the Soviet Union. This overall inclination was reinforced by Japan's desire to forge a special relationship with China on its own merits. The Japanese wish to help modernize China and contribute to its stability as well as to the bi-lateral relationship between the two countries was genuine. Japan's sense of guilt about the war calamities it had brought to China and China's historical "weight" both played an important role in shaping its China policy.

Throughout the period under examination, China took advantage of Ja-pan's pro-China inclinations in pursuit of its own interests, including strate-gic ones. In the context of this special relationship, the history issue became a potential source of ongoing tension between the two governments and peoples. Nonetheless, during the two decades under examination, the rela-tively benign, nonstrategic nature of the relationship pushed this problem to the background. Since 1989, when the end of the cold war and the Tianan-men incident affected the strategic landscape surrounding China, however, Sino-Japanese relations have entered a new post–cold war phase. This in-surmountable gap in the ways each side reflects on the history of Japanese wartime aggression was the fundamental cause of a vicious cycle. In the pres-ent post–cold war context, in which both Japan and China appear to be re-assessing their policies and adjusting to a changing international environ-ment, China's recognition of the usefulness of Japan's pro-China policy appears to be rapidly waning amid ever widening gaps in both countries' mu-tual perceptions.

Reference Matter

Notes

Chapter 1: *Michel Oksenberg, U.S. Politics and Asian Policy*

This was one of the last papers written by Michel Oksenberg, a research professor at Stanford University, before his untimely death from cancer.

Chapter 2: *Zhang Baijia, Chinese Politics and Asian Policy*

1. Robert Ross and Jiang Changbin, eds., *Re-examining the Cold War: U.S.-China Diplomacy, 1954–1973* (Cambridge, Mass.: Harvard University Asia Center, 2001), p. 74.

2. See memorandum of conversation between Mao and Nixon, February 24, 1972, in William Burr, ed., *The Kissinger Transcripts: The Top Secret Talks with Beijing and Moscow* (New York: New Press, 1999).

3. As we know, from 1949 until 1960, while China was "leaning to one side," China's foreign policy was strongly coordinated with ideology. In the process of the break with the Soviet Union beginning in 1959, China's foreign policy began to separate from ideology, but such contradictions were concealed by a more radical ideology. The main reason China gave for its opposition to the Soviet Union, besides the conflicts between the national interests of the two countries, was that the Soviet Union did not go all out to support the revolutionary movement of the people of the world: it was soft in the struggle against American imperialism, holding to the illusion that the tension between it and the United States could be alleviated and

attempting to dominate the world along with the United States. Sino-American reconciliation in the early 1970s could no longer conceal the contradiction between China's foreign policy and its ideology, although the Chinese people pretended not to know this.

4. Between 1967 and 1969, the PRC maintained a roughly $4 billion foreign trade volume each year. The following two years registered minor growth, and from 1972 onward, after the improvement of relations with Japan and the West, there was a tremendous increase. The volume of foreign trade hit a peak of $14.57 billion in 1974 but quickly dropped during 1975 and 1976, the last two years of the cultural revolution.

5. Zhang Shujun, *Da Zhuanzhe: Zhonggong Shiyijie Sanzhong Quanhui Shilu* (The Great Turning Point: A Record of the Third Plenum of the Eleventh Party Congress of the Chinese Communist Party) (Hangzhou: Zhejiang Remin Chubanshe, 1998), p. 158.

6. Speech by Li Xiannian at a conference convened by the State Council to discuss principles, September 9, 1978; speech by Hua Guofeng on Central Working Conference, November 10, 1978.

7. Li Xianqian, "Deng Xiaoping Yu Shiyijie Sanzhong Quanhui" (Deng Xiaoping and the Third Plenary of the Central Committee of the Chinese Communist Party), in Yu Guangyuan et al., *Gaibian Zhongguo Mingyun de Sishiyi Tian* (The 41 Days That Changed the Destiny of China) (Shenzhen: Haitian Publishing House, 1998), pp. 10–11.

8. For 36 days, between November 10 and December 15, 1978, the CCP Central Committee held the Working Conference, at which the major issues relevant to domestic and foreign policy were discussed. Between December 18 and 22, the Third Plenary Session promulgated a fundamental policy change, advocating that economic development should be the central task and first priority for the nation. This has generally been acknowledged as the starting point of China's "reform and opening."

9. Wu Xuewen et al., *Zhong Ri Guanxi, 1945–1994* (Sino-Japanese Relations, 1945–1994) (Beijing: Shishi Chubanshe, 1995), p. 223.

10. Han Nianlong, ed., *Dangdai Zhongguo Waijiao* (Contemporary Diplomacy of China) (Beijing: Zhongguo Shehui Kexue Chubanshe, 1988), p. 230.

11. Deng Xiaoping's talk to nine comrades, including Li Xiannian, Xu Shiyou, and Le Desheng, December 1, 1978.

12. Ye Jianying's speech on the Central Working Conference, December 13, 1978.

13. Li Xiangqian, "Zhong Mei Jianjiao Yu Quandang Gongzuo Zhaozhongdian de Zhanlue Zhuanyi" (The Establishment of Sino-American Diplomatic Relations and the Strategic Change of the Key Works of the Whole Party), *Zonggong Dangshi Yanjiu* (The Study of the History of the CCP) [Beijing], no. 1, 2000.

14. *Deng Xiaoping Wenxuan: Dierjuan* (Selected Works of Deng Xiaoping), vol. 2 (Beijing: Renmin Chubanshe, 1994), p. 91.

15. Ibid., p. 240.

16. In the 1950s, China adopted the policy of "leaning to one side," aligning with the Soviet Union against the United States; in the 1960s, it adopted the policy of "opposing two hegemonies," the Soviet Union and the United States; in the 1970s, it adopted a "one line" policy, uniting with the United States, Japan, and Western Europe against the Soviet Union; in the 1980s, it gradually developed an omnidirectional foreign policy.

17. Party History Research Institute of the Central Committee of the Chinese Communist Party, ed., *Zhongguo Gongchandang Xin Shiqi Lishi Dashiji* (Main Facts in the New Epoch of the Chinese Communist Party) (Beijing: Zhonggong Dangshi Chubanshe, 1998), p. 271.

18. Ibid., p. 280.

19. Ibid., p. 282.

20. *Deng Xiaoping Wenxuan: Disanjuan* (Selected works of Deng Xiaoping), vol. 3, pp. 311, 312, 321.

Chapter 3: *Kamiya Matake, Japanese Politics and Asian Policy*

1. For a detailed analysis of the one-party dominant system in Japanese politics since 1955, see Sato Seizaburo and Matsuzaki Tetsuhisa, *Jiminto Seiken* (Tokyo: Chuo Koron-sha, 1986).

2. This section is based mainly on the following materials: Nakano Shiro, *Tanaka Seiken 886-nichi* (Tokyo: Gyosei Mondai Kenkyujo, 1982); Nakamura Keiichiro, *Miki Seiken 747-nichi* (Tokyo: Gyosei Mondai Kenkyujo, 1981); Kiyomiya Ryu, *Fukuda Seiken 714-nichi* (Tokyo: Gyosei Mondai Kenkyujo, 1984); Kawauchi Issei, *Ohira Seiken 554-nichi* (Tokyo: Gyosei Mondai Kenkyujo, 1982); Uji Toshihiko, *Suzuki Seiken 863-nichi* (Tokyo: Gyosei Mondai Kenkyujo, 1983); Maki Taro, *Nakasone Seiken 1806-nichi*, 2 vols. (Tokyo: Gyoken, 1988); Goto Kenji, *Takeshita Seiken 576-nichi* (Tokyo: Gyoken, 2000); Watanabe Akio, ed., *Sengo Nihon no Saishotachi* (Tokyo: Chuo Koron-sha, 1995); Shiratori Rei, ed., *Nihon no Naikaku 3* (Tokyo: Shin Hyoron, 1981); Uchida Kenzo, Kinbara Samon, and Furuya Tetsuo, eds., *Nihon Gikai-Shiroku 6* (Tokyo: Daiichi Hoki, 1990); Nakamura Takafusa, *Showa-shi 2* (Tokyo: Toyo Keizai Shinpo-sha, 1993); Watanabe Akio, *Taikoku Nihon no Yuragi 1972–* (Tokyo: Chuo Koron Shin-sha, 2000).

3. Nakamura, *Showa-shi 2*, p. 584.

4. The public opinion poll conducted by *Asahi Shinbun* on August 29–30, 1972, quoted in Watanabe, *Taikoku Nihon no Yuragi*, p. 233.

5. Goto Motoo, Uchida Kenzo, and Ishikawa Masumi, *Sengo Hoshu Seiji no Kiseki* (Tokyo: Iwanami Shoten, 1982), pp. 299–300.

6. Sato and Matsuzaki, *Jiminto Seiken*, pp. 22–24.

7. Senda Hisashi, "Suzuki Zenko Naikaku," in Shiratori, ed., *Nihon no Naikaku 3*, pp. 261–63.

8. Senda, "Suzuki Zenko Naikaku," p. 258; Uji, *Suzuki Seiken 863–nichi*, p. 40.

9. Senda, "Suzuki Zenko Naikaku," p. 265.

10. Igarashi Takeshi, "Miyazawa Kiichi," in Watanabe, ed., *Sengo Nihon no Saisho tachi*, p. 429.

11. Nakamura, *Showa-shi 2*, p. 682.

12. For a typical example of this line of argument, see Kenneth N. Waltz, "The Emerging Structure of International Politics," *International Security* 18, no. 2 (Fall 1993).

13. Kamiya Matake, "Kaigai ni okeru Nihon Kaku Buso-ron," *Kokusai Mondai* 426 (September 1995).

14. For one of the best English explanations of Japan's postwar pacifism, see Thomas U. Berger, "From Sword to Chrysanthemum," *International Security* 17, no. 4 (Spring 1993). Berger uses the term "anti-militarism" instead of "pacifism."

15. Takemura Masayoshi, *Chiisaku-tomo Kirari to Hikaru Kuni, Nippon* (Tokyo: Kobunsha, 1994).

16. Kuriyama Takakazu, "Gekido no 90-nendai to Nihon Gaiko no Shin-tenkai," *Gaiko Forum* (May 1990): 16.

17. NHK Hoso Yoron Kenkyu-jo, *Zusetsu Sengo Yoron-shi Dai-2–han* (Tokyo: Nippon Hoso Shuppan Kyokai, 1982), p. 169; Eto Shinkichi and Yamamoto Yoshinobu, *Sogo Anpo to Mirai no Sentaku* (Tokyo: Kodan-sha, 1991), pp. 446–47.

18. NHK Hoso Yoron Kenkyu-jo, *Zusetsu Sengo Yoron-shi Dai-2–han*, p. 169; Eto and Yamamoto, *Sogo Anpo to Mirai no Sentaku*, pp. 446–47.

19. Uji, *Suzuki Seiken 863–nichi*, p. 189; Tanaka Zenichiro, "Suzuki Zenko," in Watanabe, ed., *Sengo Nihon no Saisho-tachi*, p. 327.

20. Since Prime Minister Sato declared the "Three Principles on Arms Export" in 1967, the Japanese government has put strict controls on exports of military weapons and military technology. In 1976 Prime Minister Miki tightened these restrictions. In 1983, Prime Minister Nakasone made the transfer of Japanese military technology to the United States possible by deciding not to apply these rules to the United States.

21. Asano Kazuhiro, "Nichibei Keizai Masatsu no Hen'yo," in Asano Kazuhiro, *Nichibei Shuno Kaidan to "Gendai Seiji"* (Tokyo: Dobunkan, 2000), p. 165.

22. Reinhard Drifte, *Japan's Foreign Policy in the 1990s: From Economic Superpower to What Power?* (New York: St. Martin's Press, 1996), p. 28; Nonaka Naoto, "Institutional Exhaustion of Strategic Thinking: Domestic Factors of the Transformation of Japan's Asian Diplomacy," paper presented at the first conference on "The China-

Japan-United States Triangle" held at Harvard University, Cambridge, Massachusetts, January 14–16, 1999, p. 16.

23. Arai Shunzo and Morita Hajime, *Bunjin Saisho Ohira Masayoshi* (Tokyo: Shunju-sha, 1982), p. 321, quoted in Muramatsu Norio, "Ohira Masayoshi," in Watanabe, ed., *Sengo Nihon no Saisho-tachi*, p. 308.

24. Ochiai Kotaro, *Kaitei Nichibei Keizai Masatsu* (Tokyo: Keio Tsushin, 1994), p. 106.

25. Ogata Sadako, *Sengo Nicchu, Beichu Kankei*, trans. Yoshihide Soeya (Tokyo: University of Tokyo Press, 1992), p. 25.

26. Tanaka Akihiko, *Nicchu Kankei 1945–1990* (Tokyo: University of Tokyo Press, 1991), p. 72.

27. Ogata, *Sengo Nicchu, Beichu Kankei*, p. 75.

28. Watanabe, *Taikoku Nihon no Yuragi*, p. 234.

29. Iizuka Shigetaro, "Fukuda Takeo Naikaku," in Shiratori, ed., *Nihon no Naikaku 3*, p. 196.

30. Watanabe, *Taikoku Nihon no Yuragi*, p. 273.

31. Kamiya Matake, "Japanese Foreign Policy Toward Northeast Asia," in *Japanese Foreign Policy Today*, ed. Takashi Inoguchi and Purnendra Jain (New York: Palgrave, 2000).

32. Kiyomiya, *Fukuda Seiken 714-nichi*, pp. 179 and 214; Iokibe Makoto, "Fukuda Takeo," in Watanabe, ed., *Sengo Nihon no Saisho-tachi*, pp. 294–95.

33. Osaki Yuji, "Arata-na Nicchu Kankei no Kochiku: Ajia Taiheiyo ni okeru Nicchu Kankei," in *Nihon, Amerika, Chugoku: Kyocho eno Shinario*, ed. Kokubun Ryosei (Tokyo: TBS Britannica, 1997), p. 180; Tanaka, *Nicchu Kankei*, p. 108.

34. Kamiya, "Japanese Foreign Policy Toward Northeast Asia."

35. Osaki, "Arata-na Nicchu Kankei no Kochiku," pp. 180–81.

36. Yomiuri Shinbun-sha Chosa Kenkyu Honbu, ed., *Yoron-chosa ni Miru Nichibei Kankei*, Yomiuri Bukkuretto no. 21 (Tokyo: Yomiuri Shinbun-sha, 2000), pp. 48–51.

37. Sekai-Heiwa Kenkyu-jo, ed., *Nakasone Naikaku-shi Shiryo-hen (Zoku)* (Tokyo: Marunouchi-shuppan, 1997), p. 21.

38. Sekai-Heiwa Kenkyu-jo, ed., *Nakasone Naikaku-shi Rinen to Seisaku* (Tokyo: Marunouchi-shuppan, 1995), p. 794.

39. Sekai-Heiwa Kenkyu-jo, ed., *Nakasone Naikaku-shi Shiryo-hen* (Tokyo: Marunouchi-shuppan, 1995), pp. 631–32.

40. For example, see Kosaka Masataka, *Nihon Sonbo no Toki* (Tokyo: Kodansha, 1992); and Kosaka, "'Gaiko o Shiranai' Futatsu no Taikoku," *Astion* (Summer 1994).

41. Sekai-Heiwa Kenkyu-jo, ed., *Nakasone Naikaku-shi Shiryo-hen*, p. 620.

42. Sekai-Heiwa Kenkyu-jo, ed., *Nakasone Naikaku-shi Rinen to Seisaku*, p. 45.

43. Ibid., p. 320.

44. Muroyama Yoshimasa, *Nichi-bei Anpo Taisei* (Tokyo: Yuhikaku, 1992), chap. 2, sec. 7, and chap. 3, sec. 4.

45. Donald C. Hellmann, "Japanese Politics and Foreign Policy: Democracy Within an American Greenhouse," in *The Political Economy of Japan*, vol. 2: *The Changing International Context*, ed. Takashi Inoguchi and Daniel I. Okimoto (Stanford: Stanford University Press, 1988), p. 377.

46. In the January 1983 poll, the approval rating of the Nakasone Cabinet was 39.6 percent. In the February poll, it dropped to 34.5 percent. Sekai-Heiwa Kenkyu-jo, ed., *Nakasone Naikaku-shi Hibi no Chosen* (Tokyo: Marunouchi-shuppan, 1996), p. 180.

47. Ibid. pp. 180, 188–89.

48. Sekai-Heiwa Kenkyu-jo, ed., *Nakasone Naikaku-shi Shiryo-hen (Zoku)*, p. 25.

49. Sekai-Heiwa Kenkyu-jo, ed., *Nakasone Naikaku-shi Hibi no Chosen*, p. 143.

Chapter 4: Robert S. Ross, U.S. Relations with China

1. This episode is discussed in Robert S. Ross, *Negotiating Cooperation: The United States and China, 1969–1989* (Stanford: Stanford University Press, 1995), chap. 2, and in Gong Li, "Chinese Decision Making and the Thawing of U.S.-China Relations," in Jiang Changbin and Robert S. Ross, eds., *Re-examining the Cold War: U.S.-China Diplomacy, 1954–1973* (Cambridge: Asia Center, Harvard University, 2001).

2. See Gong Li, *Kuayue: 1969–1979 nian Zhong Mei guanxi de yanbian* (Across the chasm: The evolution of U.S.-China relations, 1969–1979) (Henan: Henan People's Press, 1992), p. 103.

3. Ross, *Negotiating Cooperation*, p. 52.

4. Michael Schaller, "Détente and the Strategic Triangle: Or, 'Drinking Your Mao Tai and Having Your Vodka, Too'" in Ross and Jiang, eds., *Re-examining the Cold War*.

5. On China's postwar economic relationship with China, see Yoshihide Soeya, *Japan's Economic Diplomacy with China, 1945–1978* (Oxford: Clarendon Press, 1998); Chae-Jin Lee, *Japan Faces China: Politics and Economics in the Postwar Era* (Baltimore: Johns Hopkins University Press, 1976).

6. Lee, *Japan Faces China*. On Sato's China policy, see Sadako Ogata, *Normalization with China: A Comparative Study of U.S. and Japanese Processes* (Berkeley: Institute of East Asian Studies, University of California, 1988), pp. 37–40; Michael Schaller, *Altered States: The United States and Japan Since the Occupation* (New York: Oxford University Press, 1997).

7. Roger Buckley, *U.S.-Japan Alliance Diplomacy, 1945–1990* (New York: Cambridge University Press, 1992), p. 133.

8. Schaller, "Détente and the Strategic Triangle"; Soeya, *Japan's Economic Diplomacy with China, 1945–1978*, pp. 109–13. For a comprehensive discussion of the

domestic politics of Tanaka's visit, see Quansheng Zhao, *Japanese Policymaking—The Politics Behind Politics: The Informal Mechanisms and the Making of China Policy* (Westport, Conn.: Praeger, 1993), pt. 3; Haruhiro Fukui, "Tanaka Goes to Beijing: A Case Study in Foreign Policymaking, in T. J. Pempel, ed., *Policymaking in Contemporary Japan* (Ithaca: Cornell University Press, 1977).

9. Ross, *Negotiating Cooperation*, pp. 73–74.

10. Ibid., pp. 78–79.

11. Ibid., pp. 80–86.

12. This discussion draws from Lee Chae-Jin, "The Making of the Sino-Japanese Peace and Friendship Treaty," *Pacific Affairs* 52, no. 3 (Fall 1979).

13. Soeya, *Japan's Economic Diplomacy with China, 1945–1978*, chap. 7.

14. Ross, *Negotiating Cooperation*, pp. 104–7.

15. See Raymond L. Garthoff, *Détente and Confrontation: American-Soviet Relations from Nixon to Reagan* (Washington, D.C.: The Brookings Institution, 1985), pp. 100–103, 624–26, 856–57, 899.

16. Robert M. Gates, *From the Shadows: The Ultimate Insider's Story of Five Presidents and How They Won the Cold War* (New York: Simon and Schuster, 1996), pp. 122–23.

17. Lee, "The Sino-Japanese Peace and Friendship Treaty," pp. 432–33; Schaller, *Altered States*, p. 253; Zbigniew Brzezinski, *Power and Principle: Memoirs of the National Security Advisor, 1977–1981* (New York: Farrar, Straus and Giroux, 1983), pp. 216–18.

18. Soeya, *Japan's Economic Diplomacy with China, 1945–1978*, pp. 140–43; Lee, "The Sino-Japanese Peace and Friendship Treaty," pp. 432–33.

19. Robert E. Bedelski, *The Fragile Entente: The 1978 Japan-China Peace Treaty in a Global Context* (Boulder: Westview Press 1983), pp. 66, 99, 158.

20. This paragraph and the subsequent discussion draw on Ross, *Negotiating Cooperation*, chap. 6.

21. Caroline Rose, *Interpreting History in Sino-Japanese Relations: A Case Study in Political Decision-Making* (New York: Routledge, 1999), pp. 53–54.

22. Akihiko Tanaka, *Nitchu Kankei, 1945–1990* (Sino-Japanese relations, 1945–1990) (Tokyo: Tokyo Daigaku Shuppansha, 1991), cited in Rose, *Interpreting History*, pp. 55–56. On Hu Yaobang's visit, see Laura Newby, *Sino-Japanese Relations: China's Perspective* (London: Routledge, 1988), pp. 64–65.

23. Rose, *Interpreting History*, pp. 54–55.

24. The most thorough study of this episode is Rose, *Interpreting History*. For a discussion of the incident in the larger context of Sino-Japanese relations, see Hidenori Ijiri, "Sino-Japanese Controversy Since 1972 Diplomatic Normalization," in *China and Japan: History, Trends, and Prospects*, ed. Christopher Howe (Oxford: Oxford University Press, 1996), pp. 64–69; and Allen S. Whiting, *China Eyes Japan* (Berkeley: University of California Press, 1989), pp. 46–51.

25. Ross, *Negotiating Cooperation*, chap. 7.

26. This analysis is based on Robert S. Ross, "China Learns to Compromise: Change in U.S.-China Relations, 1982–1984," *China Quarterly*, no. 128 (December 1991).

27. Ross, *Negotiating Cooperation*, p. 205.

28. He Fang, "Lun Mei Su zhengdou de xin taishi" (On the new situation in the U.S.-Soviet contention), *Shijie Jingji yu Zhengzhi Neican*, no. 11 (1983).

29. This period is covered well in Ijiri, "Sino-Japanese Controversy," in Whiting, *China Eyes Japan*, and in Newby, *Sino-Japanese Relations*.

30. Newby, *Sino-Japanese Relations*, pp. 42, 71–72; Allen S. Whiting, "China and Japan: Politics versus Economics," *Annals of the American Academy of Political and Social Science* 519 (January 1992): 42.

31. For a discussion of Deng's policy retreat in 1989 and 1990, see Joseph Fewsmith, *Dilemmas of Chinese Reform* (Armonk, N.Y.: M. E. Sharpe, 1994), pp. 246–49.

32. Deng Xiaoping, *Wenxuan Disanjuan* (Selected works of Deng Xiaoping), vol. 3 (Beijing: Renmin Chubanshe, 1993), pp. 331–32.

33. This period in U.S. China policy is discussed in greater detail in Robert S. Ross, "The Diplomacy of Tiananmen: Two-level Bargaining and Great Power Cooperation," *Security Studies* 10, no. 2 (Winter 2000–2001); and Robert S. Ross, "The Origins of Engagement: The Bush Administration and China," in *Making China Policy: Lessons from the Bush and Clinton Administrations*, ed. Ramon Myers, Michel Oksenberg, and David Shambaugh (Lanham, Md.: Rowman and Littlefield, 2001).

34. See the testimony of Secretary of State James Baker to the Committee on Foreign Relations, U.S. Senate, in *Future of U.S.-Soviet Relations* (Washington, D.C.: U.S. Government Printing Office, 1989), pp. 939–40. The value of the pending loans is discussed in Committee on Foreign Affairs, U.S. House of Representatives, *Human Rights and Political Developments in China* (Washington, D.C.: U.S. Government Printing Office, 1989), p. 55.

35. *New York Times* (hereafter *NYT*), July 8, 1989; *Washington Post*, July 10, 1989; *Washington Post*, July 31, 1989; *Washington Post*, October 3, 1989; *NYT*, August 10, 1989; *Washington Post*, September 6, 1989; *NYT*, September 7, 1989; *Washington Post*, October 29, 1989; Committee on Foreign Affairs, U.S. House of Representatives, *United States Policy Toward China* (Washington, D.C.: Government Printing Office, 1990), p. 72; Committee on Foreign Relations, U.S. Senate, *U.S. Policy Toward China*, p. 54; *Los Angeles Times*, October 27, 1989; *Washington Post*, December 12, 1989; *Washington Post*, November 23, 1989; *Washington Post*, editorial, November 30, 1989; *NYT*, editorial, November 29, 1989. For congressional reaction, see *NYT*, December 1, 1989; *Washington Post*, December 10, 1989; *NYT*, December 12, 1989. On White House lobbying efforts, see *NYT*, January 25 and January 26, 1990, and the president's January 25, 1990, news conference in Office of the Federal Register, National Archives and Records Administration, *Weekly Compilation of Presidential Documents*,

January 29, 1990, pp. 114–16. Also see the president's November 30, 1989, Memorandum of Disapproval for the Bill Providing Emergency Chinese Immigration Relief.

36. Deng Xiaoping, *Wenxuan Disanjuan*, pp. 330–33, 350–51. Also see *Xinhua*, October 31, 1989; *FBIS/PRC*, October 31, 1989, p. 4; *Xinhua*, October 30, 1989, *FBIS/PRC*, October 31, 1989, pp. 4–5; *Xinhua*, November 1, 1989, *FBIS/PRC*, November 2, 1989, p. 5; *Xinhua*, November 8, 1989, *FBIS/PRC*, November 9, 1989, pp. 6–7. On the U.S. domestic response, see, for example, the editorials in *NYT*, December 12, 1989; *NYT*, December 15, 1989; *Washington Post*, December 11, 1989. On the congressional reaction, see, for example, *Washington Post*, December 10, 1989; Committee on Foreign Relations, U.S. Senate, *U.S. Policy Toward China*, pp. 32–33.

37. Interview with a Chinese government foreign policy analyst. This period is well-covered in David Shambaugh, "China and Japan Towards the Twenty-First Century: Rivals for Preeminence or Complex Interdependence?," in Howe, *China and Japan*, and in Whiting, "China and Japan: Politics versus Economics."

38. Japanese policy is discussed in Ijiri, "Sino-Japanese Controversy" and in Shambaugh, "Towards the Twenty-First Century."

39. For Japan's role in U.S.-China relations, see Seiichiro Takagi, "Human Rights in Japanese Foreign Policy: Japan's Policy Towards China after Tiananmen," in *Human Rights and International Relations in the Asia-Pacific Region*, ed. James T. H. Tang (London: Pinter, 1995), and Seiichiro Takagi, "The Role of the Asia-Pacific Region in the Formation of U.S. China Policy," paper prepared for the conference "Forging a Consensus: Making China Policy in the Bush and Clinton Administrations," Miller Center of Public Affairs, University of Virginia, December 3–5, 1999.

40. George Bush, *All the Best: My Life in Letters and Other Writings* (New York: Scribner, 1999), p. 435.

41. Interview with a Bush administration official.

42. On Chinese policy toward Japan, see Robert S. Ross, *Managing a Changing Relationship: China's Japan Policy in the 1990s* (Carlisle, Pa.: Strategic Studies Institute, U.S. Army War College, 1996). On Japan's China policy, see Michael Green and Benjamin Self, *Survival* 38, no. 2.

Chapter 5: *Jia Qingguo, Chinese Relations with the United States*

The author wishes to take this opportunity to thank Professor Ezra Vogel and the others at the Tokyo conference in January 2000 for their critical comments on this essay and their useful suggestions. The author is of course fully responsible for any errors or inadequacies.

1. Jia Qingguo, *Wei shixian de hejie: zhongmei guanxi de gehe yu weiji* (Unmaterialized rapprochement: differences and crises of Sino-American relations) (Beijing: Wenhua Yishu Publishing House), pp. 1–24.

2. Daniel S. Papp, *Contemporary International Relations: Frameworks for Understanding*, 4th ed. (New York: Macmillan College Publishing Co., 1994), p. 446; William Keylor, *The Twentieth Century World: An International History*, 2nd ed. (New York: Oxford University Press, 1992), p. 338.

3. Harry Harding, *A Fragile Relationship: The United States and China Since 1972* (Washington D.C.: The Brookings Institution, 1992), p. 36.

4. For a Chinese description of Sino-Soviet military clashes over Zhenbao Island, see Xie Yixian, ed., *Zhongguo waijiao shi: zhonghua renmin gongheguo shiqi, 1949–1979* (A diplomatic history of China: the period of the People's Republic of China, 1949–1979) (Henan: Hennan Renmin Publishing House, 1988), pp. 367–70.

5. Maurice Meisner, *Mao's China and After: A History of the People's Republic* (New York: Free Press, 1986), p. 399.

6. Ibid., pp. 350–56.

7. Xiong Xianghui, "Dakai zhongmei guanxi de qianzou" (The prelude to Sino-American rapprochement), *Xin zhongguo waijiao fengyun*, vol. 4 (Beijing: Shijie Zhishi Publishing House, 1996), pp. 7–24.

8. Zhang Xiaoming, *Lengzhan jiqi yichan* (The cold war and its legacy) (Shanghai: Shanghai Renmin Publishing House, 1998), p. 309.

9. Henry Kissinger, *Diplomacy* (New York: Simon and Schuster, 1994), p. 722.

10. Ibid., pp. 722–23.

11. Ibid., pp. 713–14; in his talk with with the Romanian Communist Party's secretary general, Nicolae Ceausescu, in 1967, Richard Nixon expressed his doubt that any true détente with the Soviets could be achieved until some kind of rapprochement could be reached with China. Richard Nixon, *RN: The Memoirs of Richard Nixon* (New York: Grosset and Dunlap, 1978), p. 281.

12. Ibid., p. 723.

13. Harding, *Fragile Relationship*, pp. 37–38; Kissinger, *Diplomacy*, pp. 723–25.

14. Gong Li, *Zhongmei guanxi redian toushi* (Analysis of the hot spots of Sino-American relations) (Heilongjiang: Heilongjiang Jiaoyu Publishing House, 1996), p. 19. According to Kissinger, the United States failed to pay attention to these two messages for various reasons. See Kissinger, *Diplomacy*, pp. 725–26.

15. Kissinger, *Diplomacy*, p. 726.

16. Gong, *Zhongmei guanxi redian toushi*, p. 21.

17. Ibid., p. 24.

18. Wang Bingnan, *Zhongmei huitan jiunian huigu* (Nine years of Sino-American ambassadorial talks in retrospect) (Beijing: Shijie Zhishi Publishing House, 1985), p. 71.

19. For a review of the ambassadorial talks, see Zhang Baijia and Jia Qingguo, "Steering Wheel, Shock Absorber and Diplomatic Probe in Confrontation: Sino-American Ambassadorial Talks Seen from the Chinese Perspective," in *Re-examining*

the Cold War: U.S.- China Diplomacy, 1954–1973, ed. Robert S. Ross and Jiang Chang-bin (Cambridge: Asia Center, Harvard University, 2001).

20. Kissinger, *Diplomacy,* p. 726.

21. Ibid., p. 727.

22. Ibid., p. 726.

23. Ibid.

24. Ibid., p. 727.

25. James Mann, *About Face: A History of America's Curious Relationship with China, from Nixon to Clinton* (New York: Alfred A. Knopf, 1999), pp. 41–46.

26. Harding, *Fragile Relationship,* pp. 373–77.

27. Nixon, *RN: The Memoirs of Richard Nixon,* p. 580.

28. Gong, *Zhongmei guanxi redian toushi,* pp. 26–27.

29. Ibid., p. 28.

30. Ibid.

31. Harding, *Fragile Relationship,* pp. 48–49.

32. Wu Qingtong, *Zhou Enlai zai wenhua da geming zhong* (Zhou Enlai During the Great Cultural Revolution) (Beijing: Zhonggong Dangshi Publishing House, 1998), p. 160.

33. Ibid., pp. 149–51; 164–67.

34. Harding, *Fragile Relationship,* pp. 46–47.

35. Xue Mouhong, ed., *Dangdai zhonggu waijiao* (Contemporary Chinese foreign policy) (Beijing: Zhongguo Shehui Kexue Publishing House, 1987), p. 225.

36. Ibid., p. 226; Harding, *Fragile Relationship,* pp. 51–52; Gong Li, *Zhongmei guanxi redian toushi,* pp. 95–99.

37. Harding, *Fragile Relationship,* pp. 62–63.

38. Ibid., pp. 74–75.

39. Hao Yufan, *Meiguo duihua zhengce neimu* (Inside story of the U.S. policy toward China, 1949–1998) (Beijing: Taihai Publishing House, 1999), p. 254.

40. Because of the time lag, it was December 15, 1978, in the United States.

41. Hao, *Meiguo duihua zhengce neimu,* pp. 263–68.

42. Ibid., pp. 282–83.

43. Marc J. Cohen and Emma Teng, eds., *Let Taiwan Be Taiwan* (Washington, D.C.: Center for Taiwan International Relations, 1990), pp. 205–6.

44. Hao, *Meiguo duihua zhengce neimu,* pp. 356–57.

45. "Candidate Ronald Reagan's Statement on Taiwan, August 25, 1980," Cohen and Teng, eds., *Let Taiwan Be Taiwan,* pp. 222–23.

46. Ibid, pp. 221–22.

47. *Renmin Ribao,* August 28, 1980.

48. Liu Liandi and Wang Dawei, eds., *Zhongmei guanxi de guiji: jianjiao yilai dashi zonglan* (The trajectory of Sino-American relations: survey of major events) (Beijing: Shishi Publishing House, 1995), p. 12.

49. Ibid., p. 220.

50. "United States-China Joint Communiqué on United States Arms Sales to Taiwan," in Harding, *Fragile Relationship*, pp. 383–85.

51. Harding, *Fragile Relationship*, pp. 116–17.

52. Xie Yixian ed., *Zhongguo waijiao shi: zhonghua renmin gongheguo shiqi, 1979–1994* (A diplomatic history of China: the period of the People's Republic of China, 1979–1994) (Henan: Hennan Renmin Publishing House, 1995), p. 33.

53. Ibid., pp. 33–35.

54. Jia Qingguo and Tang Wei eds., *Jishou de hezuo: zhongmei guanxi de xianzhuang yu qianzhan* (Difficult cooperation: the state and prospect of Sino-American relations) (Beijing: Wenhua Yishu Publishing House, 1998), p. 315.

55. Harding, *Fragile Relationship.*, pp. 208–9.

56. Ibid., p. 53.

57. Liu and Wang, *Zhongmei guanxi de guiji*, p. 277.

58. Ibid., pp. 282–83.

59. Xie Yixian, ed., *Zhongguo waijiao shi: zhonghua renmin gongheguo shiqi, 1979–1994*, pp. 41–42.

60. Ibid., p. 50.

61. Du Gong and Ni Liyu, eds., *Zhuanhuan zhong de shijie geju* (World structure under change) (Beijing: Shijie Zhishi Publishing House, 1992), pp. 110–12.

62. Harding, *Fragile Relationship*, pp. 202–3; Gong Li, *Zhongmei guanxi redian toushi*, pp. 164–65.

63. Gong Li, *Zhongmei guanxi redian toushi*, pp. 165–73.

64. Zhao Quansheng, *Jiedu zhongguo de waijiao zhengce* (Interpreting Chinese foreign policy) (Taiwan: Yuedan Publishing House, 1999), pp. 155–56.

65. Harding, *Fragile Relationship*, pp. 186–89.

66. Liu and Wang, *Zhongmei guanxi de guiji*, p. 69; Harding, *Fragile Relationship*, pp. 190–95.

67. Zhongguo shehui kexueyuan meiguo yanjiusuo and zhonghua meiguo xuehui (Institute of American Studies of the Chinese Academy of Social Sciences and Society for American Studies of China), ed., *Zhongmei guanxi shinian* (The last decade of Sino-American relations) (Beijing: Shangwu Publishing House, 1989), p. 9.

68. Ibid., p. 3.

69. Gong, *Zhongmei guanxi redian toushi*, pp. 180–83.

70. Liu and Wang, *Zhongmei guanxi de guiji*, pp. 295–96, 298.

71. *Renmin Ribao*, June 9, 1989.

72. Ibid.

73. *Deng Xiaoping wenxuan* (Selected works of Deng Xiaoping), vol. 3 (Beijing: Renmin Publishing House, 1993), pp. 302–14.

74. *Renmin Ribao*, October 4, 1989.

75. *Deng Xiaoping wenxuan*, vol. 3, pp. 330–33.

76. Liu and Wang, *Zhongmei guanxi de guiji*, pp. 296–97.

77. Ibid., p. 299.

78. Harding, *Fragile Relationship*, p. 228.

79. Ibid., p. 252.

80. Ibid., pp. 350–51.

Chapter 6: *Gerald L. Curtis, U.S. Relations with Japan*

The Japanese Center for International Exchange kindly granted permission to publish this paper.

1. Michael Schaller, *Altered States: The United States and Japan Since the Occupation* (New York: Oxford University Press, 1997), p. 225.

2. Henry Kissinger, *White House Years* (Boston: Little, Brown, 1979), p. 756.

3. Ibid., p. 1089.

4. Richard Nixon, *RN: The Memoirs of Richard Nixon* (New York: Grosset and Dunlap, 1978), p. 567.

5. Schaller, *Altered States*, p. 220.

6. Ibid., p. 230.

7. Ibid., p. 242.

8. George Shultz, *Turmoil and Triumph* (New York: Scribner, 1993), p. 173.

9. Ibid., pp. 182, 185.

10. Ibid., p. 174.

11. Jim Mann, *About Face: A History of America's Curious Relationship with China from Nixon to Clinton* (New York: Knopf, 1999), p. 240.

12. Ibid., p. 247.

13. Kissinger, *White House Years*, p. 322.

14. I. M. Destler, Fukui Haruhiro, and Sato Hideo, *The Textile Wrangle: Conflict in Japanese-American Relations, 1969–1971* (Ithaca: Cornell University Press, 1979).

15. Clyde Prestowitz, *Trading Places* (New York: Basic Books, 1988), p. 281.

16. Shultz, *Turmoil and Triumph*, p. 190.

17. Ibid.

18. Merit Janow, "Trading with an Ally: Progress and Discontent in U.S.-Japan Relations," in *The United States, Japan, and Asia*, ed. Gerald L. Curtis (New York: Norton, 1994), p. 59.

19. Leonard Schoppa, *Bargaining with Japan: What American Pressure Can and Cannot Do* (New York: Columbia University Press, 1997), p. 11.

20. See Schoppa, *Bargaining with Japan*, for a balanced discussion of what these results were.

21. Cited in ibid., p. 82.

22. See Janow, "Trading with an Ally," p. 68.

23. See Carla Hills's editorial, "Targets Won't Open Japanese Markets," *Wall Street Journal*, June 11, 1993.

24. In *Bargaining with Japan*, Schoppa goes to great lengths to demonstrate this point with careful case studies.

Chapter 7: *Nakanishi Hiroshi, Japanese Relations with the United States*

1. Paul Volcker and Toyoo Gyohten, *Changing Fortunes* (New York: Times Books, 1992), chap. 4.

2. Henry Kissinger, *Years of Renewal* (New York: Simon and Schuster, 1999), p. 695.

3. George Shultz, *Turmoil and Triumph* (New York: Scribner, 1993), p. 193.

4. Gyohten in Volcker and Gyohten, *Changing Fortunes*, p. 363.

Chapter 8: *Zhang Tuosheng, China's Relations with Japan*

1. Jiang Zemin, "Guoji Xingshi he Zhong-Ri Guanxi" (The International Situation and China-Japan Relations), a speech made at Nippon Hoso Kyokai (NHK) on July 7, 1992; Zhang Xiangshan, "Zai Zhong-Ri Youhao Ershiyi Shiji Weiyuanhui Dibaci Huiyi Shang de Jidiao Baogao" (Keynote Report at the Eighth Session of the 21st Century Committee of China-Japan Friendship Committee), September 1, 1992.

2. Zhang Xiangshan, "China-Japan Relations in the Past Twenty Years and Its Prospects," *Foreign Policy Quarterly*, no. 25 (September 1992) [English ed.].

3. Zhang Xiangshan, "Shunying Shidai Zhuchao Jixu Fazhan Zhong-Ri Youhao" (Continuously Promoting China-Japan Relations: Following the Trend of the Time), *Japan Research*, no. 3 (1992).

4. See Li Tingjiang, ed., *Zhong-Ri Guanxi Mianmianguan* (Facts of China-Japan Relations) (Beijing: China International Broadcasting Press, 1991).

5. Liu Deyou, "Ruhe Pingjia Ershiwunian Lai de Zhong-Ri Guanxi" (How to Assess China-Japan Relations in the Past Twenty-Five Years), *Peace and Development Quarterly*, no. 3 (1997): 22.

6. Japanese ODA to China includes Japanese loans with low interest, outright grants, and technical cooperation. It plays an important role in speeding up Chinese modernization and is a concrete manifestation of the Japanese government's expression of support for China's policy of reform and opening. Compared with the 1950s, China's economy recorded substantial development in the 1970s. In contrast to Soviet economic aid, which always attached political conditions, Japanese economic aid

attached no such conditions. China opens its doors to all, not just to Japan, so China is happy to receive Japan's aid and is not afraid of being controlled by others. Moreover, it is natural for some Chinese and some Japanese to believe that Japan owes China because of Japan's invasion and because China gave up its demand for war reparations. Therefore, it is considered reasonable for the economically developed Japan to offer some aid to China.

7. Liu Jiangyong, *Kua Shiji de Riben—Zhengzhi, Jingji, Waijiao Xin Qushi* (Japan at the Turn of the Centuries: New Trends in Politics, Economy, and Foreign Policy) (Beijing: Shishi Press, July 1995), pp. 499–506; Zhang, "China-Japan Relations in the Past Twenty Years and Its Prospects."

8. On September 26, 1972, Premier Zhou had a talk with Prime Minister Tanaka during which, aiming at the hope voiced by the Japanese side that the restoration of Sino-Japanese relations not affect relations with a third party, namely, the existing relations between Japan and the United States, Premier Zhou pointed out that since the objective situation for the Japan-U.S. Security Treaty had changed, the Taiwan clause in the Nixon-Sato communiqué was no longer applicable. The treaty might not have been mentioned at that time to avoid introducing any difficulties in U.S.-Japan relations. Zhou emphasized that this did not mean China had no differences with the treaty. Tanaka expressed no disagreement, which suggests that the two sides in fact reached a tacit understanding on the Japan-U.S. security treaty.

9. Some Japanese and American scholars point out that bilateral relations developed smoothly during the period because many Japanese were conscience-stricken over Japanese behavior in World War II. Thus, Japan adopted a low-key posture and was ready to provide China with some aid as, in effect, indirect war reparations. I believe this is a reasonable interpretation, but in the 1990s these attitudes have greatly changed.

10. In 1972 China and Japan reached a consensus on restoring normal relations between them in two "phases": first, to restore diplomatic relations and put an end to the abnormal relations between them, and second, to conclude the Treaty of Peace and Friendship through negotiations. After establishing diplomatic relations, the two sides could not start official treaty negotiations until January 1975 due to the delayed conclusion of four agreements on issues such as air and fishing rights. At that point, serious differences on the issue of the antihegemony clause emerged.

11. Some Japanese scholars argue that the Japanese position remained unchanged. The wording "not directed at the third party" in the Joint Statement was the Japanese way to reduce the anti-U.S.S.R. nature of the antihegemony clause. This view is not accurate, because the third party referred to in the Joint Statement was the United States, which was discussed concretely and had nothing to do with the Soviet Union. During the meetings between Zhou and Tanaka on September 21, 1972, the Japanese side also made it clear that in order to achieve the normalization,

another "third party" issue, in addition to the Taiwan issue, had to be addressed, namely, that Japan did not wish the normalization to affect Japan-U.S. relations and the Japan-U.S. security treaty. The agreement reached through these consultations is reflected in the wording of the final Joint Statement—"the normalization of relations between China and Japan is not directed at a third country"—thus replacing the Japanese draft wording "China-Japan friendship should not undermine any side's relations with its friendly countries" (obviously referring to the United States). Therefore, the Japanese side raised no opposition to the antihegemony clause at that time.

12. Zhang Xiangshan, "Comrade Deng Xiaoping and the China-Japan Treaty of Peace and Friendship," *Memories of Deng Xiaoping* (Beijing: Central Document Press, 1998).

13. Deng Xiaoping's remarks, made during a meeting with the Clean Government Party delegation, March 14, 1978.

14. Remarks made by Deng Xiaoping to a visiting Japanese delegation led by Ikeda Daisuke, April 16, 1975.

15. Some Japanese have argued that the textbook issue was not something new and that China suddenly reacted to it strongly in 1982 in an attempt to influence the settlement of the trade imbalance. This view is not supported by hard evidence. The author interviewed Luo Weilong, a correspondent then stationed in Japan, who wrote the first relevant report on the history issue. He said that the report was entirely his own idea and was written without any instructions from home or from any concerned leader. After extensive research, he felt that he possessed adequate and reliable information, and filed the report in June 1982. This report immediately sent a tremor throughout China. The Chinese reaction to the textbook issue had nothing to do with the economic friction between the two countries, since China is always against the settlement of economic friction by political pressure.

16. Liu Deyou, *Shiguang zhi Lü—Wo Jingli de Zhong-Ri Guanxi* (A Travel with Time: China-Japan Relations I Have Experienced) (Beijing: Commercial Press, 1999), p. 528.

17. Liu Deyou, "Qinqie de Jiaohui, Yan'ge de Zhidao" (Warm Care and Strict Guidance), in *A Travel with Time*.

18. Tian Heng, ed., *Zhanhou Zhong-Ri Guanxi Shinian Biao (1945–1993)* (A Chronology of Postwar China-Japan Relations, 1945–1993) (Beijing: China Social Science Press, 1994), p. 94.

19. Ibid., p. 558.

20. Liu, *Japan at the Turn of the Centuries*, p. 147.

21. Kokaryo is a five-story building in Kyoto, Japan. Not long after the end of World War II, the then government of China bought the building as a dormitory for Chinese students in Japan. After the founding of the PRC, the building was

managed by the Kokaryo Self-Governing Council. In 1960 a Kyoto court decided that the Kokaryo building belonged to the "Republic of China" on Taiwan, but so far Taiwan authorities have never been involved in the building's management. In September 1977, the court, in accordance with the fact that Japan had already recognized the People's Republic of China as China's sole legal government, decided to transfer ownership of the Kokaryo building to the PRC. However, in 1982, 1986, and 1987, the High Court in Osaka and the Kyoto court accepted appeals filed by a government official of the "ROC," finally reversing the earlier judgment and again giving ownership of the building to Taiwan. This created a legal precedent for Japan's acceptance of two governments of one country, that is, "two Chinas" or "one China and one Taiwan." This incident, therefore, was the source of a major political and legal dispute between the two countries. In March 1987, the Chinese students living in the building filed an appeal to the highest Japanese court. The court has not yet made a final ruling.

22. The talks between Premier Zhou Enlai and Prime Minister Tanaka on September 28, 1972, focused on the Taiwan issue, especially Japan-Taiwan relations after Japan severed its so-called diplomatic relations with Taiwan. Tanaka, responding to Zhou Enlai's request for "briefing beforehand," made a clear promise: "If we do anything to Taiwan, we are bound to brief your side in advance."

23. Zhang Xiangshan, *Zhong-Ri Guanxi Guankui yu Jianzhang* (Several Issues in China-Japan Relations: An Eyewitness's Point of View) (Beijing: Contemporary World Press, 1998), p. 326.

24. Deng Xiaoping, *Deng Xiaoping Wenxuan* (Selected works of Deng Xiaoping), vol. 3 (Beijing: Renmin Press, 1993), p. 230.

25. Shimata Masao, *Zhanhou Ri-Zhong Guanxi Wushinian (1945–1994)* (Postwar Japan-China Relations) [Chinese ed.] (Nanchang: Jianxi Education Press, 1998), pp. 341–42.

26. Zhang Xichang et al., *Fengluan dieqi—Gongheguo Disanci Jianjiao Gaochao* (Wave After Wave—Diplomatic Relations of the PRC) (Beijing: World Knowledge Press, 1998), p. 252.

27. *Selected Works of Deng Xiaoping*, vol. 3, p. 87.

28. Liu, *Japan at the Turn of the Centuries*, p. 499.

29. Zhang, *Several Issues in China-Japan Relations*, pp. 343–44.

30. Liu, *A Travel with Time*, p. 502.

31. *Selected Works of Deng Xiaoping*, vol. 3, p. 349.

32. Zhang Yunling, ed., *Zhuanbian Zhong de Zhong, Ri, Mei Guanxi* (The Changing Relations Among China, Japan, and the U.S.) (Beijing: China Social Sciences Press, 1997), p. 27.

33. Gong Li, ed., *Deng Xiaoping de Waijiao Sixiang yu Shijian* (Deng Xiaoping's Thinking in Foreign Policy and Its Practice) (Harbin: Helongjiang Education Press, 1996), p. 243.

34. Qu Xing, "Bashi niandai Chu Zhongguo Duiwai Zhengce de Tiaozheng" (China's Adjustment of Its Foreign Policy in the Early 1980s), in *Zhongguo Waijiao Xinlun* (*New Comments on China's Diplomacy*) (Beijing: World Knowledge Press, 1998), p. 48.

35. Zhang, *Several Issues in China-Japan Relations*, p. 48.

36. Liu, *Japan at the Turn of the Centuries*, pp. 595–96.

37. Zhang, ed., *Changing Relations*, p. 36.

Chapter 9: *Soeya Yoshihide, Japan's Relations with China*

1. The terms "strategy," "strategic," and "nonstrategic" are here used to refer to the structure of international politics as shaped by the security strategies of the "powers," which include the United States, China, and the Soviet Union. Actions and policies affecting this structure of relations among the powers are regarded as strategic.

2. Soeya Yoshihide, "Kokusai-seiji no naka-no Nitchu-kankei" (Japan-China relations in international politics), *Kokusai Mondai* (January 1998).

3. Michael J. Green and Benjamin L. Self, "Japan's Changing China Policy: From Commercial Liberalism to Reluctant Realism," *Survival* 38, no. 2 (Summer 1996).

4. I have used the same perspective in a draft paper, "U.S.-Japan Relations and the Opening to China: The Emergence of a Triangle," prepared for the Conference on Power and Prosperity: Linkages between Security and Economics in U.S.-Japanese Relations Since 1960, co-organized by the National Security Archive Project on U.S.-Japan Relations and the International House of Japan, held on January 7–10, 2000, in Tokyo. The analysis of the 1970s here draws on this draft paper.

5. Raymond L. Garthoff, *Détente and Confrontation: American-Soviet Relations from Nixon to Reagan* (Washington, D.C.: The Brookings Institution, 1985).

6. Seymor M. Hersh, *The Price of Power: Kissinger in the Nixon White House* (New York: Summit Books, 1983), p. 442.

7. Ushiba Nobuhiko, *Gaiko no Shunkan* (A moment of diplomacy) (Tokyo: Nihon Keizai Shinbun-sha, 1984), p. 134.

8. Ogata Sadako, *Normalization with China: A Comparative Study of U.S. and Japanese Processes* (Berkeley: Institute of East Asian Studies, University of California, 1988), p. 37.

9. For more detail, see Soeya Yoshihide, *Japan's Economic Diplomacy with China, 1945–1978* (London: Oxford University Press, 1998).

10. On the bureaucrats' role and involvement in the process, see Haruhiro Fukui, "Tanaka Goes to Peking: A Case Study in Foreign Policymaking," in *Policymaking in*

Contemporary Japan, ed. T. J. Pempell (Ithaca: Cornell University Press, 1977), pp. 84–90.

11. Henry A. Kissinger, "Memorandum for the President: Your Meeting with Japanese Prime Minister Tanaka in Honolulu on August 31 and September 1" (August 29, 1972), Project on U.S.-Japan Relations, National Security Archive.

12. Mainichi Shinbun-sha Seiji-bu [Political section of the Mainichi newspaper], ed., *Tenkanki no Anpo* (U.S.-Japan security in transition) (Tokyo: Mainichi Shinbun-sha, 1978), p. 208.

13. For more details, see Ogata, *Normalization with China*; Tanaka Akihiko, *Nitchu Kankei 1945–1990* (Japan-China relations, 1945–1990) (Tokyo: University of Tokyo Press, 1991); and Soeya Yoshihide, *Nihon-gaiko to Chugoku, 1945–1972* (Japanese diplomacy and China, 1945–1972) (Tokyo: Keio University Press, 1995).

14. Ogata, *Normalization with China*, p. 56.

15. Yanagida Kunio, *Nihon wa Moete-iruka* (Is Japan burning?) (Tokyo: Kodansha, 1983), p. 266.

16. Ogata, *Normalization with China*, p. 51.

17. Garthoff, *Détente and Confrontation*. The following account of international developments draws on this source unless otherwise noted.

18. Ogata, *Normalization with China*, p. 58.

19. Garthoff, *Détente and Confrontation*, p. 561.

20. Michel Oksenberg, "A Decade of Sino-American Relations," *Foreign Affairs* 61 (Fall 1982).

21. Cyrus Vance, *Hard Choices: Critical Years in America's Foreign Policy* (New York: Simon and Schuster, 1983), pp. 78–83.

22. Jimmy Carter, *Keeping Faith: Memoirs of a President* (New York: Bantam Books, 1982), pp. 193–94.

23. For Brzezinski's account of his meetings with Chinese leaders, see Zbigniew Brzezinski, *Power and Principle: Memoirs of the National Security Advisor, 1977–1981* (New York: Farrar, Straus and Giroux, 1983), pp. 211–15.

24. Garthoff, *Détente and Confrontation*, p. 711.

25. Oksenberg, "A Decade of Sino-American Relations," p. 186. Ogata, *Normalization with China*, pp. 66–71.

26. Ogata, *Normalization with China*, p. 53.

27. Brzezinski, *Power and Principle*, pp. 216–18.

28. Ogata, *Normalization with China*, pp. 88, 95.

29. Ibid., p. 84; Nagano Nobutoshi, *Ten'no to To Shohei no Akushu* (The Emperor and Deng Xiapin shaking hands) (Tokyo: Gyosei-mondai Kenkyu-jo, 1983), p. 164. Likewise, this is another key issue to be explored further.

30. Ogata, *Normalization with China*, p. 91.

31. Sonoda Sunao, "Nihon-gaiko no Tenkan wo Kokoro-mite" (Attempting to transform Japanese diplomacy), *Kikan Chuo Koron Keiei Mondai* 19, no. 1 (Spring 1980): 242.

32. David Shambaugh, "Patterns of Interaction in Sino-American Relations," in *Chinese Foreign Policy: Theory and Practice*, ed. Thomas W. Robinson and David Shambaugh (Oxford: Oxford University Press, 1994), p. 204.

33. Gene T. Hsiao, "A Renewed Crisis over Taiwan and Its Impact on Sino-American Relations," in *Sino-American Normalization and Its Policy Implications*, ed. Gene T. Hsiao and Michael Witunski (New York: Praeger Publishers, 1983).

34. Harvey W. Nelson, *Power and Insecurity: Beijing, Moscow, and Washington, 1949–1988* (Boulder: Lynne Rienner Publishers, 1989), chap. 9.

35. Kokubun Ryosei, "The Politics of Foreign Economic Policy-making in China: The Case of Plant Cancellations with Japan," *The China Quarterly*, no. 105 (March 1986).

36. Tanaka, *Nitchu-kankei*, pp. 111–12.

37. Ibid., pp. 117–19, 127–28.

38. For details see ibid., pp. 120–25, and Ijiri Hidonori, "Sino-Japanese Controversy Since the 1972 Diplomatic Normalization," in *China and Japan: History, Trends, and Prospects*, ed. Christopher Howe (Oxford: Oxford University Press, 1996), pp. 64–69.

39. Tanaka, *Nitchu-kankei*, p. 133.

40. Allen S. Whiting, *China Eyes Japan* (Berkeley: University of California Press, 1989), pp. 51–55.

41. Tanaka, *Nitchu-kankei*, pp. 137–49; Ijiri, "Sino-Japanese Controversy," pp. 69–73.

42. Tanaka, *Nitchu-kankei*, pp. 155–59; Ijiri, "Sino-Japanese Controversy," pp. 73–76.

43. Ando Masashi, ed., *Genten Chugoku Gendai-shi, Dai-8-kan, Nitchu-kankei* (Original sources modern history of China, vol. 8, Japan-China relations) (Tokyo: Iwanami-shoten, 1994), p. 269.

A Selected Bibliography on Bilateral Relations

U.S.-China Relations

Burr, William, ed. *The Kissinger Transcripts: The Top Secret Talks with Beijing and Moscow.* New York: New Press, 1998.

Garver, John W. *Face off: China, the United States and Taiwan's Democratization.* Seattle: University of Washington Press, 1997.

Harding, Harry. *A Fragile Relationship: The United States and China Since 1972.* Washington, D.C.: Brookings Institution, 1992.

Holdridge, John H. *Crossing the Divide: An Insider's Account of the Normalization of U.S.-China Relations.* Lanham, Md.: Rowman and Littlefield, 1997.

Kissinger, Henry. *Diplomacy.* New York: Simon and Schuster, 1994.

————. *White House Years.* Boston: Little, Brown, 1979.

Lampton, David M. *Same Bed Different Dreams: Managing U.S.-China Relations, 1989–2000.* Berkeley: University of California Press, 2001.

Madsen, Richard. *China and the American Dream: A Moral Inquiry.* Berkeley: University of California Press, 1995.

Mann, James. *About Face: A History of America's Curious Relationship with China, from Nixon to Clinton.* New York: Knopf, 1999.

Myers, Ramon; Michel Oksenberg; and David Shambaugh, eds. *Making China Policy: Lessons from the Bush and Clinton Administrations.* Lanham, Md.: Rowman and Littlefield, 2001.

Ross, Robert. *Negotiating Cooperation: The United States and China, 1969–1989*. Stanford: Stanford University Press, 1965.

Ross, Robert S., ed. *After the Cold War: Domestic Factors and U.S.-China Relations*. Armonk, N.Y.: M.E. Sharpe, 1988.

Ross, Robert S., and Jiang Changbin, eds. *Re-examining the Cold War: U.S.-China Diplomacy, 1954–1973*. Cambridge, Mass.: Asia Center, Harvard University, 2001.

Shultz, George. *Turmoil and Triumph*. New York: Scribner, 1993.

Swaine, Michael D. *China: Domestic Change and Foreign Policy*. Santa Monica, Calif.: Rand, 1995.

Tucker, Nancy Bernkopf, ed. *China Confidential: American Diplomats and Sino-American Relations, 1945–1996*. New York: Columbia University Press, 2001.

Tyler, Patrick. *A Great Wall: Six Presidents and China*. New York: Public Affairs, 1999.

Vogel, Ezra F., ed. *Living with China: U.S.-China Relations in the Twenty-first Century*. New York: Norton, 1997.

Zhai, Qiang. *China and the Vietnam Wars, 1950–1975*. Chapel Hill: University of North Carolina Press, 2000.

U.S.-Japan Relations

Armacost, Michael H. *Friends or Rivals: The Insider's Account of U.S.-Japan Relations*. New York: Columbia University Press, 1996.

Barnds, William J., ed. *Japan and the United States: Challenges and Opportunities*. New York: New York University Press, 1979.

Buckley, Roger. *U.S.-Japan Alliance Diplomacy, 1945–1990*. New York: Cambridge University Press, 1992.

Cha, Victor D. *Alignment Despite Antagonism: The U.S.-Korea-Japan Security Triangle*. Stanford: Stanford University Press, 1999.

Curtis, Gerald L., ed. *The United States, Japan, and Asia: Challenges for U.S. Policy*. New York: Norton, 1994.

Destler, I. M., Fukui Haruhiro, and Sato Hideo. *The Textile Wrangle: Conflict in Japanese-American Relations, 1969–1971*. Ithaca: Cornell University Press, 1979.

Funabashi, Yoichi. *Alliance Adrift*. New York: Council on Foreign Relations Press, 1999.

Green, Michael. *Arming Japan*. New York: Columbia University Press, 1995.

Green, Michael J., and Patrick M. Cronin, eds. *The U.S.-Japan Alliance: Past, Present, and Future*. New York: Council on Foreign Relations Press, 1999.

Holland, Harrison M. *Managing Diplomacy: The United States and Japan*. Stanford, Calif.: Hoover Institution, 1984.

Iriye, Akira, and Warren I. Cohen, eds. *The United States and Japan in the Postwar World*. Lexington: University of Kentucky Press, 1989.

Kitamura, Hiroshi, Ryohei Murata, and Hisahiko Okazaki. *Between Friends: Japanese Diplomats Look at Japan-U.S. Relations.* New York: Weatherhill, 1985.

LaFeber, Walter. *The Clash: A History of U.S.-Japan Relations.* New York: Norton, 1997.

Mochizuki, Mike, et al. *Japan and the United States: Troubled Partners in a Changing World.* Washington: Brassey's, 1991.

Mochizuki, Mike M., ed. *Toward a True Alliance: Restructuring U.S.-Japan Security Relations.* Washington, D.C.: Brookings Institution, 1997.

Prestowitz, Clyde. *Trading Places: How We Allowed Japan to Take the Lead.* New York: Basic Books, 1988.

Schaller, Michael. *Altered States: The United States and Japan Since the Occupation.* New York: Oxford University Press, 1997.

Schoppa, Leonard. *Bargaining with Japan: What American Pressure Can and Cannot Do.* New York: Columbia University Press, 1997.

Sigur, Gaston J., and Young C. Kim. *Japanese and U.S. Policy in Asia.* New York: Praeger, 1982.

Zhang Yuling, ed. *The Changing Relations Among China, Japan, and the U.S.* Beijing: China Social Sciences Press, 1997.

Sino-Japanese Relations

Abramowitz, Morton, Funabashi Yoichi, and Wang Jisi. *China-Japan-U.S.: Managing the Trilateral Relationship.* Tokyo and New York: Japan Center for International Exchange, 1998.

Austin, Greg, and Stuart Harris. *Japan and Greater China: Political Economy and Military Power in the Asian Century.* Honolulu: University of Hawaii Press, 2001.

Barnett, A. Doak. *China and the Major Powers in East Asia.* Washington: Brookings Institution, 1977.

Bedelski, Robert E. *The Fragile Entente: The 1978 Japan-China Peace Treaty in a Global Context.* Boulder: Westview Press, 1983.

Iriye, Akira. *China and Japan in the Global Setting.* Cambridge: Harvard University Press, 1992.

Katzenstein, Peter, and Takashi Shiraishi, eds. *Network Power: Japan and Asia.* Ithaca: Cornell University Press, 1997.

Lee Chae-Jin. *China and Japan: New Economic Diplomacy.* Stanford, Calif.: Hoover Institution Press, 1984.

———. *Japan Faces China: Political and Economic Relations in the Postwar Era.* Baltimore: Johns Hopkins Press, 1976.

Newby, Laura. *Sino-Japanese Relations: China's Perspective.* New York: Routledge, 1988.

Ogata, Sadako. *Normalization with China: A Comparative Study of U.S. and Japanese Processes.* Berkeley: Institute of East Asian Studies, University of California, 1988.

Rose, Caroline. *Interpreting History in Sino-Japanese Relations: A Case Study in Political Decision-Making.* New York: Routledge, 1999.

Soeya, Yoshihide. *Japan's Economic Diplomacy with China, 1945–1978.* Oxford: Clarendon Press, 1998.

Whiting, Allen S. *China Eyes Japan.* Berkeley: University of California Press, 1989.

Zhao, Quansheng. *Japanese Policymaking—The Politics Behind Politics: The Informal Mechanisms and the Making of China Policy.* Westport, Conn.: Praeger, 1993.

Index

Harvard East Asian Monographs
(* out-of-print)

Harvard East Asian Monographs

Harvard East Asian Monographs

Harvard East Asian Monographs

Harvard East Asian Monographs

Harvard East Asian Monographs

Harvard East Asian Monographs

Harvard East Asian Monographs